SPEAKING WORDS OF WISDOM

EDITOR
Kenneth Womack, Monmouth University

ADVISORY BOARD
Henry L. Carrigan Jr., musician and critic
Walter Everett, University of Michigan
Cheryl L. Keyes, University of California, Los Angeles
Hannah Lewis, University of Texas at Austin
Tim Riley, Emerson College
Larry Starr, University of Washington

Music shapes our world more powerfully than any other cultural product. To fully understand America, we must learn the complex, diverse history of American musical life. The books in this series tell the stories of the artists, forms, and innovations that define the musical legacy of the United States and fashion its ideals and practices.

SPEAKING WORDS OF WISDOM

The Beatles and Religion

Edited by Michael McGowan

THE PENNSYLVANIA STATE UNIVERSITY PRESS | UNIVERSITY PARK, PENNSYLVANIA

Library of Congress Cataloging-in-Publication Data

Names: McGowan, Michael (Michael W.), editor.
Title: Speaking words of wisdom : the Beatles and religion / edited by Michael McGowan.
Other titles: American music history.
Description: University Park, Pennsylvania : The Pennsylvania State University Press, [2024] | Series: American music history | Includes bibliographical references and index.
Summary: "A collection of essays by scholars of religion, music, philosophy, and culture exploring the Beatles' relationship to religion"—Provided by publisher.
Identifiers: LCCN 2024000840 | ISBN 9780271097299 (hardback) | ISBN 9780271097435 (paperback)
Subjects: LCSH: Beatles. | Beatles—Religion. | Rock music—Religious aspects.
Classification: LCC ML421.B4 S659 2024 | DDC 782.42166092/2—dc23/eng/20240123
LC record available at https://lccn.loc.gov/2024000840

Copyright © 2024 The Pennsylvania State University
All rights reserved
Printed in the United States of America
Published by The Pennsylvania State University Press,
University Park, PA 16802-1003

10 9 8 7 6 5 4 3 2 1

The Pennsylvania State University Press is a member of the Association of University Presses.

It is the policy of The Pennsylvania State University Press to use acid-free paper. Publications on uncoated stock satisfy the minimum requirements of American National Standard for Information Sciences—Permanence of Paper for Printed Library Material, ANSI Z39.48-1992.

For Magdey and Max,

who took a sad song

and made it better

Contents

ix Foreword by Anthony DeCurtis

xiii Acknowledgments

1 That Magic Feeling: An Introduction to the Beatles and Religion
MICHAEL MCGOWAN

Part I: Liverpool, Protestants, and Catholics

31 **1** Religion in the Liverpool of the Beatles' Childhoods
MELISSA DAVIS

49 **2** Born Taking Sides: Religion in the Beatles' Liverpool
DAVID BEDFORD

Part 2: The Beatles as Individuals

67 **3** The Religious Sensibility of Paul McCartney
KENNETH CAMPBELL

82 **4** John Lennon, Jesus as a Moral Model, and Imagine No Religion
EYAL REGEV

98 **5** George Harrison's Road to India
JOHN COVACH

114 **6** Don't Pass Me By: To Hell and Back with Ringo Starr
MICHAEL MCGOWAN

Part 3: The Beatles and Religious Experience

133 **7** Songs of Self-Emptying in the Beatles
SCOTT FREER

150 **8** Yeah, Yeah, Yeah: Beatlemania and the Cult of Dionysus—The Resurrection of a New Consciousness
SEAN MACLEOD

166 **9** A Religion in Fact: The Beatles as Religious Phenomenon Hidden in Plain Sight
GRANT MAXWELL

Part 4: Reception of the Beatles

185 **10** Helter Skelter: Charles Manson's (Supposed) Apocalyptic Reading of the White Album
MARK DUFFETT

201 **11** Sanctum or Artifact? The Beatles' Music in *Yesterday*
CHRISTIANE MEISER

214 **12** Necrolennonolatry: The Postmortem Adventures of John Lennon
MURRAY LEEDER

229 Conclusion: "Now and Then"—Seeking and Finding Meaning in Community
MICHAEL MCGOWAN

233 List of Contributors
237 Index

Foreword

An American singer-songwriter whom Brian Epstein was interested in managing once visited him in England and, inevitably, hung out with the Beatles. Among many riveting stories, he told me that members of the band would publicly smoke hashish, confident in that midsixties stage of their fame that they were untouchable. "They were like gods," he told me.

Soon the Beatles would be as susceptible to persecution by the British police as any other rock stars of the period, but describing them as "like gods" was very much of a piece with the general perception of them, certainly by the burgeoning counterculture. Part of the reason for their deification was purely a function of sociology. By the time the Beatles broke in America in late 1963 and early 1964, the baby-boom generation was coming of age, a huge audience of young people who had money to spend and a gathering sense of their cultural and political significance. Television had transformed, expanded, and deeply personalized young people's experience of "popular culture," a term that had yet to come into common use.

Talking with me about the shifts taking place during that era, Mick Jagger pointed out that bands weren't "talked about on any kind of intellectual level. There was no such word as 'pop culture.' None of those things existed. But with the Beatles becoming so popular, it all started to attract critical attention. Critics in broadsheet newspapers would try to explain why your children liked the Rolling Stones. They would explain why the Beatles were brilliant musicians and wrote all these songs and ask, 'Were they as good as Bach?' Albums started to be reviewed as if they were films, as if they were standing on their own as works of art—popular works of art but works of art nevertheless."

Before that, it would have been unthinkable—quite literally inconceivable—to refer to pop musicians as "artists." But their stature began to grow. Moving over from the folk music world—with its historical, literary, and political associations—Bob Dylan, of course, also brought a new seriousness to rock and roll. Folk singers addressed substantive issues in their songs and made jokes onstage about the obsession with teen romance that seemed endemic to pop music. But as folk became folk-rock, lyricists like Dylan and Paul Simon raised the stakes. Teachers in high school and college—in religion classes as well as literary ones—began examining the meanings of their songs. Young people learned to look to the artists they admired for answers to life's questions—cultural, political, and spiritual.

The currents of culture itself began to flow in different directions. While the Beatles' haircuts were initially treated as cute fads, it soon became apparent that, as a look, it was not going to disappear the way Daniel Boone caps or hula hoops had. Even the Beatles' clothes began to be commented on seriously by fashion critics, and the more colorful and experimental those clothes grew to be, the more influential they became. Respected photographers like David Bailey began to shoot rock bands, and someone like Jagger, outrageous as he was at the time, became an important figure in the fashion world.

Unlike in previous generations, trends began to move from the bottom to the top, from the streets to the runway, from young people to adults. While a decade earlier it would have been unthinkable for adults to take their style cues from the likes of Elvis Presley, that all changed in the sixties. Adult men began growing their hair longer, and women dressed in miniskirts. The Youth Quake was shaking things up, and culture would never be the same.

All this to explain why the Beatles' thoughts and experiences regarding religion became a topic that people, especially young people, wanted to learn about. Even as the Beatles were initially encouraged not to express their opinions about controversial issues, their quickness, wit, and obvious intelligence during their early press conferences clearly established them as a new order of teen idol. As the civil rights movement and protests against the Vietnam War heated up, young people came to experience their own views as important. In addition, they began to look to the musicians and songwriters they admired for insight and perspective. In 1821, Percy Shelley had declared that poets were the "unacknowledged legislators of the world." In the sixties, young people began to view the bands they loved in the same high regard.

Maureen Cleave, the journalist who knew the Beatles well enough to encourage John Lennon to be more ambitious in his lyric writing, smartly observed in her 1966 profile of Lennon for the *London Evening Standard* that "experience has sown few seeds of doubt in him; not that his mind is closed, but it's closed round whatever he believes at the time." That "whatever he believes at the time" is the key line. While Lennon was the most likely among the Beatles to express radical views about religion—as much to push buttons as for any more substantive reason—his points of view were hardly consistent. "Christianity will go. It will vanish and shrink," he famously proclaimed in Cleave's article. "I needn't argue about that; I'm right and I will be proved right. We're more popular than Jesus now."

The furor those comments caused when they appeared in America prompted a string of resentful apologies from Lennon, none of which merged into a coherent religious point of view. Which was to be expected, of course.

He was twenty-five at the time, was living a life of enormous complexity, and had plenty on his mind beyond theology. By the time of "God" on his first solo album, he was taking a purely secular view of religion: "God is a concept by which we measure our pain." It was what he believed "at the time." But none of that ever stopped him from comparing himself to Jesus, as he did in song lyrics and during this outburst in one of his last interviews, in 1980, promoting *Double Fantasy*. Infuriated by the persistent requests for the Beatles to reunite, he responded to *Playboy*'s David Sheff with a caustic string of biblical references: "If they didn't understand the Beatles and the Sixties then, what the fuck could we do for them now? Do we have to divide the fish and the loaves for the multitudes again? Do we have to get crucified again? Do we have to do the walking on water again because a whole pile of dummies didn't see it the first time, or didn't believe it when they saw it? You know, that's what they're asking: 'Get off the cross. I didn't understand the first bit yet. Can you do that again?' No way. You can never go home. It doesn't exist."

George Harrison, of course, came to value religion as a hedge against, in his view, the wild overvaluation of the Beatles and the madness that surrounded them. His friendship with Ravi Shankar introduced him to musical and spiritual worlds that provided needed perspective on the chaos of Beatlemania. He was shaken by the perils of the whirlwind surrounding the Beatles, famously remarking that the experience nearly destroyed his nervous system. His Hinduism brought him a peace that also allowed him room for elements of Christianity and the wonders revealed to him by his use of LSD. When I asked Harrison if he still felt close to Lennon after they had drifted apart after Lennon had moved to New York and distanced himself from the Beatles, Harrison responded,

> I only felt *physically* unclose to him, because we'd gone through too many things. The very first time we took LSD, John and I were together. And that experience together, and a lot of other things that happened after that, both on LSD and on the meditation trip to Rishikesh—we saw beyond each other's physical bodies, you know? That's there permanently, whether he's in a physical body or not. This is the goal anyway: to realize the spiritual side. If you can't feel the spirit of some friend who's been that chose, then what chance have you got of feeling the spirit of Christ or Buddha or whoever else you may be interested in? "If your memory serves you well, we're going to meet again." I believe that.

Ringo, predictably, has the most conventional religious views of the Beatles. Through his recovery program, he has accepted a higher power, and he has given interviews in which he has discussed how God has found a place in his life. McCartney, meanwhile, has come to something like an understanding of spiritual life that combines New Age mysticism and something like science. When I asked him in 2007 why he believed the Beatles' music still spoke to people, he replied, "I think it's basically magic. There is such a thing as magic, and the Beatles were magic. It depends on what you believe life is. Life is an energy field, a bunch of molecules. And these particular molecules formed to make these four guys, who then formed into this band called the Beatles and did all that work. I have to think that was what we humans call magic. Something metaphysical, something alchemic, something very magical happened, and I think that's what speaks."

The impressive essays in this collection explore the vast varieties of ways in which the Beatles' lives and music engaged religion. They are thorough and penetrating, and they reveal, ultimately, how, as so many of us do, the band struggled to achieve a spiritual understanding of their lives. So many listeners have looked to the Beatles' music itself to discover those answers. As the circumstances of our own lives and times change, different aspects of the Beatles' music come to the fore. That will probably never end. Perhaps the true spiritual importance of the Beatles' music lies therein. A careful listening to their songs will ensure, as their great rivals suggested, that, in spiritual terms as in so many others, you can get what you need.

—Anthony DeCurtis

Acknowledgments

This book is the product of a dispersed community of scholars, fans, and friends. First and foremost, I wish to thank the contributors to this book, who worked exceedingly hard, even during a pandemic, to be a part of this collection. If this book succeeds, it will be as a result of their efforts. Special thanks go to Anthony DeCurtis, who wrote the foreword and played an indirect role in convincing me of the need for this book. I also want to thank Kenneth Womack for being a sounding board, serving as general editor of the American Music History series, and his Beatles scholarship. I'm honored, truly.

I am also grateful for Daniel Spillman, a historian of postwar America who read portions of the book at various stages and offered indispensable historical context. I owe a debt of gratitude to Brian Wiltsey, the songwriter and producer who, at a young age, taught me the love of music from the inside. Many thanks to Adam Nevins, who introduced me to some music theory and nobly helps people struggling with poverty. And I'm thankful for Caleb Moan, fellow traveler and friend who shares the love of music.

Thank you to the staff at Penn State University Press, especially Ryan Peterson, Madison Caso, Patrick Alexander, and Alex Ramos, as well as Andrew Katz, whose painstaking copyediting is much appreciated. I owe a debt of gratitude to the great Beatles scholars, too, including Mark Lewisohn, whose next two volumes are eagerly anticipated, and Steve Turner, whose work on the Beatles' pivotal year of 1966 and the ways in which they advanced the gospel of love and freedom were both wonderful reads. A heartfelt thanks also goes to Paul Saltzman, who was willing to let us use one of his photos for the cover and whose movie *Meeting the Beatles in India* provides an intimate glimpse into the Beatles' search for meaning.

For their continual support of their faculty and students, I'm incredibly thankful for the generosity of Florida Southwestern State College, especially fellow Beatles fan and supportive dean Dr. Deborah Teed, as well as Victoria SanFilippo in the FSW library and Joe Van Gaalen in the Office of Sponsored Programs and Research.

Special thanks go to Mike and Bev McGowan, both of whom watched the Beatles live on *The Ed Sullivan Show* as kids in 1964 on opposite sides of the United States four years before they met in the middle. One of them (I won't say which) even owned a Beatles wig. And, of course, Carolyn Mortimer, for teaching the love of art.

And finally, I wish to thank the living musicians whose music and lives we are still thinking about and have benefited from: Paul McCartney and Ringo Starr. Thank you for the joy of your sound.

That Magic Feeling

An Introduction to the Beatles and Religion

MICHAEL MCGOWAN

By all accounts, the Beatles were the most innovative and commercially successful musical group of the twentieth century. Their albums sold in the hundreds of millions, they toured relentlessly, and the press was always eager to document their activities and perspectives. In short, they were something of a phenomenon. People cared about what John Lennon, Paul McCartney, George Harrison, and Ringo Starr said, paid attention to where they went, and kept track of what they were up to. And when fan appreciation morphed into fan worship, Beatlemania took on a religious significance.

But the Beatles were more than a musical group. Their career trajectory shows profound adaptation to a changing world and their ability to shape that world in their image. At times, their cultural roles put them in direct conflict with historic institutions, in relation to which the Beatles were instigators and shapers of an emerging counterculture that both intentionally and unintentionally challenged earlier forms of authority, including religious authorities. While some Americans believed the Beatles unworthy of being broadcast on the airwaves of their "God-fearing nation," many others in the United States and around the world began to look to the Beatles—their music, their commentary, their art—for meaning in a turbulent decade.

This book dives deep into the religious worlds of the band's individual members and the Beatles as a group to discern how they became reluctant modern-day sages. By taking stock of the Beatles and religion, this book also provides a case study for the ways in which consumers make culturally and religiously significant meaning from music, people, and events. The Beatles' story is the human story, in which the tension between tradition and change gives birth to some of the world's great art. It is the story of a religiously steeped Western world that was confronted with a self-consciously enlightened youth who sought answers to existential questions on their own terms and in their own way.

More Popular than Jesus

Early press coverage of the Beatles suggested they were no ordinary group. "Something significant is happening," *The New York Times* reported on December 26, 1963, as Beatlemania swept through Britain. The reaction among fans was seen by some as religiously dangerous: "Longhaired Youths with Guitars Take Charge as *Cult*."[1] Some perceived them as a threat—cellar dwellers with loose morals who would corrupt the otherwise obedient young—while others gave them religious titles and functions like "a band of evangelists" whose "gospel is fun."[2] One and a half months later, in February 1964, Ed Sullivan introduced the Beatles to the United States as one might introduce a papal entourage: "Ambassadors of Good Will." The subsequent fan worship, which had already taken hold in the United Kingdom, was no less devout than what one would find on Sunday mornings all across America and, in many cases, was more devout.

In truth, the enthusiasm with which young people experienced the band was akin to a religious experience, sometimes with the same elements as traditional religious practices. In Walnut Ridge, Arkansas, for example, the local newspaper, the *Times Dispatch*, told the story of when the Beatles stopped into the town for a brief vacation at a nearby "dude ranch," arriving late on a Friday and leaving on Sunday morning. After they left, a young girl "took her shoes off and rubbed her feet in oil that had been spilled during servicing of the plane."[3] Her self-anointing was not an isolated incident, as the Beatles received this sort of veneration wherever they went. One fan "offered a photographer $10 for the electrical cord to his camera 'because it was used to photograph the Beatles.'"[4] Fans wrote and asked band members for anything: "a lock of hair, a smoked cigarette, a thread from your coat, a button from your shirt, a piece of old toast, or a bristle from your toothbrush," and if the request were honored, fans promised, "I would treasure it forever."[5] The craze reached ridiculous proportions. People attempted to purchase shaving foam used by the Beatles and the bedsheets they slept in.[6]

When fans weren't seeking items that had been in some way connected to the band (i.e., holy relics), they forced their sick and needy onto them with the hope of healing. Beatles press officer Derek Taylor allegedly said, "It's as if they've founded a new religion. . . . Cripples threw away their sticks. Sick people rushed up to the car as if a touch from one of the boys would make them well again. Old women stood watching with their grandchildren. . . . It was as if some savior had arrived and people were happy and relieved, as if things somehow were going to be better now."[7] Whatever else this might be— hyperbole, fandom, appreciation of a musical phenomenon, and so on—one cannot deny that stories such as these suggest a deification of the band in the minds of at least some of its fans. And this type of fan was found everywhere in the world.[8] As expressed in Jonathan Miller's *Partisan Review* piece in 1964, "all over the place there are icons, devotional photos and illuminated missals which keep the tiny earthbound fans in touch with the provocatively absconded deities."[9] A great gravitational force had entered the world: crime itself, George Harrison said in the *Anthology*, stopped for the ten minutes while the Beatles were on *The Ed Sullivan Show*.[10] Their legacy endures even today, as memories still move fans on a profound (almost spiritual) level: teenage girls who were at the Walnut Ridge airport when the Beatles passed through remember the event and still speak about it with giddiness almost six decades later, according to Walnut Ridge's mayor, Charles Snapp.[11]

The deification of the Beatles and the band's relationship to religion goes further, however, as we learn something about ourselves by looking at the ways in which people discuss the legacy of the Beatles *today*. Facts and events that would be irrelevant in any other band's story become important in the Beatles story, and they are treated with an extra measure of reverence. For example, the group started and ended in religious contexts. The beginning of the band, as extensively documented by Mark Lewisohn and others, found Lennon and McCartney meeting each other for the first time at a church (St. Peter's in Woolton), where Lennon played popular rock hits with the Quarrymen.[12] And the band's ending, on April 10, 1970, after McCartney's announcement that the band was splitting up, finds Harrison being interviewed for BBC1's show about theology and the philosophy of religion, *Fact or Fantasy?*, during the "God slot" discussing "prayer and meditation."[13] Other scholars offer similarly religious assessments of the band's history, like Michael Shelden, who draws attention to the Beatles' heavenward trajectory from basement (Cavern Club) to roof (final concert).[14] Shelden also describes the forces of fate that pushed McCartney and Harrison into Lennon's art-school orbit and the impact of freakishly cold weather—colder than

Britain had seen in two hundred years[15]—that kept people home and listening to their radios in the winter of 1962–63. Here and elsewhere, language of "necessity" or "fate" is used to describe the Beatles story; these are historic philosophical and religious concepts insofar as they presume that the world is governed by some *telos*.

All of this is to say, of course, that disinterested observers saw the mythologization of the Beatles occurring right before their eyes. These are the kinds of myths we tell about religious figures, stories that confer on them greater authority than they might otherwise have. The Beatles, then, help us understand our own religiously significant meaning-making process, a conversation that includes what their lives, lyrics, and music mean *for us*.

Even the band's individual members and those in their orbit were not immune to this sort of characterization. When retelling their story in the *Anthology*, the Beatles decided to look back at their time in Liverpool with a clip from *Help!* in which they say, "let's go back to the temple." Of course, they had more appropriate lines from which to choose if they wanted to discuss their childhoods in Liverpool ("Get back to where you once belonged"), but they chose a line with religious significance, and fans often visit Liverpool as a "pilgrimage." When considering the implications of tinkering with Beatles music for use in Cirque du Soleil's show *Love*, George Martin thought it was akin to tampering with the "holy grail." Individually, too, the Beatles talked about their own religious journeys and the band's religious significance (as the essays in part 2 of this volume make clear). Harrison, for example, described the BBC's global broadcasting of "All You Need Is Love" as "a subtle bit of PR for God."[16] McCartney described his inspiration for "Yesterday" as the reason he "believes in magic"; the song came to him in a dream, as if revealed by an otherworldly source.[17] Starr's calling to the drums was similarly magical.[18] Some Beatles songs offer a similar "call and response" style that mirrors what churches practice in the recitation of liturgy (e.g., "With a Little Help from My Friends"). Harrison described Starr's addition to the band in terms of necessity; he was "the one." I could go on, but the point should be clear: the Beatles were and are treated and seen as something otherworldly, *super*natural, necessary (in the philosophical sense), and meaningful.

To explore the ways in which the Beatles relate to religion, in what follows, I situate the band in its larger historical and religious context by showing what the events of one season—spring 1966—may reveal about religious shifts under way in the 1960s and movements in the philosophy of religion and theology in the nineteenth and twentieth centuries.

Music of the Future

In the fall of 1965, as the Beatles' producer, George Martin, added his baroque touch to John Lennon's retrospective "In My Life," *Time* magazine ran a story about a fringe group of religion scholars in the United States. These self-titled "radical theologians" were willing to reconsider the most basic, axiomatic assumptions that Christian theologians had accepted for centuries. In response to the unprecedented nature of their inquiry, many in the old guard of the academic and ecclesial mainstream saw their work as dangerous, antithetical to the theologian's task. But these new, young, avant-garde thinkers drew so much attention that six months later, *Time* revisited the story. On April 8, 1966, during the same week as the Beatles began work on one of the most ambitious and forward-looking songs in pop music history ("Tomorrow Never Knows"), *Time* plastered the radical theologians' central concern as a question in bold red ink on an otherwise black cover: "Is God Dead?"[19]

By the 1960s, the "death of God" was a well-worn concept among academics. For almost a century—through a global pandemic, an economic depression, and two world wars—scholars had wrestled with the writings of Friedrich Nietzsche, who warned that Christianity was losing its moral influence in the world. A few of this book's contributors bring Nietzsche into their discussion of the Beatles and religion, and for good reason. In the spring of 1966, Lennon was certainly interested in the philosopher and religion more broadly, having (a) mused to Maureen Cleeve that Christianity "will vanish and shrink" in the infamous "more popular than Jesus" interview and (b) sought out Nietzsche's writings himself. In early March of that year, Lennon asked Barry Miles if the Indica Bookshop in London had any works by "Nitz Ga," an accidental mispronunciation of the surname "Nietzsche."[20] As Miles scanned his shelves, Lennon perused a recent addition to the bookshop's inventory, *The Psychedelic Experience*, Timothy Leary's "how to" guide for LSD trips, designed to facilitate the taker's mystical "ego death" in a nonthreatening way based on the *Tibetan Book of the Dead*. Miles also sold him *The Portable Nietzsche*, a popular anthology of Nietzsche's "greatest hits," as it were. We can see clearly the influence of *The Psychedelic Experience* on Lennon's lyrics, but the extent to which Nietzsche influenced Lennon is less clear, certainly not as overt as in the cases of, say, Jim Morrison or Robert Plant, both of whom openly embraced Nietzsche, either in a Dionysian stage persona or as an intellectual interest.[21]

We do know, however, that Lennon's sentiments regarding religion are of one mind with Nietzsche's and that the Beatles, more than the Doors or Led

Zeppelin, participated in the "death of God" drama that Nietzsche saw coming. By "death of God," Nietzsche means that, although people once had the stable and predictable presence of God around which to orient their lives and in accordance with which to make moral choices, Christianity's central claims became increasingly incredible and its practices unlivable. Like a madman shouting in a peaceful marketplace, Nietzsche warned that Christian faith will eventually cease to speak words of wisdom to receptive hearts and minds, leading to an inevitable collapse into nihilism.[22] He speaks of it as if it already happened. "What I relate is the history of the next two centuries," Nietzsche writes in 1888, and it "can no longer come differently.... Necessity itself is at work here. This future speaks even now in a hundred signs, this destiny announces itself everywhere; for this *music of the future* all ears are cocked even now."[23]

Does Nietzsche's assessment of the situation fit the facts on the ground in the tumultuous 1960s? Was Christianity losing influence in the Western world? In the United Kingdom, this shift was accelerated (if not partially brought about) by a confluence of antiestablishment factors: a youth culture engaged in a mutually invigorating relationship with the Beatles and their music, the scandalous behavior of some of Britain's public servants (e.g., the Profumo Affair), the expansion of liberties to include family planning (the pill), and the loosening strictures on artists that gave them freedom to push the boundaries of what was considered socially acceptable (e.g., *Lady Chatterley's Lover*). Moreover, a younger generation benefited from the postwar economic boom (especially in the United States), which led not only to the liberal purchasing of albums and other memorabilia but also to the diminishing force of the values of older generations.[24] Christian faith was less compelling when people lived in peace and had many of their financial needs met.

In *The Religious Crisis of the 1960s*, Hugh McLeod sees in British and US history that the "long sixties" (1958–74), which closely resemble the years of the Beatles from their founding until their official dissolution, stand out as an example of shifting religious sensibilities. "In the religious history of the west," McLeod writes, "these years may come to be seen as marking a rupture as profound as that brought about by the Reformation."[25] He portrays the decade as "the end of Christendom," which resulted in "the journey from Christian country to civilized country."[26] Across the Atlantic, the United States was undergoing religious shifts as well. In *America Divided: The Civil War of the 1960s*, Maurice Isserman and Michael Kazin make a bold claim: "Nothing changed so profoundly in the United States during the 1960s as American religion," a claim that they realize is "a startling statement."[27]

Within the "long sixties," two years were particularly disruptive and, therefore, pivotal. These two years, moreover, track with significant events in the Beatles' history. First, Callum Brown argues that 1963, the same year as Beatlemania erupted in Britain, was "when Christian culture, as a hegemonic feature of British society, died and instigated sharpened gradients of decline in virtually all statistical indicators of religiosity and social conservatism."[28] Second, McLeod identifies 1967 as the pivotal year of religious change—the year of "Strawberry Fields Forever" and "Penny Lane," *Sgt. Pepper* and the Summer of Love, "All You Need Is Love" on *Our World*, the first visit with the Maharishi Mahesh Yogi in Wales, and the conclusion of the Beatles engagement with psychedelia in the various *Magical Mystery Tour* releases.[29] These religious shifts were felt in the United States, too. In *The Sixties Spiritual Awakening*, Robert Elwood says, "1967 was a hinge year, a time of epochal turning for American religion." He proceeds to describe the "smoldering year" as the time when "modern civil religion turned decisively to radical pluralism."[30]

Other historians go further, making the link between religious change in the 1960s and the Beatles more explicit. For example, Adrian Hastings suggests that the correlation between major Beatles events and shifts in religion do in fact suggest causation, as he lays some of these religious changes squarely at the feet of the Beatles and their "anti-structured world of class" that resulted in "a movement of basic secularization—a decline in any sort of Church commitment by ordinary people."[31] And some historians of religion even separate epochs by pre-Beatles and post-Beatles visits to their country, like David Hilliard. When discussing religion on the Australian landscape in the 1960s, Hilliard says, "In Australia, the 'remembered sixties' may be taken to begin in 1964, with the visit to Australia of the Beatles."[32]

Survey data support these contentions that significant religious shifts were under way during the pivotal decade.[33] Organized (Christian) religious beliefs and practices noticeably declined in the 1960s. McLeod says, "nearly every Western country saw a drop in church-going, and in some cases the drop was dramatic."[34] Not only church attendance but other aspects of religious life were changing, too: decreasing proportions of couples marrying in a church, fewer baptized children in relation to birth rates, falling rates of men willing to become clergy (which, therefore, resulted in fewer ordinations), and "a modest increase in the numbers of those professing other religions."[35] Christian worldviews, like all totalizing metanarratives of the time, were losing their influence.[36]

Nowhere to Go

While scholars agree that the 1960s were a pivotal decade for religion in Europe and America, and while they agree that the Beatles were involved, understanding their role in relation to religious shifts is a matter of debate. Were the Beatles simply responding to events "on the ground" and, therefore, acting as a mirror to the changing cultural and religious landscapes? Or were they shaping the (counter)culture in distinct antireligious ways during the 1960s? Several essays in this book attempt to answer these questions, and most argue that it was some combination of the two. That is, the Beatles were *both* responsive to and instigators of a shift in religious sensibilities during the period.

As a way to understand the context and the "new" thing the Beatles offered, consider the world out of which the Beatles came, as described in part 1 of this volume. The Beatles were born into and as children played among war ruins. Other than London, Liverpool was the second-hardest-hit by German air raids in the Second World War, the war itself being the largest global conflict in history. A distinct theological perspective emerged from the global calamity and became dominant in the interwar period—neo-orthodoxy, also known as the "theology of crisis"—with popular figureheads like Karl Barth in Europe and Reinhold Niebuhr in America. Niebuhr, of course, has been credited with the composition of the Serenity Prayer, the opening line of which sums up the basic outlook of the period: "God, grant me the serenity to accept the things I cannot change." One of the radical theologians mentioned above, William Hamilton, finds it understandable that people would gravitate toward neo-orthodoxy, because "just as we were learning despair and tragedy from daily events, the theological equipment was there to help us interpret what was happening. Neo-orthodoxy was in part a pessimistic theology" that, even though it began as a "radical protest against liberal conformism, became one of the fashionable ideologies for the Eisenhower period in American intellectual life."[37]

However, for the 1960s youth, freed from mandatory National Service in the United Kingdom or having grown up with financial stability in the postwar United States, "pessimism doesn't persuade anymore."[38] People wanted not lower but *higher* expectations of what a unified society could do, and they saw that kind of optimism in many places: Kenneth Boulding, Marshall McLuhan, Lionel Trilling, John Cage, and importantly, the Beatles. After seeing *A Hard Day's Night*, Hamilton and other radical theologians saw kindred spirits in the Fab Four, who escaped "from the prison-like television studio, where worldly men are trying to get them to perform properly, and flee to an open field for a few surrealistic moments of jumping, dancing, abandon. This movie," Hamilton continues, "and perhaps even the famous Beatles' sound, is part of this mood of celebration and rejoicing."[39] The movie itself, in the words of a *New Republic* film critic, "floats above despair and alienation."[40] Like the Beatles, the radical theologians see themselves as "the not-havers, whose undialectical *yes* to the world is balanced by a *no* to God."[41] So, one explanatory framework (or "model") for understanding the relationship between the Beatles and religion locates them in a decades-long struggle to find meaning in a world that used to find its purpose, its *telos*, its meaning from without (i.e., from God) but was now contending with secularization, economic prosperity, and the advancement of the sciences.

But what of the religious impulse so firmly rooted in the human mind and heart? What of the desire for transcendence? One would expect it to linger. The world's great wisdom traditions, many of which are rooted in a belief that this world is not all there is, gave people a target for their religious impulses. The impulse to be devoted to something greater than oneself is, if not universal, certainly widespread. But what does one do when the religious impulse has no credible supernatural entity to which it can attach itself? What does one do when "that magic feeling" has "nowhere to go"?

Nietzsche argues that people overcome nihilism by forging new values. In the vacuum left by Christianity's absence, people would have to choose for themselves what ultimate authority they would recognize, and the search for an authority will inevitably give rise to revolutionary figures who will lead the society toward those new values. In the 1960s, society's gaze drifted from heaven to earth and the possibility of creating a Great Society here and now. Many worthy contenders emerged to stand in as substitutes. Each provided a way for people to channel the religious impulse toward solving specific social problems, ways in which social upheaval created conditions under which old values were replaced by activism in the name of "new values."[42]

For 1960s radical theologians, progress in these social causes shows a secular gospel at work in several areas. First, the United States in the 1960s reinvigorated its religious impulse by channeling it toward the critique of the materialism of "godless communism" through unfettered commercial production and a Cold War national pride. This left the United States in an interesting religious situation: instead of defending a distinctively "Christian" United States, leaders defended something more closely resembling a broadly construed "theism," according to which capitalists believe in God and communists do not. The Beatles, for their part, pushed against this sort of othering, collapsing an "us versus them" distinction by humorously describing the humanity of a Russian spy in "Back in the USSR," a song written from the perspective of a grateful operative returning back to the motherland while at the same time modeling the benefits of living in a free society.[43] History records the Beatles as having an enormous influence on these religio-political conflicts.[44] The former general secretary of the Communist Party Mikhail Gorbachev allegedly offered this remarkable assessment of their influence: "More than any ideology, more than any religion, more than Vietnam or any war or nuclear bomb," he said, "the single most important reason for the diffusion of the Cold War was . . . the Beatles."[45] Second, the sixties also offered the struggle for civil rights as a pathway for channeling religious devotion toward a positive social outcome.[46] The Beatles were involved in collapsing racial distinctions as well. They used their influence to join the cause by refusing to play to segregated audiences, which had the immediate and consequential result of an integrated concert in Jacksonville, Florida, on September 11, 1964. Third, one could channel one's religious impulse toward causes that support gender parity. Following the 1963 publication of Betty Friedan's *The Feminine Mystique*, sales of the book soared in 1964, giving voice to and permission for women to liberate themselves from their quiet discontent. The Beatles, too, entered this arena, but inconsistently and not in their personal lives.[47] Rather, it was in their music that they described strong women exercising their agency.[48]

In a sense, then, the Beatles became Nietzsche's *Übermenschen*, the "super men" who "laid out a few paths for people to follow."[49] However noble and necessary the social causes were into which people poured their energies, they were not the routes that all people took in the 1960s. For many at that time, particularly young women, the religious impulse was directed at the Beatles themselves, which is to say, a not insignificant portion of British and US society deified the Beatles (as the essays in part 3 of this book make clear). Young Americans needed a target for their worship, and they found it in February 1964, when the Beatles played *The Ed Sullivan Show*. Stephen Prothero, in his book *Religious Literacy*, illustrates one of the downstream effects of the Beatles' deification vis-à-vis traditional Christianity: "A few years ago no one in Jay Leno's *Tonight Show* audience could name any of Jesus' twelve apostles, but everyone, it seemed, was able to list the four Beatles."[50]

Of course, paradoxically, even though the Beatles spoke honestly about moments they understood to be magical or spiritually significant, they also separated themselves from the notion that they were always steering the ship themselves. The band's members recognized that "the Beatles" was always greater than the sum of its parts. The band's name towers over its members in the opening credits of the *Anthology*. Band members came to see their creation ("the Beatles") as a fan might, as "a remote thing," or as "those other Beatles" (Lennon's attempt at quelling the "Jesus Controversy"). McCartney has said in several interviews that the Beatles took on a life of their own: "You just did it, and you weren't aware of any significance. It was just a band." And only when his children brought home history books did it dawn on him that he was involved in something much, much greater than himself.[51] Harrison, too, described the disconnect between the public perception of the band and what they were actually doing: "We're not trying to do anything. That's the big joke. . . . But we don't plan anything. We don't do anything. All we do is just keep on being ourselves. It just comes out. It's the Beatles."[52]

What would Nietzsche think? The religious phenomenon of the Beatles would probably have confounded Nietzsche rather than ameliorate his worries over nihilism's march. While it is true that Nietzsche was one of the "people we like," considered for inclusion on the cover of *Sgt. Pepper*, and while Lennon's "Nowhere Man" bears striking resemblance to Nietzsche's "last man," in other areas the Beatles were decidedly anti-Nietzschean.[53] The use of mind-altering drugs, for example, would probably have disappointed Nietzsche. The philosopher argued that one should accept reality at all costs (per his "eternal recurrence" doctrine), to take joy in the actual world, not a fictitious, escapist world.[54] Half the group (Lennon and Starr) seriously struggled with substance abuse, while the other half saw drugs as an enhancement to life. Harrison was on a real quest for spiritual wisdom, and McCartney "took [LSD] with a deliberate purpose in mind: to find the answer to what life is all about."[55] That is to say, Harrison and McCartney were less interested in escaping reality and more in augmenting it, *adding to* rather than detracting from. And for the two of them, it worked.[56]

In sum, religious sensibilities were shifting in the 1960s away from traditional (i.e., Christian) worldviews, and a number of worthy social causes rushed in to fill the gap. For a large number of Americans, the Beatles themselves came to occupy a sacred role normally reserved for religious figures. But the Beatles were nothing if not always on the move, and in response to their deification and its convoluted aftermath, they stopped touring, invested heavily in the studio, and sought wisdom elsewhere.

Go East, Young Men

While there were certainly members of minority religious communities in Liverpool in the mid-twentieth century, the city offered two main religious options, both of which were Christian (Protestant and Catholic). Part 1 of this book looks at how the Beatles were shaped by these identities. However, these traditional forms of faith failed to speak to the Beatles; indeed, some of their fans conferred on them religious authority that they never asked for or wanted. Lennon saw the rise of interest in alternative spiritualities in the broader context of the diminishing influence of the Western Christian religious establishment: "The youth of today are really looking for some answers—for proper answers the established church can't give them, their parents can't give them, material things can't give them."[57] In looking to the wisdom traditions of Asia, especially India, for spiritual insight, the Beatles facilitated a transcultural communication unseen throughout modern history. They, perhaps more than any of their predecessors, opened up the modern West to Hinduism and its syncretic offshoots.

The story of the Beatles' relationship with India is a long one, stretching back into their early years.[58] It began as a childish fascination with the "crazy guy" on television, the Maharishi Mahesh Yogi, who traveled around trying "to heal the world" with Transcendental Meditation (TM), a practice of focused, auditory entrancement devised and adapted from the *Yoga Sutras* and other Indian texts. A young Paul McCartney loved his "giggly" laugh.[59] Mahesh's later influence on the Beatles is due in part to the marriage of George Harrison and Patti Boyd. Harrison was intrigued by the sitar on the set of the movie *Help!*, and not long after *Rubber Soul*'s "Norwegian Wood," the first commercially successful song with Indian instrumentation, Harrison and Boyd traveled to Mumbai. Harrison eventually asked the world-renowned sitar player Ravi Shankar for lessons. In 1967, Boyd heard Mahesh speak, and in August of that same year, she convinced all four Beatles to join her for another speech in London. After his talk, they were invited to Wales for a "study session" with the Maharishi, which was cut short by the unexpected and untimely death of their friend and manager, Brian Epstein. Mahesh offered some words to help them cope with the tragic loss, and they planned to visit his private retreat in Rishikesh, India, the following winter. Other celebrities joined them there: Mike Love of the Beach Boys, Mia Farrow (and sister Prudence), Donovan, and others. They also met a young seeker named Paul Saltzman, who later documented the experience in his 2020 film *Meeting the Beatles in India*. Saltzman's documentary provides a firsthand account of their time in Rishikesh: he recounts private conversations and sacred moments (e.g., a worshipful musical experience with Harrison). He also tapped the eminent Beatles scholar Mark Lewisohn to accompany him to India and discuss *The Beatles* (the White Album).

What was it about Indian spirituality that resonated so deeply with Harrison and at least caught the attention of the other Beatles for a time? To answer this question, consider how the interests and history of the Beatles dovetail with the thrust of Hinduism and Asian religions more broadly. Most obviously, the Beatles endorsed a moral law of cause and effect (i.e., the principle of *karma*) in what might be the most enduring swan song in rock music history from *Abbey Road*: "The love you take is equal to the love you make."

Additionally, the Hindu tradition posits four aims or goals of life, the first two of which fall on the Path of Desire and were well familiar to the Beatles. The first aim is pleasure: pure, unalloyed, sensory stimulation, like food, drink, drugs, and sex. This was no doubt the mood or spirit of the Beatles in Hamburg. Unlike some rigid religious sects, in the Hindu tradition, pleasure is not inherently bad or evil; in fact, the religion offers suggestions on how to attain it if, indeed, that is what one wants. "Hinduism was valued as being inclusive," Hugh MacLeod writes in *The Religious Crisis of the 1960s*, "as emphasizing individual experience more than dogma, and as having a positive view of sex."[60] However, the Hindu tradition also suggests that focusing one's life on pleasure will be ultimately unsatisfying because pleasure is fleeting and overly concerned with the self. The Harrison who was deported from Hamburg matured into the Harrison who visited San Francisco in the middle of the Summer of Love and was disheartened. Instead of finding young wisdom seekers in "a brilliant place," he found the Haight-Ashbury "full of horrible, spotty, drop-out kids on drugs." Reflecting on the disconnect between his expectations and reality, Harrison later said, "It turned me right off the whole scene.... It was terrible."[61] India tells us why: if people's focus is on themselves and their own wants/desires, their focus is too small.

If one moves from pleasure to the next goal on the Hindu Path of Desire—success—one has three avenues in which to pursue it: wealth, power, and fame. Beatlemania, of course, gave the Fab Four all three, and, again, Hinduism says that these measures of success are not bad in themselves. But just as with pleasure, if one pursues success exclusively, one will not be satisfied. Midcareer, just before the Beatles' artistic ambitions were unleashed, one can see the truth of this assertion in the forlorn faces gracing the cover of *Beatles for Sale*. Success had not satisfied the Beatles, and Hinduism offers an explanation: the problem is not desire itself but, rather, desiring things at the wrong time or for an inappropriate duration. Moreover, wealth, power, and fame are competitive values. Worse still, success itself is fleeting, and the drive for it is insatiable. The image of a donkey moving forward because its driver has mounted a carrot atop its harness originated in ancient Hindu texts.[62] "Unlike mental and spiritual values," Huston Smith writes, wealth, power, and fame "do not multiply when shared; they cannot be distributed without diminishing one's own portion."[63] Harrison "felt that there was much more to life than the considerable wealth which he was accumulating as a Beatle."[64] The Beatles, more than most, knew that worldly success does not ultimately satisfy.

Only when one makes the journey from the Path of Desire to the Path of Renunciation does one begin to make progress in Hinduism, but here three of the Beatles lost interest. Only after the breakup did they approximate something resembling the third goal of life, duty to others, or the fourth: liberation from the cycle of birth, death, and rebirth. Between Desire and Renunciation, the Beatles' Romantic sympathies took over, and they strove for artistic excellence by pushing their music forward. With the exception of Harrison, the Beatles' interest in Indian religion dwindled.

With respect to Rishikesh, scandal engulfed Mahesh when he faced (unproved) accusations of sexual impropriety and financial compensation unbecoming of a spiritual leader. Following the scandal, the Beatles left the retreat center one by one. Lennon resolved to prevent his money from being stolen by a man he perceived to be a fraud.[65] McCartney was more interested in the novel sounds of Indian instrumentation than in the religion or culture of India. He watched as his friend Lennon strolled around with Mahesh in a manner more "like school" than a vacation or a spiritual retreat.[66] Starr was uncomfortable being separated from his growing family for so long a time, and he disliked the food in India; cans of baked beans filled his suitcase, and he left the ashram as soon as his supply was gone.

Harrison's search was only just beginning, however, and he did not leave India so easily. Some Hindu ideas made their way into his Beatles songs, like *Sgt. Pepper*'s "Within You, Without You." Reflecting on the superficiality of worldly success, Harrison asks what good it is for people to "gain the world" but "lose their soul." George Martin's score blends musical ideas in an almost conversational back and forth between Western and Eastern stringed instruments, while the lyrics express the notion of the self as part of something larger. Whereas you may have been ignorant of your true essence, hiding "behind a wall of illusion," you are, nevertheless, able to see "beyond yourself," and "then you may find peace of mind" by realizing that "it's all within yourself." Of course, this resonates with a key concept that leads to liberation in Indian philosophy of religion, that one's inner *atman* (roughly translated "soul") is identical with the God of the universe, *Brahman*. And in fact, if one can peel away layers of ignorance, one can find this God deep inside a person and at the same time cosmically underpinning everything that exists; God is *simultaneously* "within you and without you." Metaphors break down, even for the two characters discussing the matter in sacred Hindu texts (e.g., a conversation between Svetaketu and his father in the *Upanishads*), but like salt disappearing into water, the taste illustrates the soul's continued existence, and yet it cannot be seen or touched. "An invisible and subtle essence is the Spirit of the whole universe. That is Reality. That is Truth," says Svetaketu's father, and "Thou art that." When a person realizes that *atman* is *Brahman*, they find release: "I shall wander in this world until I attain liberation; but then I shall go and reach my Home" (*Chandogya Upanishad* 6.12–14). Or, in Harrison's own words from his 1968 *Rolling Stone* interview, people "haven't been able to see God because he is hidden in themselves. All the time people concentrate their energies and activities outwards on this surface level that we live on," but "it's only by turning your concentration and directing it inwardly, in a form of meditation, that you can see your own god in there."[67]

For Harrison more than the others, the faith that began in his Beatles years continued throughout his life, inspiring not only charity and activism but also the cultivation of lifelong relationships. Ravi Shankar came to visit Harrison shortly before Harrison died in 2001. When he did pass, Harrison was surrounded by family and Krishna devotees, and his ashes were scattered in the Ganges. A friend of his remarked, "He was a very spiritual person, who was unafraid to die," and he "passed from this world with the scent of incense in his nostrils, while his friends chanted the praises of Krishna. His body was covered with a yellow silk blanket, and sprinkled with rose petals and holy water."[68]

The Beatles' relationship with the Maharishi was mutually beneficial while it lasted: the Beatles brought Mahesh some money and a wider audience, while Mahesh brought TM to the Beatles and a sense of peace and quiet in early 1968, during which they wrote dozens of songs that ended up on the White Album. "I thought he made a lot of sense. I think we all did," McCartney recalled later. "He said that with a simple system of meditation . . . you could improve the quality of life and find some sort of meaning in doing so."[69]

Another explanation of TM's appeal is that it let the Beatles do and believe as they pleased. For Harrison, TM permitted a Hindu/Christian hybrid: "It was only through India and through Hinduism and through yogis and through meditation that I learned about Christ and what Christ really meant and stood for. . . . The Christ-consciousness is like the Krishna-consciousness, which is absolute and it is in every speck of creation."[70] Notwithstanding incompatible metaphysics (cyclical versus linear time), Harrison subscribed to them both simultaneously. Contradictions such as these have given rise to a criticism of

TM, namely, that it lacks any actual religious content. It is "not really a Hindu practice," Paul Oliver explains in *Hinduism and the 1960s*, but rather "a form of secular meditation without any spiritual content" that has an "absence of scriptures, and of a clear belief system."[71] So, even though the Beatles engaged with the ancient Asian wisdom tradition of Hinduism (and flirted with Taoism[72] and Buddhism[73]), between the Hindu paths of Desire and Renunciation, the Beatles took a detour, making India just one stop on a longer journey.

Models and Significance

Despite multitudes of books on the Beatles, even those written or authorized by the Beatles themselves, "something mysterious remains," as noted by Adam Gotnip in the *New Yorker*. And "that mysterious thing, as always in the lives of artists, is how they did what they did." As mentioned above, "There is something fated about the Beatles."[74] One of these mysteries lies in the Beatles' relationship to our highest values, which, borrowing from Paul Tillich, is to say their relationship to the things that concern us ultimately or, simpler still, their relationship to religion.

To help elucidate the relationship between the Beatles and religion, one may construct various "models" of their relationship. These models act as explanations of their religious significance in much the same way as John Godfrey Saxe's "Blind Men and the Elephant," a story in which six blind men attempt to describe an elephant based on what they can experience through touch alone. The subject can and should be looked at from multiple angles, which, taken together, provide a more complete picture of the relationship between the Beatles and religion. Each model should offer a response to at least one of three questions, which recur throughout this book: First, did the Beatles have a religious (or *anti*religious) message they sought to convey? Second, what does it say about *us*—our desire for certainty, our search for significance, our need for prophets and leaders—that we looked to the Beatles for meaning in an otherwise incomprehensible decade? Third, how far do the Beatles' intentions for their own music go toward explaining their religious significance? Many of this book's contributors assume that audience reception is as fruitful an inquiry as their own goals when looking for the meaning of a particular lyric, song, or album.

The first model, described above, suggests that the Beatles were the most significant artistic expression of the search for meaning amid the decline of traditional Western Christianity. Call this the "meaning-making" model (or the

"Lennon model," since it was he who gave voice to it and spawned the Jesus Controversy in the US South). Allegiances shifted from traditional forms of faith to the Beatles themselves. As Robin Sylvan argues in *Traces of the Spirit: The Religious Dimensions of Popular Music*:

> Observers of culture and scholars of religion have said many things about the slow decline of religion and the death of God in Western civilization. Yet for millions of people... religion and God are not dead, but very much alive and well and dancing to the beat of popular music; the religious impulse has simply migrated to another sector of the culture, a sector in which religious sensibilities have flourished and made an enormous impact on a large portion of the population. Right under our noses, a significant religious phenomenon is taking place, one which constitutes an important development in the Western religious and cultural landscape.[75]

It is not the case that the religious impulse has disappeared altogether. Rather, Sylvan suggests, it has "migrated" to popular music in the wake of the Beatles. "I can lose myself in music," Morgan Freeman says in *The Story of God*. "I hear it. I feel it. And it transports me to another time and place. Some would call it a religious experience. Can't say that I disagree."[76]

Interestingly, the "meaning-making" model is problematized by the responses of some members of Britain's clergy to the Beatles phenomenon. When young people became infatuated with the band (and not church), religious leaders faced a choice: either adapt their methods or wither on the vine. Facing dwindling numbers, some chose to engage the youth by attempting to bring Beatles enthusiasm into their services instead of risking extinction. Cognizant of this fact, the archbishop of Canterbury, for example, said the Beatles' appeal "has to be understood and lived with," not ignored.[77] Other ministers were far less measured, however, and they attempted to hijack the Beatles to serve religious ends. Bishop Ian Ramsey said that for some fans, "the Beatles might be one stage in the progress toward a cosmic disclosure."[78] Other ministers, like Rev. Robert Bailey, gave sermons about Beatles' songs and occasionally even wore a Beatles wig. Ronald Gibbins, a Methodist minister, believed "the Beatles could save religion or found a religion of their own," and he invited them to discuss his ideas with younger members of his congregation.[79] These and other religious figures adapted their style and message to reinvigorate their diminishing platforms, latching onto the Beatles' rising star so as to not disappear entirely. That is to say, some liberal Christian leaders rode the coattails of the Beatles out of irrelevance.

Such efforts led to further divisions in the faith writ large, as Christian churches splintered between those with "seeker"-friendly goals and those that had a "faithful" or "traditional" self-understanding. To the "faithful," using the Beatles in church appeared as a shameless marketing ploy, placing religion on the shelf as another product alongside Beatles memorabilia. Anne Scott-James urged a reorientation back to Christianity's essence when she suggested that "if a person cannot win a congregation with dignity, he might as well give up."[80] Similar critiques cautioned Christians against losing their souls in a "desperate anxiety to be modern at all costs."[81] And the division between seeker-friendly and traditional churches persists to this day.

A second model wrestles with the "message" question, asking whether the Beatles actually were a "band of evangelists" with a gospel to share. While joining Paul Saltzman for the filming of *Meeting the Beatles in India*, the eminent Beatles historian Mark Lewisohn says, "The Beatles didn't preach any message. And those who read messages into their work are barking up the wrong tree because they were not 'message givers' particularly." Rather, "they were just writing for themselves." Even without a message, he says, their music helped others come into their own: they "empower people to think for themselves, to express themselves differently."[82] If Lewisohn is correct, the Beatles never sought to persuade anyone of any specific message, religious or otherwise, and efforts to understand what they were "really saying" are misguided. Lennon poked fun of those who sought some deeper meaning in their work: "I was just having a laugh, because there had been so much gobbledygook writing about *Sgt. Pepper*. People were saying, 'Play it backwards while standing on your head, and you'll get a secret message . . .' So this was just my way of saying, 'You are full of shit.'"[83] Interestingly, however, the words and actions of the Beatles challenge this interpretation. In the wake of the Jesus Controversy, Lennon argued against those who sent him spiteful letters, telling *Datebook*'s editor, Art Unger, "They don't want to know what's going on. You're lucky to get rid of them. So are we. . . . Let them move on. We obviously can't get through to them."[84] Lennon clearly wanted to "get through" to the readers of *Datebook*, if only for exculpation. Or look at the music itself; on the plain reading of several lyrics, an agenda is at work: "I'm here to show everybody the light" ("The Word"). Later, Lennon's "Hair Peace, Bed Peace" campaign was intended to change minds as well. Or consider Lennon's generational anthems (e.g., "Imagine" and "Give Peace a Chance"), which are nothing if not attempts to convey a message.

Convincing people to think for themselves (contra traditional authorities) and the promotion of peace are messages with religious significance, which leads to Steve Turner. In his thorough and fascinating book *The Gospel According to the Beatles*, Turner presents a "shaman model" for explaining the relationship between the Beatles and religion. He notes, "Although there were no precedents in Western pop music for musicians as spiritual leaders, there were in other cultures. The most pertinent was the tradition of the shaman in areas such as Africa, South America, and Siberia."[85] According to the "shaman model," the Beatles experienced a sort of hell and heaven (in that order) and reported back to their listeners what they had seen and heard on the journey. Turner's thesis is, of course, an echo of an earlier assessment of the relationship between the Beatles and religion coming from one of their contemporaries, Allen Ginsberg, whose engagement with India predated the Beatles' by several years. According to Ginsberg, the 1960s facilitated "breakthroughs of community spirit." He said, "Among the young we find a new breed . . . entering trance states to the electric vibrations of the Beatles who have borrowed shamanism from African sources."[86]

From the perspective of "religious studies," what exactly is the "shaman" role in the world's religions? Huston Smith, distinguished scholar of religion at Syracuse University for years and member of the 1960s Harvard Psychedelic Club that included Timothy Leary, has an answer.[87] According to Smith, the shaman can "bypass symbolism and perceive spiritual realities directly." One can "think of shamans as spiritual savants, savant being defined as a person whose talents . . . are exceptional to the point of belonging to a different order of magnitude."[88] As an explanation of the Beatles' songwriting talent, so far so good. But Smith also notes that shamans are "subject to severe physical and emotional traumas in their early years," and they "are able to heal themselves and reintegrate their lives in ways that place psychic if not cosmic powers at their disposal. These powers enable them to engage with spirits, both good and evil, drawing power from the former and battling the latter where need be. They are heavily engaged in healing, and appear to have preternatural powers to foretell the future and discern lost objects."[89] If the shaman role necessarily entails overcoming severe trauma in one's early years, perhaps Turner's model applies more to Lennon than to the other Beatles. Contrarily, if the shaman model relies on summoning supernatural powers instead of just heightened natural powers, it would apply least of all to Lennon, whose maturing atheism preventing such beliefs.

Still, comments by the individual Beatles seem to support this model. Harrison explains, "We're in a position to try things, to show people. . . . We can jump around and try new things which others can't or won't. Like drugs. People doing ordinary jobs just couldn't give the time we did to looking into all that."[90] For Turner, the Beatles played the role of shamans during 1966–70, promoting transcendence by advancing messages of love and freedom. He recognizes that some people will disagree with his model, thinking it "preposterous" that "the Beatles had any kind of gospel to spread."[91] Within this "message-giving" model, then, a debate exists between Lewisohn, who argues that the Beatles never intended to present a message, religious or otherwise, and on the other side, Turner, who argues that they acted as shamans to achieve transcendence and convey a message of love. (Of course, some of this debate can be attributed to inconsistency in the Beatles' own comments.)

A third model highlights the fact that the Beatles were the most commercially successful band at the same time that they were the world's most innovative band, and their experimentation in three areas (music, drugs, religion) all pushed toward the same deeply religious realization. Call this the "mystical union" model. Harrison's interest in Asian religion was complemented by Lennon's interest in "turning on" (i.e., dropping acid) and McCartney's interest in London's avant-garde art scene. A central feature of psychedelic drug use is the experience of an "ego" death and the merging of one's self into a larger sea of selves. This is what made the *Tibetan Book of the Dead* a fitting source for Timothy Leary on which to base *The Psychedelic Experience*. Both Hinduism and LSD drove this same point home: one can experience unity with something greater than oneself, and we are all connected, one to another.

McCartney's interest in London's avant-garde music of the time had the same result: to remove distinctions between "us" and "them," between what is "art" and what is not, such that sounds not normally considered "music" are reinterpreted as part of the show. George Martin says, "Paul was heavily into Stockhausen and John Cage and all the avant-garde artists."[92] One of the radical theologians mentioned above, William Hamilton, says that Cage's music serves as a kind of life-affirming "purposeless play" that has a distinct function, namely, "to remind people of the fact that *every* sound they hear is potentially music, if listened to in the right way."[93] This resonates with the interview the Beatles gave two days after their first *Ed Sullivan Show* performance, in which McCartney attempts (unsuccessfully) to help his interviewer recognize the ubiquity of music. "It's music, isn't it?" McCartney says, at which point he proceeds to make sounds that other people would not consider musical: "Bumm Bumm Bumm. . . . We try not to define our music because we get so many wrong classifications of it. It's no use. We just call it—music?" he says cheekily, "even if you don't."[94] The category of "music" is broad enough to include not only audience sounds but also tape loops, as in "Tomorrow Never Knows," which was inspired by Stockhausen's *Gesang der Jünglinge* (Song of the youths), which Stockhausen sought to perform as a religious song in religious contexts. McCartney was infatuated with Stockhausen and this song, as well as with John Cage.[95] "I heard about people like John Cage," he said, "and that he'd just performed a piece of music called 4′33″ (which is completely silent) during which if someone in the audience coughed, he would say, 'See?' Or someone would boo and he'd say, 'See?' It's not silence—it's music. I was intrigued by all of that. So those things started to be part of my life."[96]

From the avant-garde London underground, McCartney saw that music is a much broader category than hitherto assumed and that audience and performer merge into one. From India, Harrison learned that his soul (*atman*) was identical with the God of the universe (*Brahman*) and, in a sense, all is one in God. From psychedelics, Lennon learned that the "ego," which so often gets in the way of unity with others, could be chemically circumvented. Each of these interests drive toward the same deeply religious end: unity and oneness. Michael Baur identifies the Beatles' philosophy as "ideological monism," according to which "all existing things are modes or expressions of a single essence or substance which is essentially mental or spiritual in nature."[97] The idea of mystical union is not new; it has been a central feature of religious experiences throughout history. In the words of Walter Stace, "in this general experience of a unity, which the mystic believes to be in some sense ultimate and basic to the world, we have the very inner essence of all mystical experience."[98] Similarly, William James describes his experience with mystical union by saying, "The keynote of it is invariably one of reconciliation. It is as if the opposites of the world, whose contradictoriness and conflict make all our difficulties and troubles, were melded into a unity.... [This] monastic insight, in which the *other* in its various forms appears absorbed into the One," constitutes "the keynote of all mysticism."[99] So, according to the mystical union model, the interests of the three principal songwriters of the Beatles were all geared toward facilitating oneness with others and that which is ultimately real, which made their combination especially powerful.

These three models—meaning-making, message-giving, and mystical union—are not necessarily incompatible or mutually exclusive. Rather, they are mutually illuminating. In the meaning-making model, the Beatles were artistic manifestation of the search for values while Christianity was losing some of its influence. While they searched, the Beatles were simply being themselves and encouraging others to do the same (Lewisohn), but when their search yielded novel experiences and/or answers to existential questions, they could then relate their insights and experiences to others (Turner). And the most important insight they received, coming at them from all angles, was the value of oneness and unity (mystical union), which led to their efforts to collapse distinctions, to see others as a "Thou" and not an "it."

The Beatles and America

In *Speaking Words of Wisdom: The Beatles and Religion*, leading voices from a number of fields (religious studies, musicology, sociology, history, literature, media studies, philosophy) explore the subject of religion in the Beatles' lives, music, reception, and legacy.[100] As subsequent scholars look for the meaning of the Beatles phenomenon in the twentieth century, our hope is that this volume will provide a launching-off point for future academic research and popular appreciation by those who are interested in the ways in which the Beatles relate to religion. We explore the themes of tradition and change, Western societies (especially the United States) encountering Asian religious traditions, fundamentalist reactions to the Beatles' open-mindedness, the Beatles' attacks on organized religion, the metaphysics of selfhood in light of psychedelics, the deification of popular figures, and others.

Scholarly interest in the Beatles is rising. Young scholars, some of whom are included in this collection, have begun looking at the Beatles for what their story tells us about the place of the 1960s in the twentieth century, which is to say, as history. The Beatles were active during a pivotal decade in American history that is eerily similar to the times in which we currently live: political unrest, institutions under threat, failures of religious and political leadership, and so on. By looking at how the Beatles offered a counternarrative to the dominant religious and political leaders of their time, this book sheds light on the ways in which one might navigate current societal challenges. And the Beatles offer an opportunity to ask about human nature and the ways in which we individually and collectively look for and make meaning.

While it may initially seem odd that a book on a British band should be included in a book series called American Music History, for many reasons the Beatles belong in the American story just as much as they do in Britain. The band's early influences were clearly American: country music, rock music, soul. Not only were their influences American, but the Beatles are obviously major contributors to American music culture, as seen through the success of their early tours, Beatlemania, *Sgt. Pepper* inaugurating the "Summer of Love," and so on.

Furthermore, the relationship of the Beatles to their fans was different in the United States than it was in Britain. Jonathan Gould points out that "a great many more young people in America than in Britain really did regard the Beatles as the quasi-mythic figures depicted in the film [*Yellow Submarine*]."[101] This was different than the British view of the band, as noted by Nik Cohn in 1968: "In America and England they have become two entirely different things: in the States, where pop is followed with great solemnity by almost everyone intelligent under the age of thirty, there are still a great many people who take them seriously, who see them as divinities and hang upon their every utterance; in England, where pop remains mostly entertainment, they're seen as cranks, millionaire eccentrics in the grand manner—vaguely regrettable, maybe, but quite harmless."[102] Their outsized influence in the United States threatened those who would wish to divide people on the basis of arbitrary factors like race, gender, sexual orientation, and of course, religion. Hopelessly unaware of the irony, for example, robed Klansmen in the US South denounced the band's negative impact on the youth of the sixties.

In short, the United States has been the most significant and enduring audience for the Beatles. At the same time, it has also hosted some of the most vigilant, religiously themed opposition to them. In 1966, disk jockeys in the US South organized boycotts and bonfires of Beatles albums and memorabilia after Lennon said the Beatles were "more popular than Jesus." Of course, it went underreported that many of the DJs involved were simply attempting to raise their public profile. An interviewer asked the DJ who organized the largest of these public bonfires, "Do you feel you've accomplished all your goals in this campaign?" The DJ responded, "Yes. We've shown the Beatles we won't tolerate such foolishness. Besides, it put our little station on the map. Advertising income is up 36 percent."[103] Exploring the Beatles as part of the American Music History series permits both sorts of questions to be asked—veneration of them and opposition to them—in search of a better understanding of the relationship between the Beatles and religion.

NOTES

1. "Liverpool Cellar Clubs Rock to Beat Groups."
2. Quoted in Szatmary, *Rockin' in Time*, 114.
3. Tillman, "Life in Arkansas."
4. "Gambling City Liked Beatles."
5. M. Starr, *Ringo*, 89.
6. Greene, "Hotel Stripped Its Bed."
7. Aronowitz, "Return of the Beatles." Taylor regretted this statement, according to Turner, *Gospel*, 93, but his was not the only voice suggesting that what America was witnessing was religious in nature. See also Gould, *Can't Buy Me Love*, 340–43.
8. Woodhead, *How the Beatles Rocked the Kremlin*. Woodhead quotes many Russians who understood the Beatles in religious ways. "The Beatles turned tens of

millions of young people to another religion," one interview subject says, "and by the end of the eighties, the whole of Soviet ideology and Soviet power disappeared like a fog in the morning" (135).

9. Quoted in Gould, *Can't Buy Me Love*, 341.

10. Beatles, *Anthology*, 119.

11. Telephone correspondence with author, January 25, 2021.

12. Lewisohn, *Tune In*, 127–33.

13. Lewisohn, *Complete Beatles Chronicle*, 349.

14. Shelden, "Triumph of the Beatles."

15. S. Jones, "Coldest Winters."

16. Beatles, *Anthology*, 257.

17. Heinzerling, *McCartney 3, 2, 1*, episode 6.

18. R. Starr, "Meet Your Instructor," in *Drumming and Creative Collaboration*.

19. Elson, "Is God Dead?"

20. Spitz, *Beatles*, 600. See also Turner, *Beatles '66*, 135–36.

21. Huckvale, *Music for the Superman*, 188. See also Flynn, "Celebrating the Agony of Life."

22. Nietzsche, *Gay Science*, 181–82.

23. Nietzsche, *Will to Power*, 3.

24. Staley, *Beatles and Economics*, 5.

25. McLeod, *Religious Crisis*, 1.

26. Brown, "What Was the Religious Crisis?," 469.

27. Isserman and Kazin, *America Divided*, 241.

28. Brown, *Death of Christian Britain*, 1. See also Brown, "What Was the Religious Crisis?," 472.

29. McLeod, *Religious Crisis*, 259.

30. Elwood, *Sixties Spiritual Awakening*, 176–77. It is worth noting that others locate the tumultuous year of 1968 as the latter hinge of history; see, e.g., Jenkins, "Religious World Changed."

31. Hastings, *History of English Christianity*, 515–16, 551.

32. Hilliard, "Religious Crisis," 210.

33. Brown, "What Was the Religious Crisis?," 469–70. See also McLeod, *Religious Crisis*, 212.

34. McLeod, *Religious Crisis*, 1.

35. Ibid., 1.

36. For a prescient philosophical explanation of the phenomenon, see Lyotard, *Postmodern Condition*.

37. Hamilton, "New Optimism," 158.

38. Ibid., 158.

39. Ibid., 163.

40. Quoted in ibid., 164.

41. Ibid., 169.

42. Nietzsche, *Will to Power*, 4.

43. Unexpectedly, the anticollectivist sentiment animating anticommunism turned the United States into a semicollectivist nation of its own, guided by possibility and optimism, as noted by Tillich in *Courage to Be*, 108: "The typical American, after he has lost the foundations of his existence, works for *new foundations*. This is true of the individual and it is true of the nation as a whole" (emphasis added). See also Allitt, *Religion in America*, 28.

44. Woodhead, *How the Beatles Rocked the Kremlin*.

45. Sandler, *How the Beatles Changed the World*, 151.

46. Allitt, *Religion in America*, 44, 59.

47. See, e.g., Lewisohn, *Tune In*, 207–8, for an example of how some of their interactions with women would rightfully be targets of the #MeToo era today.

48. Kenneth Womack argues that in 1965, the Beatles "created a very specific type of female character who would think for herself and did not need a man." See Pazzanese's interview with Womack, "Baby, You Can Drive My Car." At the time, it was "revelatory, really": "We have many songs that begin to appear at this point that are highly progressive about women living their own interests and aims and pleasure, as opposed to serving some undefinable other."

49. Heinzerling, *McCartney 3, 2, 1*, episode 3.

50. Prothero, *Religious Literacy*, 7.

51. See McCartney's interview in Howard, *Beatles: Eight Days a Week*.

52. Turner, *Beatles '66*, 5.

53. Nietzsche, *Thus Spoke Zarathustra*, 17.

54. Huckvale, *Music for the Superman*, 189.

55. Beatles, *Anthology*, 255.

56. See Huckvale, *Music for the Superman*, 189–92, for ways in which "Eleanor Rigby" and "Imagine" represent Nietzschean concerns in pop music.

57. Beatles, *Anthology*, 260.

58. The seeds of the relationship may have been planted before the Beatles' births, as

Mona Best spent significant time there and probably shared stories with the young Beatles around the time they played at the Casbah Club with her son, Pete Best.

59. See Beatles, *Anthology*, 260. See also Heinzerling, *McCartney 3, 2, 1*, episode 3.
60. McLeod, *Religious Crisis*, 133.
61. Beatles, *Anthology*, 259.
62. Smith, *World's Religions*, 16.
63. Ibid., 15.
64. Oliver, *Hinduism and the 1960s*, 62.
65. Tillery, *Cynical Idealist*, chapters 6–7.
66. Jackson, *Beatles: Get Back*.
67. N. Jones, "*Rolling Stone* Interview."
68. Doggett, *You Never Give Me Your Money*, 331–32. See also Oliver, *Hinduism and the 1960s*, 67.
69. Beatles, *Anthology*, 260.
70. MacLeod, *Religious Crisis*, 131.
71. Oliver, *Hinduism and the 1960s*, 61.
72. The "gently weeps" portion of Harrison's "While My Guitar Gently Weeps" was borrowed from a line in a book that Harrison pulled off the shelf at random. He did so on the ancient Chinese suggestion in the *I-Ching* that life is determined, not random. See Davies, *Beatles Lyrics*, 274; and Turner, *Hard Day's Write*, 255.
73. The *Tibetan Book of the Dead*, on which Timothy Leary based *Psychedelic Experience*, was then cribbed by Lennon for "Tomorrow Never Knows." This text is part of the (Mahayana) Tibetan Buddhist tradition.
74. Gopnik, "Long Play."
75. Sylvan, *Traces of the Spirit*, 3.
76. Freeman, "Who Is God?"
77. Collins, *Beatles and Sixties Britain*, 69.
78. Ibid., 69.
79. Ibid., 70.
80. Ibid., 70.
81. Ibid., 70.
82. Saltzman, *Meeting the Beatles in India*.
83. Dowlding, *Beatlesongs*, 225.
84. Turner, *Gospel*, 35.
85. Ibid., 5.
86. *International Times*, January 30–February 12, 1967, quoted in McLeod, *Religious Crisis*, 125. Others have also highlighted the connection between the "shaman" role and popular musicians, like U2's Bono in his introduction to *Book of Psalms* (see Allen and Carlin, "Hold On to Love," 69).
87. Smith, *Cleansing the Doors of Perception*, 10; Smith, *Tales of Wonder*, 170–76; Partridge, *High Culture*, 226–27; Lattin, *Harvard Psychedelic Club*.
88. Smith, *World's Religions*, 382.
89. Ibid., 382.
90. Turner, *Gospel*, 7.
91. Ibid., 11.
92. Beatles, *Anthology*, 210.
93. Hamilton, "New Optimism," 163 (emphasis added).
94. Spangler, "Beatles Interviews."
95. Spitz, *Beatles*, 601.
96. Beatles, *Anthology*, 212; Peel, *Unknown Paul McCartney*, chapters 2–3.
97. Baur, "And the Time Will Come," 14.
98. Stace, *Mysticism and Philosophy*, 132.
99. James, *Varieties of Religious Experience*, 388, 389, 405.
100. For the purposes of this collection, the difference between "religion" and "spirituality" is insignificant. However, for the interested reader, "religion" can be seen as the category of institution that enables spirituality to thrive. Religion is, in the words of Huston Smith in *Why Religion Matters*, "institutionalized spirituality" (96).
101. Gould, *Can't Buy Me Love*, 506.
102. Quoted in ibid., 507.
103. Lovinggood, "Burn, Beatles, Burn!," 4.

BIBLIOGRAPHY

Allen, Nicola, and Gerry Carlin. "Hold On to Love: U2's Bespoke Exorcism of the 1960s." In *U2 and the Religious Impulse: Take Me Higher*, edited by Scott Calhoun, 63–74. New York: Bloomsbury, 2018.

Allitt, Patrick. *Religion in America Since 1945: A History*. New York: Columbia University Press, 2003.

Aronowitz, Alfred G. "The Return of the Beatles." *Saturday Evening Post*, August 8, 1964.

Baur, Michael. "And the Time Will Come When You See We're All One: The Beatles and Idealistic Monism." In *The Beatles and Philosophy: Nothing You Can Think That Can't Be Thunk*, edited by Michael Baur and Steven Baur, 13–24. Chicago: Open Court, 2006.

Beatles. *The Beatles Anthology*. San Francisco: Chronicle Books, 2000.

Brown, Callum G. *The Death of Christian Britain: Understanding Secularization, 1800–2000.* London: Routledge, 2000.

———. "What Was the Religious Crisis of the 1960s?" *Journal of Religious History* 34, no. 4 (December 2010): 468–79.

Collins, Marcus. *The Beatles and Sixties Britain.* Cambridge: Cambridge University Press, 2020.

Davies, Hunter. *The Beatles Lyrics: The Stories Behind the Music.* New York: Little, Brown, 2014.

Doggett, Peter. *You Never Give Me Your Money: The Beatles After the Breakup.* New York: HarperCollins, 2009.

Dowlding, William. *Beatlesongs.* New York: Simon and Schuster, 1989.

Elson, John. "Is God Dead?" *Time,* April 8, 1966.

Elwood, Robert. *The Sixties Spiritual Awakening: American Religion Moving from Modern to Postmodern.* New Brunswick, NJ: Rutgers University Press, 1994.

Flynn, Erin E. "Celebrating the Agony of Life." In *Led Zeppelin and Philosophy: All Will Be Revealed,* edited by Scott Calef, 173–86. Chicago: Open Court, 2009.

Freeman, Morgan, host. "Who Is God?" Season 1, episode 3, of *The Story of God with Morgan Freeman.* Series. National Geographic Channel, 2016.

Frontani, Michael R. *The Beatles: Image and the Media.* Jackson: University Press of Mississippi, 2007.

"Gambling City Liked Beatles." *Hope Star* 65, no. 260 (August 22, 1964).

Gopnik, Adam. "Long Play: The Charmed Lives of Paul McCartney." *New Yorker,* April 26, 2016.

Gould, Jonathan. *Can't Buy Me Love: The Beatles, Britain, and America.* New York: Harmony Books, 2007.

Greene, Bob. "Hotel Stripped Its Bed and Now Must Lie in It." *Chicago Tribune,* August 18, 1993.

Hamilton, William. "The New Optimism—from Prufrock to Ringo." In *Radical Theology and the Death of God,* by William Hamilton and Thomas J. J. Altizer, 157–70. New York: Bobbs-Merrill, 1966.

Hastings, Adrian. *A History of English Christianity, 1920–1985.* London: Collins, 1986.

Heinzerling, Zachary, dir. *McCartney 3, 2, 1.* Hulu, 2021. Series.

Hilliard, David. "The Religious Crisis of the 1960s: The Experience of the Australian Churches." *Journal of Religious History* 21, no. 2 (June 1997): 209–27.

Howard, Ron, dir. *The Beatles: Eight Days a Week: The Touring Years.* London: Apple Corps, 2016. Film.

Huckvale, David. *Music for the Superman: Nietzsche and the Great Composers.* Jefferson, NC: McFarland, 2016.

Isserman, Maurice, and Michael Kazin. *America Divided: The Civil War of the 1960s.* New York: Oxford University Press, 2000.

Jackson, Peter, dir. *The Beatles: Get Back.* Disney+, November 2021. Series.

James, William. *Varieties of Religious Experience: A Study in Human Nature.* London: Longmans Green, 1929.

Jenkins, Philip. "The Religious World Changed in 1968, but Not in the Ways We Think." *ABC Religion and Ethics,* July 31, 2018.

Jones, Nick. "The *Rolling Stone* Interview with George Harrison." *Rolling Stone,* February 24, 1968. http://www.rollingstone.com/music/music-news/the-rolling-stone-interview-george-harrison-part-2-231245/.

Jones, Sam. "The Coldest Winters in the UK." *Guardian,* January 5, 2010.

Lattin, Don. *The Harvard Psychedelic Club: How Timothy Leary, Ram Dass, Huston Smith, and Andrew Weil Killed the Fifties and Ushered in a New Age for America.* New York: HarperCollins, 2010.

Lewisohn, Mark. *The Complete Beatles Chronicle.* New York: Harmony Books, 1992.

———. *Tune In: The Beatles—All These Years.* Vol. 1. New York: Crown Archetype, 2013.

"Liverpool Cellar Clubs Rock to Beat Groups: Long-Haired Youths with Guitars Take Charge as Cult." *New York Times,* December 26, 1963.

Lovinggood, Sutton L. "Burn, Beatles! Burn!" *Gazette Leader Post* (Medina, OH), August 29, 1966.

Lyotard, Jean François. *The Postmodern Condition: A Report on Knowledge.* Translated by Geoff Bennington and Brian Massumi. Minneapolis: University of Minnesota Press, 1979.

McLeod, Hugh. *The Religious Crisis of the 1960s.* New York: Oxford University Press, 2007.

Nietzsche, Friedrich. *The Gay Science: With a Prelude in Rhymes and an Appendix of Songs.* Edited and translated by Walter Kaufmann. New York: Vintage Books, 1974.

———. *Thus Spoke Zarathustra: A Book for All and None.* Translated by Walter Kaufmann. New York: Penguin, 1966.

———. *The Will to Power.* Edited and translated by Walter Kaufmann. New York: Vintage Books, 1968.

Oliver, Paul. *Hinduism and the 1960s: The Rise of a Counter-culture.* London: Bloomsbury, 2014.

Partridge, Christopher. *High Culture: Drugs, Mysticism, and the Pursuit of Transcendence in the Modern World.* New York: Oxford University Press, 2018.

Pazzanese, Christina. "Baby, You Can Drive My Car." *Harvard Gazette*, December 10, 2019.

Peel, Ian. *The Unknown Paul McCartney: McCartney and the Avant-Garde.* London: Reynolds and Hearn, 2002.

Prothero, Stephen. *Religious Literacy: What Every American Needs to Know—and Doesn't.* New York: HarperOne, 2007.

Saltzman, Paul, dir. *Meeting the Beatles in India.* Toronto: Sunrise Films Limited, 2020. Film.

Sandler, Martin W. *How the Beatles Changed the World.* London: Bloomsbury, 2014.

Shelden, Michael. *England, the 1960s, and the Triumph of the Beatles.* Great Courses, 2020. https://www.thegreatcourses.com/courses/england-the-1960s-and-the-triumph-of-the-beatles.

Smith, Huston. *Cleansing the Doors of Perception: The Religious Significance of Entheogenic Plants and Chemicals.* New York: Penguin, 2000.

———. *Tales of Wonder: Chasing the Divine.* New York: HarperCollins, 2009.

———. *Why Religion Matters: The Fate of the Human Spirit in an Age of Disbelief.* New York: HarperOne, 2006.

———. *The World's Religions: Our Great Wisdom Traditions.* New York: HarperCollins, 1991.

Spangler, Jay. "Beatles Interviews: Washington Coliseum 2/11/1964." February 11, 1964. Transcript: http://www.beatlesinterviews.org/db1964.0211.beatles.html. Video: https://youtu.be/CNagjxDKhVk.

Spitz, Bob. *The Beatles: The Biography.* New York: Little, Brown, 2005.

Stace, Walter. *Mysticism and Philosophy.* Los Angeles: JP Tarcher, 1987.

Staley, Samuel R. *The Beatles and Economics: Entrepreneurship, Innovation, and the Making of a Cultural Revolution.* London: Routledge, 2020.

Starr, Michael Seth. *Ringo: With a Little Help.* Milwaukee: Backbeat Books, 2015.

Starr, Ringo. *Drumming and Creative Collaboration.* Online class. MasterClass, 2021.

Sylvan, Robin. *Traces of the Spirit: The Religious Dimensions of Popular Music.* New York: New York University Press, 2002.

Szatmary, David P. *Rockin' in Time: A Social History of Rock and Roll.* Upper Saddle River, NJ: Prentice Hall, 2004.

Tillery, Gary. *The Cynical Idealist: A Spiritual Biography of John Lennon.* Wheaton, IL: Quest Books, 2009.

Tillich, Paul. *The Courage to Be.* New Haven: Yale University Press, 1952.

Tillman, J. C. "Life in Arkansas." *Baxter Bulletin* (Mountain Home, AR), October 1, 1964.

Turner, Steve. *Beatles '66: The Revolutionary Year.* New York: HarperCollins, 2016.

———. *The Gospel According to the Beatles.* London: Westminster John Knox Press, 2006.

———. *A Hard Day's Write: The Stories Behind Every Beatles Song.* New York: MJF Books, 2009.

Woodhead, Leslie. *How the Beatles Rocked the Kremlin: The Untold Story of a Noisy Revolution.* New York: Bloomsbury Academic, 2013.

PART I

LIVERPOOL, PROTESTANTS, AND CATHOLICS

CHAPTER I

Religion in the Liverpool of the Beatles' Childhoods

MELISSA DAVIS

Any consideration of the Beatles in relation to or within the context of religion requires a familiarity with the milieu of the city into which they were born. The population of Liverpool at the beginning of the 1930s, when their parents—born between 1902 and 1914—were meeting, marrying, and starting their families, was at its apex: 846,302—the second largest city in Britain.[1] As with most ports, it was home to a wide array of nationalities and races, but Liverpool was unique: within it was the largest Black community in Britain and the oldest Chinese center in Europe.[2] Its residents included those relocating from member nations of the British Empire as near as Ireland and as far as the Caribbean and India. Migrants also came to Liverpool from Europe and the Middle East.

Although the city faced the expected challenges posed by such a large and diverse population—housing, employment, health and sanitation, education, and crime—the religious-based animosity between the Catholic and Protestant faithful in the city that had been a fact of life in Liverpool during the previous century was ever so slightly giving way in the face of shared experiences and cultural and societal movement. The ill will bordering on hatred had influenced the everyday lives of generations of Liverpudlians in ways ranging from the most significant—where they lived, where and how they worshiped, and whom they married—to the everyday, such as their favorite pub.

Physical segregation with bright-line borders had meant that walking on the "wrong" street could result in a beating. Annual parades didn't just end in violence; they were expected to do so. Job discrimination based on religion was common, and a "mixed" marriage between the two faiths could, if it occurred at all, lead to a lifelong schism within families. In fact, marriage between a "mixed" couple—Protestant and Catholic—could be difficult to even arrange, as often neither church would pronounce them man and wife. This might account for the number of the nonmarried unions—called "problematic" by Mark Lewisohn—in the Beatles' respective family trees.[3] Harrison's maternal grandparents were not married despite having seven children.[4] Lennon's father was the twelfth child of an unwed couple, and his maternal grandparents didn't marry until they had their third child, Mary Elizabeth, after seven years of cohabitation; she would forever be known as John's Aunt Mimi in the Beatles story.[5]

Compounding the problem, institutions that might have been expected to prevent or at least lessen the violence and heal the divisions—the clergy of both faiths and the government—could often be found at the forefront of the trouble, stoking tensions. The press, which at the time numbered more than two dozen daily and weekly newspapers in Liverpool and the surrounding county of Lancashire, reported the poverty and disease, violence and vice, unemployment and crime, as well as the politics and pronouncements of city officials and faith leaders in the unrestrained, often florid prose of the time and always through the prism of religion, inflaming passions even further.

In the spring of 1835, even before the famine sent Irish Catholics to Liverpool by the tens and hundreds of thousands, the *Liverpool Standard* newspaper had already decided what was wrong with the city: "Two thirds of the rates [taxes] of this town are spent on Irish mendicants. Irish papists infest our streets, worm their way into our local establishments, sit on our civic boards and deprive Englishmen of employment" (April 28, 1835). "Papist" was a dirty word synonymous with poverty, beggars, infestations, worms, and the inability of Liverpudlians to feed their own families.

It was in this Liverpool that many of the Beatles' forbearers made their homes and raised their families. The four Beatles would each have been exposed to the legacy of religious prejudice and tension in their schools and on their playgrounds, in their neighborhoods, and, to varying degrees, in their homes. How this impacted them as individuals and later as a group and influenced their associations, their attitudes, and the role of religion in their music and lyrics will be discussed throughout this book. This chapter provides the background necessary for an understanding of how Liverpool became the "town where they were born."

Three of the four Beatles—Lennon, McCartney, and Harrison—were born into religiously "mixed" families—Catholic and Protestant. Starkey seems to have come from exclusively Protestant stock, but his father's unofficial adoption by a partner of his mother makes tracing the family lineage impossible.[6] How those families came to Liverpool and how they lived once they arrived is a story of many elements, not only religion. Geography, economics, agriculture, and nationality each contributed, but politics and prejudice, amplified by the press, also played their roles. The combination fueled a partisanship unrivaled in Britain during the nineteenth and early twentieth centuries, even in London or other cities like Glasgow and Manchester, which were also impacted by Irish migration. A virulent sectarianism took hold, and an "us against them" viewpoint grew over time, coloring life within the city and its reputation beyond.

Proximity and Heritage

From Liverpool's earliest days in the thirteenth century—it was granted a charter in 1207 by King John—proximity made the city a destination for Irish seeking work. It has a westward-facing port—at a distance of 136 miles, Liverpool is closer to Dublin than it is to London, which is 178 miles to the southwest. Still, in 1685, the Irish Catholic population of the city was minuscule. A series of events originating in Ireland would change that in the space of less than a decade.

In 1688, the unpopular reign of James II, a Catholic, led to his deposition in favor of his daughter Mary and her Dutch-born Protestant husband, William of Orange. As a condition, they were obliged to swear an oath to maintain the Protestant faith and "preserve inviolable the settlement of the Church of England, and its doctrine, worship, discipline and government."[7] The practical effect was the official domination over Irish Catholics by the English and Irish Anglicans loyal to the monarchy. Irish Catholics found themselves required to tithe to the Protestant Church while barred from owning firearms, voting, or holding public office.

Later, the failure of a brief and bloody rebellion in 1798 in Ireland led to an uptick of migration to Liverpool; the Irish arrived with their disappointment and their bitterness toward the Protestant English. Little more than fifty years later, when the entire population of the city was 376,065,[8] 22 percent of its people (83,813) were Irish-born.[9]

The Irish migrants, the majority of whom were Catholic, settled close by where they docked on the River Mersey. As with most migrants, they sought out the familiar language, songs and stories, customs and comfort of their homeland and faith. The beginning of an Irish ghetto took hold, forming the identity of the Liverpool Irish Catholics, both in their own eyes and in those of the existing, mostly Protestant community.

That identity was soon met by an opposing force in the form of the Orange Order, a Protestant group with roots in the Reformation, reemergent in Ireland during the Rebellion of 1798 and revitalized in England as a response to the influx of Irish Catholics. The necessary elements of religious sectarianism, of "us against them," were in place, and the two sides became instantly recognizable—orange versus green.[10]

"Orange-ism" reaffirmed the Protestant identity for its members who believed the Orange Lodge would preserve Protestant culture and community, while protecting their faith from the perceived threat of Catholics, the distrust of whom formed the basis for the rising membership. Lodges paraded the colors each July 12 ("The Twelfth") in celebration of William of Orange's defeat of James II. These were showy displays of loyalty to Protestantism and the monarchy intentionally designed to offend Irish Catholics, but the Irish Catholics had their own parades.[11] Years later, Beatle drummer Richard Starkey, better known as Ringo Starr, would recall, "On 17 March, St. Patrick's Day, all the Protestants beat up the Catholics and on 12 July, Orangeman's [sic] Day, all the Catholics beat up the Protestants. That's how it was."[12]

Liverpool prospered in the first decades of the nineteenth century, but in the mid-nineteenth century, circumstances and events created a state of open and acknowledged hostility between the Protestants and Irish Catholics of Liverpool that would taint life for both groups in the city for the next 150 years.

In the mid-1840s, successive failures of the staple crop of Ireland, the sole sustenance for tenant farmers, devastated Ireland; the West Counties were hit especially hard. Subsequent years of crop failures and deliberately harsh economic policies led to starvation, creating an exodus across the waters to England, North America, and Australia, changing people, nations, and communities forever. What became known as the Great Potato Famine had begun.

An Gorta Mór

Simply put, "An Gorta Mór,"[13] the Great Hunger, was caused by a fungus—*Phytophthora infestans* (infesting plant destroyer).[14] The soil in western Ireland was particularly suitable for growing potatoes, which constituted almost the entire diet of the poor; the fungus attacked the tuber in the soil, rotting the farmers' source of food while it was still in the ground.

With the first crop failure of 1845, Irish tenant farmers and their Anglo-English landlords believed the next year's crop would be better. It wasn't. After another failure in 1846–47, combined with a hard winter, farmers reneged on rents. Some ate seaweed and raw shellfish to survive; thereafter, the year was known as "The Black Forty-Seven."[15]

Potato crops continued to fail, and death from malnutrition and disease rose in appalling numbers.[16] Victims were buried in mass graves, and landlords pressed evictions. Relief was slow: private charities proved inadequate, and government soup kitchens were discontinued in September 1847 after only six months. Internment in disease-ridden government workhouses was contingent on harsh terms: eviction from leaseholds, mandatory hard labor, separation of families, and the renunciation of the faith.[17] The expression "taking the soup" meant renouncing Catholicism in exchange for food.[18]

Help from far-off London was not forthcoming. The government adopted a laissez-faire reliance on an eventual, natural resolution to the problem. Policies requiring continued export of corn and meat worsened the famine. A false rumor that Queen Victoria donated £5 from her personal accounts for Irish famine relief—in fact, the amount was £2,000, the equivalent of £61,000 or $83,000 using the July 2021 rate—was held up as proof of the casual cruelty of the ruling Protestants.[19] Escape became the only option for millions of Irish, and once again, the proximity of Liverpool made it the natural destination.

An estimated two million Irish headed across the Irish Sea to Liverpool between 1845 and 1854.[20] Most eventually boarded "coffin" ships to cross the Atlantic, but many stayed on in Liverpool at a time when the city already faced rampant unemployment, squalor, and disease.[21] The Irish believed life in Liverpool would be an improvement, and in some ways, it was: charitable and government relief were at least available in Liverpool, but the limited resources of the city were insufficient to address the needs of the native poor, let alone the sudden flood of starving migrants.

One-third of the relief provided to the Liverpool poor went to the newly arrived Irish Catholics.[22] Soon, the initial sympathy turned to resentment. In the winter of 1847, the *Liverpool Mercury* put it bluntly: "Thousands of hungry and half naked wretches are wandering about, not knowing how to obtain a sufficiency of the commonest food nor shelter. . . . The numbers of starving Irish men, women, and children daily landed on our quays is appalling; and the Parish of Liverpool has, at present, the painful and most costly task of keeping them alive, if possible."[23] The *Times* put it more succinctly: "Every English working man carries an Irish family on his shoulders."[24]

The city was unable to absorb the migrants; housing was scarce and substandard, employment at a premium. In the opinion of many educated Brits at the time, the Irish had to be taught to stand on their own feet and "unlearn" their dependence on government.[25] Many of the Irish found their way to the Rainhill Asylum—then known as the Rainhill Lunatic Asylum—for food and shelter. The commissioners of the asylum reported, "A very large proportion of the patients are Irish, and of the lowest strata in the population of Liverpool."[26] And "resorting to voluntarily going to Rainhill proved a deeply traumatic and enduring aspect of the Irish migration experience."[27]

The penniless Irish sheltered where they could, living with other families in cellars, breaking into condemned structures without water, sanitation, or light. Crowded conditions and infestations of rats compounded the spread of disease. Poverty and everything it entailed—hunger, disease, ignorance, hopelessness, and death—were the everyday reality of those who lived in the slums, and although the Protestants also faced privation, the newly arrived Irish Catholics lived and died in the worst of it.

Conditions worsened, and antipathy grew into outrage as outbreaks of disease spread from Irish streets into Protestant ones. Epidemics of cholera and typhus broke out. As many as sixty thousand Liverpudlians contracted typhus, and another forty thousand were struck with dysentery during the epidemic of 1847.[28] City authorities estimated that 88 percent of the sick and dying were Irish.[29] The city tried to isolate the diseased in sheds and warehouses, turning ships into lazarettos (floating hospitals), but many Irish Catholics refused to be separated from their families.[30]

Lacking the scientific understanding that poor living conditions, malnourishment, and lack of medical care breed disease among any people, the newly arrived became the scapegoat; the contagion was labeled "Irish fever."[31] Future outbreaks of disease—cholera in 1866 and smallpox in 1871–72—only served to reinforce the perceptions of the Irish Catholics as disease-ridden.

Liverpool was no longer a backwater on the River Mersey but rather a growing city, and the migrants, mostly illiterate potato farmers lacking the skills needed to earn a living in a port or at sea, were willing to compete for any unskilled job. This drove down wages and job opportunities, further increasing hard feelings. Women and even young girls often had no recourse other than prostitution.[32] In such an atmosphere of hopelessness, alcohol consumption ran to alcoholism, and not surprisingly, fighting in public—as near sport—was common. Tensions continued to grow.

Irish Catholics had different customs, spoke a different language, and even looked different. Generations of malnutrition had left them small and stooped-shouldered, prematurely aged, "their rags, and malnutrition, in their missing teeth, matted hair, body smells, and [in] other visible signs which clearly set them apart."[33]

Irish Catholics' main distinguishing characteristic, however, was their faith. To Protestants whose religion was born of the Reformation, Catholicism was in stark contrast to their own faith. Elements such as the Latin Mass, the doctrine of transubstantiation, rosaries, and incense were not viewed merely as a different way to worship the same Christian God but as sinister superstitions. Worse still in the eyes of many Protestants was the Catholic allegiance to the pope in Italy, anathema to those who swore their loyalty to the English monarch in London.

Consequently, "Orangeism" continued to grow as a response to what was perceived as a near invasion. The Irish Catholics, in turn, looked to their parishes not only for worship but also for schools for their children. Catholics and Protestants lived segregated lives in distinct streets and neighborhoods, worshiped in different churches, sent their children to different schools, socialized in their own pubs, and did not mingle. Anger and resentment, fear and ignorance, and the clash of cultures became centered around religion, and the divisions crystallized into sectarianism.

This is the Liverpool of the Beatles' forbears. For the families, both Protestant and Catholic, their streets and neighborhoods—Saltney, Vauxhall, Wavertree, Toxteth, Everton, Fazakerley, and the lower end of Scotland Road—demarcated their worlds, and the boundaries were understood and observed. Mark Lewisohn documents the frequent moves of the Beatles' families from one street to the next but rarely out of "their" area; Lennon's great-grandparents had eight children, each of whom was born at a different address.[34]

Religious sectarianism continued to roil as unemployment rose, with job scarcity again causing friction. Long-standing tensions erupted in June 1909 when Protestants reacted to rumors about a proposed march by members of a Catholic church; not surprisingly, the violence occurred near Scotland Road. With this, Liverpool became known as "The Belfast of England," but it can be argued that 1909 represented at once the height of sectarianism and the beginning of a slow waning of violence.[35]

The Apex of Violence and Shared Experience

Just two years later, a general transport strike created a temporary alliance between predominantly Catholic dockworkers and mainly Protestant carters, as shared desperation over unemployment and low wages provided common ground. When police used excessive force to control a large but peaceful crowd of strikers and their supporters in August 1911, troops were called in, and gunboats were moored in the Mersey, but the clashes were between the strikers and law enforcement, rather than Protestant and Catholic. Sectarian divisions began a gradual shift from religion to class.[36]

Experiences shared by both sides of the religious divide followed: two world wars with a decade-long economic depression in between. Popular culture gained traction with the advent of liberated fashion for women, with bobbed hair, short skirts, and rouged knees; more revealing swimsuits and beauty contests became widespread and common. Women exercised their right to vote, drive, and access higher education, adding a bit of rebellion with smoking and drinking. Couples enjoyed a new genre of music, jazz, dancing the Charleston with abandon, and "talking" movies featuring exotic plotlines and idols like Clara Bow and Rudolph Valentino. These were viewed as decadent by adults and other authority figures, thus adding to their appeal, especially to youth. Even more impactful in the lives of women and couples was the publication of educational books about sexual relations and the freedom gained by the provision of family-planning information and methods through maternity and child welfare clinics via a directive from the Ministry of Health in Britain.[37] There were increased employment opportunities outside the home beyond that of "domestic," and a limited group of women gained suffrage in the United Kingdom in 1918, with even more added to the rolls in 1928.[38] These changes served to lessen strict religious adherence: in the 1930s, attendance at church was nearly halved from that of 1901.[39]

Liverpudlians of all faiths suffered losses with the high number of military dead in World War I, and unemployment soared again following the global economic collapse of 1929. Just over 52 percent of all married men in Liverpool received public assistance in 1931, the year George Harrison's parents welcomed their first child; his father would spend two years on the dole in the middle of the "Hungry Thirties."[40]

With the declaration of war against Germany in September 1939, many of the unemployed men left to serve in uniform, Catholic and Protestant side by side. Those who remained behind due to age or disability found war-related work defending the same homeland. Paul McCartney's father, Jim, thirty-seven years old and partially deaf, became an inspector at a shell-casings company and served as a volunteer fireman during bombing raids.

Liverpool, the natural destination for shipments of men and materiel from the United States, received special attention from the Luftwaffe, second only to that showered on London. Four thousand civilian lives were lost; the docks and the site of the incomplete Catholic cathedral were hit. In one seven-night period in May 1941, over 6,500 homes were destroyed and another 190,000 damaged by Luftwaffe bombers.[41] Seven hundred water mains and eighty sewers were compromised, as were gas, electricity, and telephone lines.[42] It was a unifying experience: 70,000 people became homeless in that single week.[43] Protestant, Catholic, and Jew, as well as every ethnic minority of Liverpool, suffered together because it was *their* city that suffered.

"Mixed" Families

More than a century and a half of immigration and oppositional reaction, suffering and survival, religious sectarianism, and tentative steps toward truces created the religious environment the Beatles were born into. All four of the Beatles were "war babies"—Lennon and Starkey in 1940, McCartney in 1942, and Harrison in 1943. Their "mixed" families—one parent Protestant, the other Catholic—represented the devout, the lapsed, and the agnostic. John Lennon might have been fascinated to learn that there was a Fr. William Lennon in his family tree.[44] Occasionally, conversions took place, but often for nontheological reasons: Lennon's paternal grandmother stopped having her babies baptized Catholic after the first seven died in infancy, taking them instead to the font at a nearby Protestant church.[45] She later had John's father "converted" to gain acceptance at a Protestant orphanage-school.[46] Harrison's Protestant paternal grandmother had his sister baptized in that faith while his mother, Louise, was still recovering from the birth. Three years later, Louise "corrected" things.[47] In families such as these, there could not have been much room for religious rigidity; tolerance and acceptance would have been a necessary part of the everyday home lives of the boys as they grew up.

There is no reason to believe that the Beatles' families were unique in their mixed-faith unions and easing of strict religious adherence in the first half of the twentieth century. To a large extent, the "mixed" nature of their families mirrored changes in Liverpool itself.

Religious affiliations remained strong as two cathedrals rose at either end of Hope Street—the huge, traditional Anglican anchoring one end and the modern Catholic at the other. However, the sectarian violence that had once been synonymous with the city's name, the virulent rhetoric in the press, and the "us versus them" atmosphere began to abate. By an ironic and happy coincidence, the architect of the Catholic cathedral was Protestant.

When the Irish Republican Army (IRA) launched a bombing campaign throughout Britain in early 1939, Liverpool was hit, but this was distinguishable from previous violence in the city: the bombings were orchestrated from Ireland, not homegrown, and were political without religious affiliation or target. Instead, the blasts were intended to create fear in the general populace by targeting infrastructure such as electrical pylons and utilities. The Trocadero Theater, where Julia Stanley Lennon sometimes worked as an "usherette," was hit. And although anti–Irish Catholic sentiment ran high for a time and was compounded once again by unemployment, the Irish population of the city, both Catholic and Protestant, was equally at risk. In fact, the perpetrators found little succor or sympathy among Irish Catholic Liverpudlians, who were angered that suspicion had been brought on them through no fault of their own.[48]

The Jewish Community in Liverpool

Irish Catholics were not the only religious group immigrating to Liverpool. Jews also made their way to the port as early as the eighteenth century, when the Methodist leader John Wesley noted the "excellent relations" between the two groups.[49] While some Jews were undoubtedly fleeing antisemitism, others saw opportunity in the thriving port and opted to make it their home. Unlike the Irish Catholic migrants, however, most Jewish migrants at that time did not arrive starving or suffering from disease. Nor were the majority uneducated, unable to make a living in an urban setting. Some may have been persecuted in their homeland, but they were not without skills—many were merchants, businesspeople, and clergy.

Arriving by train from the east rather than the Irish Sea, many Jews chose to settle near Lime Street station, far from the slums. They assimilated—establishing congregations, schools, and businesses—becoming part of the economic and civic life of the city. The Lewis family was among Liverpool's foremost philanthropists. Charles Mozley became Liverpool's first Jewish mayor in 1863.[50]

In the latter half of the nineteenth century, driven by the Russian pogroms, the Jewish population of Liverpool grew, second only to London by 1860.[51] A teenaged Isaac Epstein was among the immigrants, and his grandson—Brian Epstein—would be at the helm of the Beatles' success.

Antisemitism may have been rife in London, but according to at least one historian, it stemmed from resentment held by the Radical wing of the Liberal Party "against the growing visibility of successful businessmen in national life."[52] No antisemitic riots took place in Liverpool. No newspaper campaigns debased the Jewish immigrant or blamed the city's economic woes and health crises on the non-Christian newcomers. Instead, as the historian and former chairman of the Liverpool Jewish Historical Society Arnold Lewis notes, "What's remarkable is the social acceptance of Jews. There was very little anti-Semitism. . . . Another indication of the social acceptance of Jews in Liverpool is they were accepted to become members of the Athenaeum, a very high cultural society, . . . an indication of the city's cosmopolitan tolerance."[53] (A brief spasm of smashing and burning occurred throughout Britain, especially in the north, during a bank holiday weekend in 1947, precipitated by events in Israel involving Palestinians. No injuries were reported, and it was soon forgotten.)[54]

The Jewish community thrived, weaving its way through the Liverpool that the Beatles and their families knew. Isaac Epstein founded a household-furnishings store that offered such reasonable terms that it became possible for families like the McCartneys to own a piano.[55] The art-college students John Lennon and Cynthia Powell, like many couples, met under the Jacob Epstein statue *Liverpool Resurgent* (better known as "Dickie Lewis") hanging—prominently—on the front of Lewis's department store, founded in 1856 by a Jewish family. In all likelihood, the Beatles would have been taken to see Father Christmas at the store's "Christmas Grotto" when they were little boys; six-year-old Lennon posed for a set of holiday photographs at Lewis's.[56]

When the Epstein family's artistically frustrated son, Brian, decided to manage a rock and roll group, the family was appalled, but the Beatles' families were not. McCartney acknowledged that the stereotype was a positive factor: "Everyone knew Jewish people were good with money," but the young men also said they were impressed by the Epstein family's contacts with record companies in London and the possibility that he could secure better-paying gigs around town (the "posh" car probably didn't hurt, either).[57] Harold Harrison and Jim McCartney signed the management contract on behalf of their underage sons.

Reforms and Shared Outcomes

Social reform measures in the Labour government of the postwar period also served to ameliorate some of the conditions that had fueled sectarian violence. The National Health Service improved the physical well-being of all residents, and the Education Act of 1944 brought local schooling within national control, creating a universal standard and providing the opportunity for children to meet, play, and become friends with those of other faiths at an early age. These advances would have impacted each of the Beatles well before their tenth birthdays.

The removal of war rubble allowed for slum clearance in some areas, blurring and even removing old religious boundary lines. Newly established housing developments away from the city center created new neighborhoods lacking old religious sectarian associations. McCartney and Harrison shared a half-hour bus ride from Speke, a new area to the south of the city, to their high school near the religiously segregated area in the city where their grandparents had lived.

The city's two enormously popular football teams may also have played a role in diluting the religious sectarianism.[58] Although it is often thought that Liverpool is "Catholic" and Everton "Protestant," in fact, Methodists started professional football in the city, and neither has ever been officially affiliated with any religion (other than winning). It was the ability and toughness of the player, the level of play, and the aptitude of the managers that commanded the loyalty of the fans, rather than any perceived association of either team with a particular faith. The Beatles were not football fans, but a shift from religious rivalries to sports-based ones would have had an impact on their families, friends, and the city as a whole.

Religion in the Beatles' Family Homes

The religious strife that had played such a significant role in the life of the city and the lives of the Beatles' parents, grandparents, and great-grandparents seems not to have taken hold in the family sons. There is little mention of religion in their childhood homes, no photographs of them appearing as Magi in nativity plays or wearing uncomfortable confirmation suits.

When McCartney's mother died, she was buried with her rosary. At age fourteen, he experienced a crisis of faith when his prayers went unanswered: "Daft prayers, you know, if you bring her back, I'll be very, very good for always. I thought, it just shows how stupid religion is. . . . The prayers didn't work, when I really needed them to."⁵⁹ He had been baptized Catholic but, like all the Beatles, attended a state school. Harrison had also been baptized Catholic and later said he enjoyed the stained glass and incense of his parish church,⁶⁰ but his older sister remembered the family turning the radio off to avoid the priest at the door on his weekly collection rounds.⁶¹ Starkey remembers his mother belonging to an Orange Lodge for a brief time in her youth, but at one time, he committed to converting, a prerequisite to an anticipated engagement to a Catholic Liverpool girl, and wore a St. Christopher medal given to him by a relative.

That Lennon had been confirmed at St. Peter's Church might have helped the sixteen-year-old convince the vicar to allow his high school group, the Quarrymen, to play at a summer fête in July 1957. His uncle, George Smith, was buried a few yards away from where fifteen-year-old Paul McCartney would first see his future musical partner playing rock and roll.

For each of the Beatles, by the time they were adolescents making their own choices about whom they became friends with, played music with (increasingly one and the same), dated, drank, and partied with, little evidence exists that religious affiliation figured into the equation. Whether someone received communion at an Anglican or Catholic altar (or received it at all) did not matter if they could demonstrate a guitar chord, share a new record, or play the drums. Similarly, if someone with business acumen and a staunch belief in the group wanted to serve as their manager, his Jewish faith was not an impediment but rather an asset. Nor did bearing the name of the Prophet Mohammad, as was the case with Lennon's art-college classmate Jeff Mohammad, outweigh friendship in his mind.

Competence and an unwavering faith in Lennon, McCartney, Harrison, and Starkey collectively or as individuals seem to have taken precedence over any preconceived prejudices absorbed in either the home or the community. In a 1967 letter Harrison sent to his mother, a devout Catholic, he explained the Beatles' interest in Transcendental Meditation: "God is not divided into different sects as our religious leaders here make out by their prejudices. It [TM] doesn't affect my dedication to Sacred Heart in any way. It only strengthens it."⁶²

In terms that are familiar at the time this chapter is being written but that were not in use during the Beatles' youth, inclusiveness and nonjudgmental acceptance seemed to have governed their opinions, whether consciously or not. Their understanding of and belief in the tenets of religion could be found in their music and lyrics.

The Role of Faith in the Beatles' Lyrics and Music

Faith has traditionally played two key roles: it has provided hope to counter fear and offered solace when fears have been made manifest. One cost of religious sectarianism is that differences in outward symbolism and rites can obscure the foundational beliefs that the faiths have in common. The practices of religion—when to sit, stand, or kneel (or not), what and when to sing, how to make the sign of the cross or genuflect—have to do with visible and physical demonstrations of the profession of faith rather than inner belief.

It is in the inner realm that the Beatles' music and lyrics reveal and demonstrate faith—for themselves, as well as for their audience. The foundational tenets of faith in their family backgrounds and the city of their birth can be seen to have left a more indelible imprint on them in relation to their music rather than to the outward demonstration of either religion.

The group's first public comment on religion came in a February 1965 interview in *Playboy* magazine just a year after they debuted in America:

McCartney: We probably seem antireligious because of the fact that none of us believe in God.
Lennon: If you say you don't believe in God, everybody assumes you're antireligious, and you probably think that's what we mean by that. We're not quite sure *what* we are, but I know that we're more agnostic than atheistic.
Playboy: Are you speaking for the group, or just for yourself?
Lennon: For the group.
Harrison: John's our official religious spokesman.
McCartney: We all feel roughly the same. We're all agnostics.[63]

Harrison's wry statement aside, it would be Lennon's famous "Jesus" remark eighteen months later that would unleash a firestorm of disapproval on them, especially in the US South. Yet, in 2021, McCartney acknowledged, "Many of our influences were spiritual, which was good."[64]

In their lyrics, the Beatles can be seen as advocating sacred principles of faith: "Blessed are the *peace*makers" (Matthew 5:9 KJV) and "*Love* one *another*" (John 15:12 KJV). The word "love" appears repeatedly in their lyrics, evolving from a purely romantic meaning to a universal one, such as in "All You Need Is Love" and "The End," the final track on their final album ("And in the end, the love you take is equal to the love you make"). If faith feeds hope, reassurances in lyrics such as "It's getting better all the time," "Take a sad song and make it better," "We can work it out," "Here comes the sun," "Take these broken wings and learn to fly," and "When the night is cloudy, there is still a light that shines on me" (echoing the light shining in the darkness in John 1:5 KJV) speak of a faith that things will not always be as bleak as they may seem.

Hope and solace are also in the music, not merely in the lyrics. The repetition of the mantra-like final chorus of "Hey Jude" lasts longer than the body of the song itself, and it inspired audience participation even from the song's 1968 debut on national television in both the United States and the United Kingdom. Over half a century later, the "sing-along" remains the highly anticipated—and expected—finale of McCartney's solo concerts. Audience members, thousands of strangers, with arms wrapped around each other, sing the refrain at venues around the globe. No translation is required; the hopefulness of the message transcends nationality, language, or religion.

In the midst of the Vietnam War era, Lennon released an anthemic plea for the world to "give peace a chance," as he did later with "imagine all the people living life in peace," even as he encouraged imagining a world without religion. The overriding emphasis in these songs had to do with peace. As solo artists, Lennon and McCartney each wrote songs in support of Irish independence.[65] Starkey has long requested that fans acknowledge his birthday with greetings of "Peace and Love," seizing any opportunity to spread that particular gospel.

Lyrics touching on religious figures—Lady Madonna, Mother Mary (McCartney's mother's name but also, of course, that of Christ's mother), Fr. McKenzie, and Jude, the patron saint of lost causes—are too obvious to be mere coincidence given the presence of the Catholic faith in McCartney's childhood home. As a Beatle, Harrison sang of "The Inner Light" in 1968; his solo work began with "My Sweet Lord."[66] His actions also demonstrated a commitment to another tenet of the faith: charity. His 1971 effort to raise funds for and awareness of dire conditions in Bangladesh gave birth to "rock philanthropy," leading to such subsequent fund-raising charitable events as Live Aid, Band Aid, Farm Aid, We Are the World, and many others. Harrison's last words were "Love one another."[67]

Harrison's religious pluralism and his strong inclination for tolerance may have been learned at his family home on 12 Arnold Grove in Liverpool; his parents joined the Beatles in attending the funeral of their Jewish manager at a London synagogue. A revealing moment occurred in 1964, when a group member used a Jewish epithet overheard by, but not directed toward, a young journalist, Larry Kane. Offended, Kane confronted them, convinced he would lose press access to the group during their first North American tour but adamant nonetheless. Instead, according to Kane, each Beatle approached him to "normalize" the awkwardness; Lennon seized the opportunity for what Kane calls "a real conversation about the religious attitudes—and jargon—prevalent in Liverpool." Kane and Lennon formed a friendship that lasted until Lennon's death.[68]

And in the End . . .

Regardless of the impressions of religious conflict that the Beatles might have received in their homes, in their experience of organized religion, and in their city while growing up, positive religious themes are evident in their music and lyrics. The tenets of love, peace, hope, and charity are present in their songs. The Beatles *sang* their faith. And it is precisely *because* those songs have been sung communally around the world and played without interruption for more than half a century that the Beatles' declaration of faith has always been evident and will remain so for generations to come.

NOTES

1. GB Historical GIS, "Liverpool District Through Time."
2. Liverpool City Council et al., "World Population Review."
3. Lewisohn, *Tune In*, 47.
4. Ibid., 46.
5. Ibid., 20, 25.
6. Ibid., 51.
7. Maer and Gay, "Coronation Oath."
8. Farrer and Brownbill, *Lancaster*, 37–38.
9. Irish Genealogy Toolkit, "Irish Immigration to Britain."
10. McSweeney, "Liverpool."
11. Roberts, "Rise and Fall," 97.
12. Sounes, *Fab*, 7.
13. Lexilogos, "Scottish Gaelic Dictionary," https://www.lexilogos.com/english/gaelic_scottish_dictionary.htm.
14. Donnelly, *Great Irish Potato Famine*, 10.
15. Ó Gráda, *Black '47*, 3.
16. Crowley, Smith, and Murphy, *Atlas*, 13–17.
17. McCarthy, "Disturbing Origins."
18. Ibid.
19. Mulraney, "Real Story."
20. Embassy of Ireland USA, "About Us."
21. Irish Genealogy Toolkit, "Irish Immigration to Britain."
22. Lowe, *Irish*.
23. *Liverpool Mercury*, January 15, 1847.
24. *Times*, May 6, 1847, quoted in Neal, *Sectarian Violence*, 109.
25. Donnelly, "Irish Famine."
26. Cox, Marland, and York, "Emaciated, Exhausted and Excited."
27. Hand, "Poverty, Welfare and Insanity."
28. Cox, Marland, and York, "Emaciated, Exhausted and Excited."
29. Belchem, *Irish, Catholic and Scouse*, 60.
30. Neal, *Black '47*, 87.
31. Cox, Marland, and York, "Emaciated, Exhausted and Excited."
32. Roberts, *Liverpool Sectarianism*, 302.
33. Kerrigan, *Bowl of Scouse*, 220.
34. Lewisohn, *Tune In*, 21.
35. Neal, *Sectarian Violence*, 1.
36. "Liverpool's Fatal 1911 Riots Remembered."
37. Simms, "Parliament and Birth Control," 83–88.
38. Representation of the People Act 1918 and Equal Franchise Act 1928.
39. Branson and Heinemann, *Britain in the 1930s*, 269–70.
40. Boyer, *Winding Road*.
41. "Liverpool May Blitz Remembered"; Imperial War Museums, "Liverpool Blitz."
42. Imperial War Museums, "Liverpool Blitz."

43. National Museums Liverpool, "Maritime Museum."
44. Lewisohn, *Tune In*, 19.
45. Ibid., 21.
46. Ibid., 22.
47. Ibid., 48.
48. Evans, "Fear and Loathing in Liverpool."
49. Gilman, "Jewish Traveler."
50. Jewish Virtual Library, "Liverpool."
51. Cesarani, "Jews of Bristol and Liverpool."
52. Endelman, *Jews of Britain*.
53. Quoted in Dawson, "Celebrating Liverpool's Jewish History."
54. Trilling, "Britain's Last Anti-Jewish Riots."
55. Lewisohn, *Tune In*, 25.
56. Ibid., 112.
57. Beatles, *Anthology*, 65. McCartney said, "At that age, we were very impressed by anyone with a suit or a car."
58. Roberts, *Liverpool Sectarianism*.
59. Davies, *Beatles Authorized Biography*, 127.
60. Womack, "How George Harrison's Lifelong Quest."
61. Louise Harrison Caldwell, interview with author, April 10, 2009.
62. Beatles, *Anthology*, 18.
63. Shepherd, "Candid Conversation."
64. Heinzerling, *McCartney 3-2-1*, episode 3.
65. Paul McCartney, "Give Ireland Back to the Irish (Don't Make Them Have to Take It Away)," Wings single (EMI, 1972); John Lennon and Yoko Ono, "The Luck of the Irish," on *Some Time in New York City* (Apple, 1971).
66. George Harrison, "The Inner Light," Beatles single (Apple, 1968); Harrison, "My Sweet Lord," on *All Things Must Pass*, recorded May–October 1970 (Apple, 1970).
67. Bernstein, "Beatle George Harrison Dies."
68. Kane, interview with the author, July 14, 2021.

BIBLIOGRAPHY

Beatles. *The Beatles Anthology*. San Francisco: Chronicle Books, 2000.
Belchem, John. *Irish, Catholic and Scouse: The History of the Liverpool-Irish, 1800–1939*. Liverpool: Liverpool University Press, 2007.
Bernstein, Adam. "Beatle George Harrison Dies." *Washington Post*, December 1, 2001.
Boyer, George R. *The Winding Road to the Welfare State: Economic Insecurity and Social Welfare Policy in Britain*. Princeton: Princeton University Press, 2019.
Branson, Noreen, and Margot Heinemann. *Britain in the 1930s*. New York: Praeger, 1971.
Cesarani, David. "The Jews of Bristol and Liverpool, 1750–1850: Port Jewish Communities in the Shadow of Slavery." *Jewish Culture and History* 7 (2012): 141–56.
Cox, Catherine, Hilary Marland, and Sarah York. "Emaciated, Exhausted and Excited: The Bodies and Minds of the Irish in Nineteenth-Century Lancashire Asylums." *Journal of Social History* 46, no. 2 (2012): 500–524.
Crowley, John, William Smith, and Mike Murphy, eds. *Atlas of the Great Irish Famine*. Cork: Cork University Press, 2012.
Davies, Hunter. *The Beatles Authorized Biography*. London: Heinemann, 1968.
Dawson, Lisa. "Celebrating Liverpool's Jewish History." *BBC*, October 5, 2005.
Donnelly, James. *The Great Irish Potato Famine*. Stroud, UK: Sutton, 2002.
———. "The Irish Famine." *BBC Online*, February 17, 2011.
Embassy of Ireland USA. "About Us." An Roinn Gnóthaí Eachtracha Department of Foreign Affairs. Accessed November 11, 2020. https://www.dfa.ie/irish-embassy/usa/about-us.
Endelman, Todd M. *The Jews of Britain, 1656 to 2000*. Oakland: University of California Press, 2002.
Evans, Bryce. "Fear and Loathing in Liverpool: The 1939 IRA Bombing Campaign in Merseyside." *Transactions of the Lancashire and Cheshire Historical* 161, no. 1 (2012): 25–45.
Farrer, William, and John Brownbill, eds. *A History of the County of Lancaster*. Vol. 4. London: Victoria County History, 1911.
GB Historical GIS, University of Portsmouth. "Liverpool District Through Time: Population Statistics." In *A Vision of Britain Through Time*. Accessed December 31, 2021. https://www.visionofbritain

.org.uk/unit/10105821/cube/TOT_POP.

Gilman, Lois. "The Jewish Traveler: Liverpool." *Hadassah Magazine*, August–September 2006.

Hand, Jane. "Poverty, Welfare and Insanity Amongst Irish Migrants." University of Warwick, Centre for the History of Medicine, June 18, 2014. https://warwick.ac.uk/fac/arts/history/chm/outreach/migration/backgroundreading/poverty.

Heinzerling, Zachary, dir. *McCartney 3-2-1*. Hulu, 2021. Series.

Imperial War Museums. "The Liverpool Blitz." Accessed December 31, 2021. https://www.iwm.org.uk/history/the-liverpool-blitz.

Irish Genealogy Toolkit. "Irish Immigration to Britain." Accessed December 31, 2021. https://www.irish-genealogy-toolkit.com/Irish-immigration-to-Britain.html.

Jewish Virtual Library. "Liverpool." Accessed December 31, 2021. https://www.jewishvirtuallibrary.org/liverpool.

Kerrigan, J. P. *A Bowl of Scouse: The Forgotten People and Hidden Events Beneath the Surface of Liverpool's History*. Birkenhead, UK: Countyvise, 2009.

Lewisohn, Mark. *Tune In: The Beatles—All These Years*. Vol. 1. New York: Three Rivers, 2013.

Liverpool City Council, Office for National Statistics, and World Urbanization Prospects. "World Population Review." 2023. https://worldpopulationreview.com/world-cities/liverpool-population.

"Liverpool May Blitz Remembered with Parade and Ceremony." *Liverpool Echo*, April 30, 2011. https://www.liverpoolecho.co.uk/news/liverpool-news/liverpool-blitz-remembered-parade-ceremony-3378851.

"Liverpool's Fatal 1911 Riots Remembered." *BBC News*, August 16, 2011.

Lowe, W. J. *The Irish in Mid-Victorian Lancashire*. Bern: Peter Lang, 1989.

Maer, Lucinda, and Oonagh Gay. "The Coronation Oath." House of Commons Library, August 27, 2008. https://researchbriefings.files.parliament.uk/documents/SN00435/SN00435.pdf.

McCarthy, Gerard. "The Disturbing Origins of the Irish Famine Term 'Take the Soup': How Poor Irish Catholics Were Forced to Choose Between Converting to Protestantism or Starvation During Ireland's Great Hunger." *Irish Central*, February 20, 2020.

McSweeney, Declan. "Liverpool and the Orange Lodges Parading Season." *Guardian*, June 21, 2012.

Mulraney, Frances. "The Real Story of Queen Victoria and the Irish Famine." *Irish Central*, April 26, 2020.

National Museums Liverpool. "Maritime Museum." Accessed December 31, 2021. http://www.liverpoolmuseums.org.uk/maritime/exhibitions/blitz/may.aspx.

Neal, Frank. *Black '47: Britain and the Famine Irish*. London: Palgrave Macmillan, 1998.

———. *Sectarian Violence: The Liverpool Experience*. Manchester: Manchester University Press, 1988.

Ó Gráda, Cormac. *Black '47 and Beyond: The Great Irish Famine in History, Economy, and Memory*. Princeton: Princeton University Press, 1999.

Roberts, Keith Daniel. *Liverpool Sectarianism: The Rise and Demise*. Liverpool: Liverpool University Press, 2017.

———. "The Rise and Fall of Liverpool Sectarianism: An Investigation into the Decline of Sectarian Antagonism on Merseyside." PhD diss., University of Liverpool, 2015.

Shepherd, Jean. "A Candid Conversation with England's Mop-Topped Millionaire Minstrels." *Playboy*, February 1965.

Simms, Madeleine. "Parliament and Birth Control in the 1920s." *Journal of the Royal College of General Practitioners* 28 (February 1978): 83–88.

Sounes, Howard. *Fab: An Intimate Life of Paul McCartney*. Boston: Da Capo, 2010.

Trilling, Daniel. "Britain's Last Anti-Jewish Riots: Why Have the 1947 Riots Been Forgotten?" *New Statesman*, December 22, 2012.

Womack, Kenneth. "How George Harrison's Lifelong Quest for Spiritual Enlightenment Shaped His Music and Life." *Salon*, February 25, 2021.

CHAPTER 2

Born Taking Sides

Religion in the Beatles' Liverpool

DAVID BEDFORD

In Liverpool, you are born taking sides: you have to choose your tribe, whether it is football or religion. In fact, you have to choose both. I remember at the age of ten being asked by a complete stranger, "Liverpool or Everton?" That was my choice of football teams, which for me was Liverpool Football Club. It still is. He then asked me the religious question: "Catholic or Protestant?" In Liverpool, this is not a question where your interrogator is checking to see if you are an evangelist looking to share the "good news" about your faith. It has very little to do with any belief system or personal faith. In fact, it is like choosing the football club with which you share your affiliation. It is with this tribe that you attend your place of worship (like the football stadium) and you sing your hymns together (like the football anthems). It is a congregation of like-minded people who gather every weekend to worship their team. So how did I answer the question about religion? It was quite easy, because my father was a vicar at the local St. Philemon's Church, which was part of the Church of England. I was brought up in a Christian household and attended church every Sunday, something that I still do to this day, though in a Methodist/United Reformed Church.

My father's church, opposite St. Silas School, was officially entitled the Parish Church of St. Philemon with St. Silas. The original St. Silas Church had been demolished following damage during the Second World War, though not before a young Richy Starkey had occasionally attended choir practice and the odd official service there.

So there it was: choose the Protestant Church of England or the Roman Catholic Church. It was easy for most people, as they followed the religion of their parents. It was supposedly part of your DNA, and you are rarely given a choice in childhood as to which to follow. Belief was incidental: your religion was a way of life. They were certainly the two dominant religious denominations in Liverpool, but in my local area of South Liverpool, they weren't the only choices. In fact, Liverpool has a religious history as diverse as its population and none more so than the area around where Ringo Starr grew up.

Young Richy's walk to school took him from his Admiral Grove home, along High Park Street, where St. Silas Church had stood. It was bombed, along with the surrounding area, on October 19, 1940, just three months after Richy was born. As he continued his walk along High Park Street, he would pass Our Lady of Mount Carmel Roman Catholic Church, where a young Gerry Marsden, who would form Gerry and the Pacemakers, was a member. He would then pass St. Peter's Methodist Church. Opposite him was Wellington Street Baptist Church.

Turning left down Park Road, he was heading to heart of the Dingle and his school, Dingle Vale Secondary Modern School. One of the buildings he passed was Peel Hall, where, with his friends in the Eddie Clayton Skiffle Group, he would make his musical debut. It was affiliated with the Protestant Order of the Orange Lodge, of which Richy and his family were members. Known as the "Orange Lodge," they were at the heart of the sectarian battles that divided a lot of Liverpool. Just beyond Peel Hall was the Ancient Chapel of Toxteth Park, which linked Liverpool with America's Pilgrim fathers.

The Ancient Chapel of Toxteth Park

Officially known as the Toxteth Unitarian Chapel, the Ancient Chapel is the oldest building in the Dingle area. This church became one of the most rebellious religious buildings in Liverpool in the seventeenth century. Founded around 1618, it was established on the land belonging to one of Liverpool's rich landowners, Sir Richard Molyneux. His land became home to the Puritans, who wanted to escape the religious persecution that was prevailing in England at the time. With the founding of the Church of England in the sixteenth century following King Henry VIII's disagreement with the pope over his wish to have his marriage annulled, there was sustained persecution of the Catholics. However, the Church of England didn't just persecute Catholics but sought to control all forms of public worship. The Puritans sought to purify the structures and the practices within the Church of England. These Puritans were seen as dissidents, and as in the case of Toxteth Park, they had some religious freedom to follow their own forms of worship. But the Church of England was cracking down on the dissidents and would later make it illegal for anyone over the age of sixteen to follow any forms of religious worship outside the Book of Common Prayer, the official liturgical guide for the Church of England. Sensing the change, many Puritans left England for the new world across the Atlantic.

One of the first schoolmasters of the Ancient Chapel of Toxteth was Richard Mather, a prominent Puritan. Objecting to persecution, Mather headed for the south coast of England. It was there that Mather followed in the wake of the Pilgrim fathers and sailed for America. The family settled in Boston, Massachusetts, where Mather continued to preach. Richard Mather had a son, Increase, who followed his father into the ministry, becoming the president of Harvard College for twenty years. Increase's son, Cotton, was also a minister in Boston and became a prolific author and scientist; however, he is most famously remembered for his part in the Salem Witch Trials.

Richard Mather is remembered in Liverpool with a road named after him, Mather Avenue, from which Paul McCartney would catch his "bus in seconds flat" to take him to his high school, the Liverpool Institute, every day. Mather Avenue leads to Allerton Road and through Penny Lane.

To demonstrate the diversity of religious organizations in Liverpool, within a one-mile radius of Ringo's house were the following religious organizations and denominations: Our Lady of Mount Carmel Roman Catholic Church, St Peter's Methodist Church, St. Philemon's Church of England, Belvedere Independent Baptist Church, the Sailors Chapel, Ancient Chapel of Toxteth Park, Toxteth Tabernacle Baptist Church, St. Malachy Roman Catholic Church, St. Gabriel's Church of England, St. Cleopas Church of England, St. Margaret's Church of England, Christian Science Third Church, Greek Orthodox Church, Princes Road Synagogue, Unitarian Church; United Reformed Church, St. Paul's (Church of England), St. James (Church of England), and others. Just over one mile away was the German Lutheran Church, Liverpool Chinese Gospel Church, Swedish Seamans Church, and the Anglican Cathedral, which was still under construction.

However, with many of these churches being independent or in the smaller collection of free churches, Liverpool was dominated by the two major Christian denominations: the Church of England, part of the worldwide Anglican

Communion, and the Roman Catholic Church. These two religious institutions would play a significant part in the family lives of John, Paul, George, and Ringo.

The years that followed King Henry VIII's argument with Rome led to the dissolution of the monasteries and the Protestant persecution of Catholics, apart from a few years under Queen Mary, a Catholic, who persecuted the Protestants in return. There were ritual burnings at the stake for heresies, depending on who was calling the shots on the throne at the time. Is it any wonder there were tensions between the two churches? Whatever happened to love thy neighbor as thyself? It seemed like the faith at the heart of Christianity had little to do with the religious traditions. But that was hundreds of years ago. Why should that matter?

The Church of England has been the official denomination since Queen Elizabeth I, who was the queen of England and Ireland from 1558 to 1603. Every monarch since then has the title of "Defender of the Faith" and is the de facto head of the Church of England. The fact that monarchs were also the ruler of Ireland is significant to what happened next, the ramifications of which are still felt in Liverpool today and impacted the lives of the Beatles.

A Dutch sovereign, King William III, known as William of Orange, ascended to the throne of England, Scotland, and Ireland in 1689. He left his mark on British history in 1690 when he led an English army across the Irish Sea to quell the Irish rebellion. The battle was between King William III and the deposed King James of England, Ireland, and Scotland. Known as the Battle of the Boyne, the conflict took place close to Drogheda on the River Boyne and was fought to defend Protestantism. After the battle, King William—often referred to as "King Billy" by Protestants to this day—marched into Dublin. This battle is still commemorated on July 12 every year, especially in Belfast in Northern Ireland, Glasgow in Scotland, and Liverpool. It has often led to sectarian division, fighting, and the Irish nationalism that resulted in the formation of the IRA, the Irish Republican Army, founded in 1917.

In 1920, the British government passed the Government of Ireland Act, which partitioned Ireland and split it into Northern Ireland, which was predominantly Protestant and loyal to the United Kingdom, known as Unionists, and what became the Republic of Ireland, which was mainly the home of Irish nationalists, who were Catholic and believed in a united Ireland. Prompted by the massacre known as "Bloody Sunday" between the British Army and protesters in 1972, Paul McCartney wrote the song "Give Ireland Back to the Irish," which was banned by the BBC.

The "Orange Lodge"

Following the victory at the Battle of the Boyne, those cities with a large Irish population, like Belfast, Glasgow, and Liverpool, hold marches on July 12 by the "Orange Lodge." Its official title is the Loyal Orange Institute, though it is more commonly known as the Orange Order, but it is always referred to in Liverpool as either the "Orange Lodge" or just the "Lodge." Although it is well-known in the cities with the highest Irish population, the Orange Order has lodges or meeting places across the United Kingdom and Commonwealth and in the United States. Liverpool is the only English city to have an Orange Lodge, though it is also the most Catholic city in the United Kingdom by numbers of parishioners. These are the tensions that have caused many a street battle.

Although the "Lodge" commemorates the Battle of the Boyne in 1690, the Orange Order wasn't founded until over a century later, following continued Protestant-Catholic sectarian fighting. As an organization, it was founded to protect and promote the superiority of the Protestant Church of England over the Roman Catholic Church, as well as the Unionist support for the British monarch. One of its key tenets is that you must be a member of the Protestant Church of England, and you may not marry a Roman Catholic.[1] This becomes especially important in understanding the relationships within the families of Paul McCartney, George Harrison, and Ringo Starr.

This mixed marriage of Protestant and Catholic affected my wife's family. Her family were members of the Orange Lodge and, therefore, forbidden to marry a Catholic. However, one of my mother-in-law's sisters fell in love with and decided to marry a Catholic. The family were forbidden to attend the wedding, the daughter was disowned by her parents, and the rest of the family had to follow suit. My mother-in-law decided to ignore that advice and attended her sister's wedding, but she was punished when she got home. That is how seriously the Catholic/Protestant distinction was taken in the 1960s.

The Protestant Orange Lodge marches that Ringo took part in were still a huge spectacle in the 1970s and 1980s. One of my abiding memories of growing up in the Dingle was on July 12, when the Orange Lodge would parade from the nearby Southern Area Memorial Hall (known locally as SAMS) on Mill Street, the headquarters of the local lodge. They would have a full parade, with a drum major leading the way, throwing his mace in the air in front of the band that followed him. He was immediately followed by the men carrying the flags of their local lodge. The music was provided by a band made up of drums, pipes, bugles, vibraphones, and other instruments. The men would be wearing a traditional white shirt, plus a tie, with white gloves and a ceremonial apron, similar to those worn in similar organizations, like the Masons.

Following the band would be the men in their white shirts, without jackets, wearing their orange sashes, usually over both shoulders, connected by the waist at the front. A small carriage carries children dressed up as King William (of Orange) and Queen Mary, celebrating their victory at the Battle of the Boyne. Occasionally, fights would break out during the July 12 parades in areas divided by Protestants and Catholics, especially when the Orange Lodge marched past Catholic churches or through Catholic areas.

One of my abiding memories was as a young teenager, marching with the Boy's Brigade from my dad's church in the Dingle. As we passed an apartment block, we were pelted with objects from on high! One of those, a metal fork, landed between me—playing the snare drum—and my friend banging the bass drum. We were obviously mistaken for the Orange Lodge, and it could have turned out badly if that fork had embedded itself in our heads!

The Great Famine

In the 1840s, the "Great Famine" (also known as the "Potato Famine") resulted in the deaths of around one million people in Ireland. Between tenants being kicked off the English landowners' plots and the need for paid work, approximately 1.3 million Irish people came to Liverpool, Ireland's nearest major port and a well-known transatlantic gateway to the United States and Canada. A large proportion of Irish American immigrants can trace their journey back through Liverpool. However, around sixty thousand Irish migrants settled in Liverpool. Many didn't speak English, most had run out of money, and they had no jobs. It is not surprising, then, that many of those Irish migrants died soon after arriving in Liverpool.

The Irish author Greg Quiery has written an excellent book on the Irish migration, called *In Hardship and Hope*. He explains how migration shaped Liverpool. Even though many Irish now considered Liverpool their home, Irish immigrants retained a sense of themselves as Irish. However, they were only able to continue with some of the culture they had brought with them, because elements like the Irish language died out, as the only schoolteachers available were English speakers.

Although traditions like gathering as a family to celebrate birthdays and Christmas were continued, many of those traditional musical skills that had traveled from Ireland were, sadly, not passed on to the next generation.

However, at the large family gatherings, everyone had to know their song and be ready to sing it. Thankfully, argues Quiery, the passing on of their Irish history was retained within the families. "The Irish way was also one of oral tradition. This was how you passed on history and tradition, especially in poor communities, where you couldn't afford a piano or fiddle, or where they were illiterate; this was how you passed it on to the next generation."[2] If one wants to understand where the attitude, rebellious nature, and musical influence of the great Lennon/McCartney songwriting partnership began, then it is within those Irish migrants who helped to shape modern Liverpool and the Beatles, as all of the Fab Four had Irish roots, as did former Beatles drummer Pete Best.

Although the Orange Lodge had the July 12 as its parade day, the Catholics had their own day of celebration as well, and nowhere in the United Kingdom is it celebrated in more style than in Liverpool. St. Patrick's Day, March 17, was always celebrated by Irish Catholics as they honored their patron saint who, it is believed, set sail from Liverpool when he crossed over to Ireland to begin his mission. Not so much a Catholic celebration any more, St. Patrick's Day has become a day when people with even the smallest Irish heritage—mine is about 3 percent—come out, don big green hats, and drink Guinness, Dublin's finest export. Mostly enjoyed by students and young people, it has become a day of drinking and partying and enjoying the craic!

As Liverpool had suddenly received a large Irish and Catholic population in the 1840s, the very nature of Liverpool was changed. By the 1850s, over 20 percent of Liverpool's population was Irish. It is for this reason that they had such an effect on the city's culture, language, and outlook. There was then a second Irish migration to Liverpool in the 1950s and 1960s.

Although the Northern Ireland "Troubles" of the 1970s rarely affected Liverpool, there was still a sectarian division. Thankfully, after the violence of the 1970s and 1980s, the Anglican bishop David Sheppard and the Roman Catholic archbishop Derek Worlock decided to work together to heal the divide between the two religious communities. The enormous impact of what was achieved by Sheppard and Worlock cannot be underestimated. Their work was incredible and brought healing and almost a complete end to the sectarianism in Liverpool. A statue of them was erected in 2005, paid for by the people of Liverpool, to commemorate their work.

With Liverpool having a large Protestant and Catholic population, the city has two cathedrals: the Anglican cathedral was designed by a Catholic, Sir Giles Gilbert-Scott, and the Roman Catholic cathedral was designed by a

Protestant, Sir Frederick Gibberd. To add to the beautiful irony, they stand at either end of Hope Street. That sign of hope now sees the statue of both great clergymen on Hope Street, and every year, a large group of Christians walk from one cathedral to the other to hold a joint service of Protestants and Catholics. The cathedrals take turns hosting the ceremony.

John Lennon: "The Luck of the Irish"

Why did John Lennon feel inspired to write "The Luck of the Irish"? The name Lennon is an "Anglicized" derivative of the Irish "O'Lennon," which comes from the ancient Gaelic "Ó Leannáin." John's great-grandfather James Lennon hailed from County Down, south of Belfast, and moved to Liverpool with his future wife, Jane McConville, and her family sometime in the 1840s during the Potato Famine. They lived in Saltney Street, North Liverpool, close to the dock where they first landed. On John's mother's side of the family, Julia Lennon's grandmother Elizabeth Gildea was born in 1851 in Omagh, County Tyrone, Ireland. So, John has Irish ancestry on both sides of his family, from both the North and South. Is it any wonder he wrote about Ireland and planned to retire in Ireland on the island of Dornish? Sadly, he never got to realize that dream. From a religious point of view, he was brought up in the Church of England.

John's two Irish songs, "Luck of the Irish" and "Sunday Bloody Sunday," featured on his 1972 album *Sometime in New York City*, focused on the Northern Ireland conflict as well as the controversial 1972 Bloody Sunday massacre. "Luck of the Irish" sets out the history from the point of view of the downtrodden ancestors whom he believed had been badly treated, reminiscent of those first Irish migrants who landed in Liverpool in the 1840s:

> You should have the luck of the Irish
> And you'd wish you was English instead.

He was under no illusion as to who was to blame:

> A thousand years of torture and hunger
> Drove the people away from their land
> A land full of beauty and wonder
> Was raped by the British brigands.

As usual, John didn't mince his words. He also referred to what he had been told, presumably by his family, of what happened to his great-grandparents and their fellow migrants:

> In the 'pool they told us the story
> How the English divided the land
> Of the pain and the death and the glory
> And the poets of auld Eireland.

One line in particular summed up what John felt about the cause of the trouble: "Why the hell are the English there anyway?"[3]

He was also incensed by the Bloody Sunday massacre in 1972 as he was preparing for his new album. His song "Sunday Bloody Sunday" left the listener in no doubt as to what he was writing about, but how many have heard that song and not realized the significance and power of the lyrics?

> Well, it was Sunday Bloody Sunday
> Oh, when they shot the people there
> The cries of thirteen martyrs filled the free Derry air
> Is there any one amongst you, dare to blame it on the kids?
> Not a soldier boy was bleeding when they nailed the coffin lids.

He even picks up on the marches that the "Orange Lodge" made when they walked into Catholic areas, which he, along with the Catholics, saw as inflammatory: "When Stormont bans our marches, they've got a lot to learn." He even made his views very clear on what should happen:

> How dare you hold to ransom, a people proud and free
> Keep Ireland for the Irish, put the English back to sea.[4]

When talking about the violence in Ireland, John was naturally torn. "I understand why they're doing it, and if it's a choice between the IRA or the British army, I'm with the IRA. But if it's a choice between violence and non-violence, I'm with non-violence. So it's a very delicate line. . . . Our backing of the Irish people is done, really, through the Irish Civil Rights, which is not the IRA. Although I condemn violence, if two people are fighting, I'm probably gonna be on one side or the other, even though I'm against violence."[5] John and Yoko donated the proceeds from their two Irish songs to the civil rights movements in Ireland and New York.

One has to wonder, though, if John's mother, Julia, ever told him about the night she survived an IRA bomb. Liverpool was usually immune from any IRA attacks due to its substantial Irish population. However, just before World War II broke out, the IRA exploded two bombs in Liverpool. First, on April 5, 1939, on Menlove Avenue, close to Calderstones Park, an IRA bomb exploded, causing panic and terror in the area. On May 3, 1939, teargas bombs were planted and detonated at the Trocadero cinema, where Julia worked. Although the bombs were only planted to cause alarm and make a statement, the moviegoers weren't to know that and quickly exited the cinema. There was a further explosion at the Tatler Cinema in Liverpool City Centre at the end of May 1939.

The IRA campaign in Liverpool ended when a far greater enemy was at the door. On September 1, 1939, Germany invaded Poland. Two days later, Great Britain declared war on Germany. It was during the second war of that generation that the Beatles were born.[6]

So even John Lennon, who was supposedly a "working-class/middle-class" boy from the very English village of Woolton, had Ireland in his roots, which he brought into his songwriting. When you understand the fact that John had grown up with the divisions of religions, sectarianism, and religious prejudice by people hijacking a faith supposedly about loving one another, is it any wonder he wrote, "Imagine there's no religion"? He didn't say "no faith" but "no religion."

John was brought up at St. Peter's Church in Woolton, where in 1957 he met Paul McCartney. A regular in Sunday school from the age of five, he also sang in the choir and was part of the church youth group. He was, however, thrown out of the church choir for stealing fruit from the Harvest Festival. The other choirboys started giggling, and the thief was soon identified. John and his partner in crime, Pete Shotton, were expelled from the choir and also barred from the church.[7] It seems that Jesus—or at least his representatives—were bigger than Lennon.

Paul McCartney: "Give Ireland Back to the Irish"

Paul McCartney's family were also firmly rooted in Ireland on both his mother's and father's side. His maternal grandfather, Owen Mohan (sometime changed to Mohin), was born in Tullynamalrow, County Monaghan. Although we know that his paternal ancestors came from somewhere in Ireland, we also know that the Irish McCartneys emigrated to Scotland from Ireland before settling in Liverpool. "On his mother's side," says the historian Greg Quiery, "the Mohins were active republicans, for example. Irish families who came to Liverpool would be not putting an emphasis on republicanism. You might have an uncle who fought in the war of Irish independence, but the family in Liverpool might keep that quiet. You couldn't keep some of that being passed on to the next generation, even subliminally."[8]

McCartney also commented, "Half of Liverpool comes from Ireland. That was the shocking thing: It felt like we were fighting us, and that we'd killed them, and it was all very visibly on the news."[9] McCartney's family were probably the most Irish of all the Beatles, with strong roots on both sides. However, they were not Catholic on both sides, which brought complications. Jim McCartney's family were Protestants, while Mary McCartney (née Mohan/Mohin) were Catholic. Although most mixed marriages are thought of as interracial, there is a religious mixed marriage, which is of significance in Liverpool. The marriage between a Protestant and a Catholic can have significant difficulties, including how the children will be raised and which school they will go to—state, Church of England, or Catholic—decisions that can be a strain on any marriage.

Jim and Mary, however, managed to make it work without too much trouble, with Mary's Catholicism a greater influence than Jim's Protestantism. That religious tolerance didn't extend to indoctrination, as Mary felt that sending her boys, Paul and Mike, to Catholic School would be too much. The two boys were, therefore, baptized Catholic but sent to state schools. In fact, Paul joined the choir at St. Barnabas Church (at the top of Penny Lane), which was part of the Church of England.

"When he was twelve, Owen Mohin left for Glasgow, Scotland," remarked Mike McCartney, "and at the age of 25 settled down in Liverpool where he married Mary Teresa Danher (aged 26) in St. Charles R. C. Church, Toxteth Park. After the death of his wife in 1919 he took his three children (Wilf, Mum and Bill) back to Eire."[10] Owen then returned to Liverpool with the family.

Paul reflected his religious upbringing, particularly in his song "Let It Be," which mixed the imagery of the Virgin Mary, so prominent in the Roman Catholic Church, with his own mother, Mary, who tragically died when Paul was only fourteen years old. "Let it be" is also, in its Hebrew form, translated as "Amen." He also repeated these images in "Lady Madonna," again reflecting on the name for the Virgin Mary as the Madonna. Much of Paul's religious philosophy was based on watching Protestant and Catholic speakers arguing with each other down at the Pier Head. It was always about the two religions arguing, though he never took sides. His parents' wisdom in not enforcing their religious views gave Paul a balanced upbringing.

Mike McCartney's abiding memory of his mother just before she died was of her crying in his bedroom. "She was holding a crucifix and a picture of one of her Catholic priest relatives."[11] It was only about a month later that she died. Mary knew what was wrong, but by the time she went to the doctor, her breast cancer was too far gone. "Before she died, she received the last rites and allowed the Catholic head of the clinic where she worked to tie rosary beads round her wrists, and admitted to Brother Bill's wife Auntie Dill, 'I would have liked to see the boys growing up.'"[12]

That Irish heritage instilled by Paul's mother, Mary, was always with him. With the strength of his Irish Catholic background, it is no wonder that he was incensed by the Bloody Sunday massacre in 1972, which he reflected in his song "Give Ireland Back to the Irish."

> "I wasn't really into protest songs—John had done that—but this time I felt that I had to write something, to use my art to protest," he said. Talking about the controversial stance that the Wings took, McCartney explained: "From our point of view, it was the first time people questioned what we were doing in Ireland. It was so shocking. I wrote 'Give Ireland Back to the Irish,' we recorded it and I was promptly phoned by the Chairman of EMI, Sir Joseph Lockwood, explaining that they wouldn't release it. He thought it was too inflammatory. I told him that I felt strongly about it and they had to release it. He said, 'Well it'll be banned,' and of course it was. I knew 'Give Ireland Back to the Irish' wasn't an easy route, but it just seemed to me to be the time (to say something)."[13]

Paul showed that his way of writing protest songs was very different from John's. Whereas Lennon was very angry and outspoken, McCartney was more diplomatic and assertive, still making his point:

> Give Ireland back to the Irish
> Don't make them have to take it away
> Give Ireland back to the Irish
> Make Ireland Irish today
> Great Britain you are tremendous
> And nobody knows like me
> But really what are you doin'?
> In the land across the sea.[14]

George Harrison: French Irish

George's Irish roots came through his maternal grandfather, John French, who was from Wexford in southeastern Ireland. Unlike the Lennons and McCartneys, he did not come over in the Great Famine. French journeyed to Liverpool after selling off the family's smallholding in the early twentieth century. Also unlike Lennon, who made frequent childhood trips to Scotland to visit family, George made several family trips to Ireland in his childhood, encouraged by his mother, Louise. "George had cousins living in Drumcondra and he made a point of visiting them when they went over to play in 1963." George was already a regular on that ferry across the Irish Sea because, in the late 1940s and early 1950s, the family would get the boat from Liverpool to Dublin to stay with the cousins and go to places like Malahide beach. "I have photos of him there and (of him) walking down O'Connell Street with his mother. So there was a strong connection from the family point of view," says Damian Smyth, coauthor of *The Beatles and Ireland*.[15]

George Harrison's father, Harold, described himself as a "lapsed Anglican," while his mother, Louise, was Catholic—another mixed marriage, similar to the McCartneys. Louise wanted George to be baptized into the Roman Catholic Church at Our Lady of Good Help in Wavertree, just down the road from their Arnold Grove home. George also joined the Boy Scouts movement at St. Anthony of Padua Catholic Church in Mossley Hill. When George was enrolled in Dovedale Primary School, a recent law change allowed Louise and Harold to exclude four-year-old George from the daily religious instruction, which made him stand out at an early age and may have contributed to his religious rebellion. This was probably prompted by what happened to George's sister, Louise, after returning from evacuation. "When I came back, the school had received bomb damage. We were sent to the local Roman Catholic convent to be taught by the nuns. Mum didn't think I was doing as well as I could, as all I was learning was the catechism."[16] She was soon moved to a non-Catholic school, where she thrived.

George's exclusion from daily religious assembly also occurred at the Liverpool Institute, as observed by his school friend Ray O'Brien.

> One of the other ways of standing out from the crowd was morning religious assembly. Every morning on the dot of nine o'clock, all the boys would gather in the hall for assembly. If you were late, then at the end of the assembly, you were paraded down the middle of the hall to

the front and made to stand in front of the whole school: being named and shamed. This was supposed to be a deterrent, which worked for many boys. George would often be in this group. As well as the latecomers, there were the boys excused from the religious service. This group included those boys who were from either Jewish or Catholic families, and George was often with them.[17]

Following his mother's more liberal stance toward the Catholic Church, George, in an interview with *Rolling Stone* in 1968, described his views of the Catholic Church: "You know, this is the Catholic trick—they nail you when you're young and brainwash you, and then they've got you for the rest of your life."[18] His last album was titled *Brainwashed*, which indicates that he held this view for most of his life.

George was always the one seen as the "spiritual" Beatle because of his embrace of Eastern religion in his time with the Beatles. He was the one encouraging his fellow band members to travel to India with him, he was friends with Ravi Shankar, and he introduced the sitar to Beatles songs. Where did this come from?

First, George's mother listened to Radio India during her pregnancy with George, which she felt was a contributory factor. Second, another great influence on George's embrace of Eastern philosophies came from Mona Best, the mother of Pete Best and the female entrepreneur behind the Casbah Coffee Club. Mona's father, Major Thomas Shaw, was Irish and was stationed in India, where Mona was born and grew up. It was there that Mona discovered the Eastern religions. In those early days at the Casbah, Mona would regale the lads, including John, Paul, and George, with tales of India, Eastern religions, and philosophies. George picked up on those influences, and in the 1960s, when those Eastern religious ideas came up again with the Maharishi, he would have recalled those discussions with Mona.

Richy "Ringo" Starkey: Orange or Not?

Ringo, like his fellow Beatles, also had Irish roots, though not as strong. He had an Aunt Mary, who came from Mayo in Ireland. For a time, Richy's family were involved with the Orange Lodge in the Dingle, with the venue where Richy and his friends made their debut, Peel Hall, being their local Orange Lodge. Young Richy started to learn the accordion and occasionally marched with the band.

Although members of the Orange Lodge weren't supposed to have anything to do with Catholics, Richy's mother, Elsie, was not a typical member of the lodge. Richy's childhood friend Marie Maguire was the daughter of Elsie's best friend. "I was brought up a Catholic by my mum," said Marie, "and Elsie was a member of the Orange Lodge—staunch Protestants who normally hate the Catholics. However, mum and Elsie celebrated the 12 July (Orange Lodge celebration) and 17 March (St. Patrick's Day for the Irish Catholics). They would sing the songs together and enjoy the day, and proved that not all Protestants and Catholics had to hate each other."[19]

Ringo's memories of his religious influences were quite straightforward: "I was a Protestant—my mother had been a member of the Orange Lodge for a while although not for long. On 17 March, St Patrick's Day, all the Protestants beat up the Catholics because they were marching and on 12 July, Orangeman's Day, all the Catholics beat up the Protestants. That's how it was, Liverpool being the capital of Ireland, as everybody always says."[20] The family affiliation with the Orange Lodge didn't last long, but Richy was well aware of the religious tensions between the Protestants and Catholics locally. Religion wasn't something that raised its head in Ringo's life, even though he attended the ashram in Rishikesh with his fellow Beatles. He did, however, return to religion later in his life, which he announced at the Grammy Museum in 2010. "For me, God is in my life. I don't hide from that. . . . I think the search has been on since the '60s."[21]

Those Liverpool-Irish roots of the Beatles were rooted in the sectarian divisions between the Protestants and Catholics that went back centuries, affecting their beliefs, their families, and their music. Liverpool people are born taking sides, whether it is football, religion, or, since the birth of the Fab Four, being a fan of the Beatles. The religion of their families played a huge part in the lives, music, and spirituality of John, Paul, George, and Ringo.

NOTES

1. McGarry and O'Leary, *Explaining Northern Ireland*, 180.
2. Quoted in Bedford, *Country of Liverpool*, 36.
3. Lennon and Ono, "Luck of the Irish."
4. Lennon and Ono, "Sunday Bloody Sunday."
5. Blaney, *John Lennon*, 114.
6. Lewisohn, *Tune In*, 25.
7. Norman, *John Lennon*, 47.
8. Quoted in Bedford, *Country of Liverpool*, 46.
9. Kielty, "Story."
10. McCartney, *Thank U Very Much*, 17.
11. Ibid., 22.
12. Ibid., 22.
13. Dasgupta, "Paul McCartney's Song."
14. McCartney and McCartney, "Give Ireland Back to the Irish."
15. Butler, "How George Harrison."
16. Louise Harrison, interview with David Bedford, 2015.

17. Quoted in Bedford, *Liddypool*, 88.
18. Jones, "*Rolling Stone* Interview."
19. Quoted in Bedford, *Liddypool*, 96.
20. Beatles, *Anthology*, 36.
21. Hough, "Beatles' Drummer."

BIBLIOGRAPHY

Bedford, David. *The Country of Liverpool: Nashville of the North*. Liverpool: David Bedford Books, 2020.

———. *Liddypool: Birthplace of The Beatles*. Liverpool: Liddypool, 2017.

Blaney, John. *John Lennon: Listen to This Book*. N.p.: Paper Jukebox, 2005.

Butler, Jonathan deBurca. "How George Harrison—Who Had Strong Irish Connections—Was Far from the Quiet Beatle." *Independent*, February 26, 2018.

Dasgupta, Pubali. "Paul McCartney's Song in Support of Northern Ireland." *Far Out*, February 2021.

Hough, Andrew. "The Beatles' Drummer Ringo Starr Admits: 'I Have Found God.'" *Daily Telegraph*, February 3, 2010.

Jones, Nick. "The *Rolling Stone* Interview: George Harrison, Part 2." *Rolling Stone*, February 24, 1968.

Kielty, Martin. "The Story of Paul McCartney's 'Give Ireland Back to the Irish.'" *Ultimate Classic Rock*, February 19, 2017. https://ultimateclassicrock.com/paul-mccartney-give-ireland-back-to-the-irish.

Lennon, John, and Yoko Ono. "Luck of the Irish." *Some Time in New York City*. Apple/EMI, 1972.

———. "Sunday Bloody Sunday." *Some Time in New York City*. Apple/EMI, 1972.

Lewisohn, Mark. *Tune In: The Beatles—All These Years*. Vol. 1. New York: Little, Brown, 2013.

McCartney, Mike. *Thank U Very Much: Mike McCartney's Family Album*. London: Arthur Baker, 1981.

McCartney, Paul, and Linda McCartney. "Give Ireland Back to the Irish." Single. Apple, 1972.

McGarry, John, and Brendan O'Leary. *Explaining Northern Ireland: Broken Images*. Chichester, UK: Blackwell, 1995.

Norman, Philip. *John Lennon: The Life*. New York: HarperCollins, 2008.

Quiery, Greg. *In Hardship and Hope: A History of the Liverpool Irish*. Liverpool, UK: G and K, 2017.

PART 2

THE BEATLES AS INDIVIDUALS

CHAPTER 3

The Religious Sensibility of Paul McCartney

KENNETH CAMPBELL

In *The Beatles Anthology*, Paul McCartney reflects on his religious upbringing, saying, "I was exposed to many religious arguments on the pierhead, and I came to the conclusion that 'God' is just the word 'good' with the 'o' taken out, and Devil is the word evil with a 'D' added. Really, all that people have done throughout history is to personify the two forces of Good and Evil."[1] Such an insight seems strikingly simple on the one hand but reflects a somewhat mature and profound religious sensibility on the other, reflecting the notion held by many spiritual masters throughout the centuries that God, whatever God might be, is not the anthropomorphized entity so familiar to people raised in the Judeo-Christian tradition. Yet, does this statement represent the sum total of McCartney's views on religion or the approach to religion taken in both his life and work? This chapter argues that McCartney's religious sensibility has evolved over the course of his life and that this evolution has manifested itself in both his life and his music, sometimes consciously, other times less so. McCartney might not have thought of religion in conventional terms or have aspired to the levels of spirituality sought, if not attained, by George Harrison, but this does not mean that he neglected his spirituality altogether or that he lacked a religious sensibility. For example, the profound insights McCartney shared in a song like "Eleanor Rigby" easily match any contributed by Harrison to the Beatles oeuvre. In addition, however, this chapter also explores the limitations of McCartney's religious sensibility, focusing especially on his fear of death and general level of discomfort with the topic. Attitudes toward death and the afterlife need not have religious overtones, but they frequently do. McCartney's uneasiness about death manifested itself most prominently when, shortly after the death of John Lennon, he responded to a question about that tragic event with the seemingly flippant comment, "It's a drag"—a response that elicited a great deal of criticism and later self-reproach on McCartney's part. This did not necessarily mean, however, that McCartney lacked a religious sensibility or that this comment reflected his final word on the subject of death. In fact, this chapter argues that religious and spiritual considerations frequently crop up in his songwriting beginning in the early stages of his career and that these considerations prepare the way both for a more mature approach to death and spirituality as he aged and for his ability to compose such an explicitly Christian work in his *Liverpool Oratorio* in 1991.

The Beatles Years

In the early years of the Beatles' recording career, their music did not generally display much in the way of a concern for religious concepts, at least not in terms people would generally recognize as such. McCartney's songs, in particular, displayed a sunny disposition that bordered on solar worship, as in "I'll Follow the Sun," from *Beatles for Sale*, which foreshadowed his later "Good Day Sunshine," not to mention Harrison's masterpiece, "Here Comes the Sun," and John Lennon's "Sun King," both from the Beatles' last recorded album, *Abbey Road*. Joe Robinson calls "Good Day Sunshine "euphoric, exuberant sun worship at its efflorescent best, reflecting and refracting the summer of heat which came before the summer of love."[2] Most early Beatles songs, however, consisted of catchy, if sophisticated, pop tunes that abound with the euphoria, longing, and travails associated with young love.

McCartney, like many young men in their twenties, especially those who have not grown up in a particularly religious household, felt no need for organized religion or even an overarching religious philosophy. Asked to mull the topic by the journalist Maureen Cleave in 1963, he replied, "I don't feel I have to be religious. I may need it as I get older to comfort me when I die. But now, as far as I'm concerned, I can rot."[3] When asked about his religious views two years later, McCartney said of the Beatles, "We all feel roughly the same. We're all agnostics."[4] A juxtaposition of these two quotations suggests two interesting aspects of McCartney's thinking about religion though, beyond his relative indifference to it at the time. First, both quotations imply uncertainty, a youthful acknowledgment of his egocentric perspective, tempered by a willingness to reserve judgment. "I don't feel," "as far as I'm concerned," "We all feel"—McCartney is saying this is the way I or we see the world, not necessarily the way it is. Second, they imply an openness to change in the future—"I may need it when I get older," McCartney says, while agnosticism implies an open mind as well as uncertainty. The statement was an admission on McCartney's part that neither he nor the Beatles had all the answers, but it would soon become clear that they had not finished searching for them. At this point, McCartney was simply reflecting the perspective he had learned both at home and on the docks of Liverpool that variation in religion had stirred up too many disputes and too much hatred and that it was better to remain indifferent, while adopting an attitude of tolerance toward those who might hold differing viewpoints. His own family provided an excellent example of this, since his mother was a Catholic and his father a Protestant, although not much of a practicing one, who had to look past each other's religious backgrounds to forge a successful marriage.

McCartney was seemingly more buoyant and optimistic than Harrison and Lennon, who both displayed dark sides to their personalities and a skeptical approach to fame and fortune relatively early. McCartney convincingly bobbed his head and smiled infectiously any time the Beatles performed anywhere and seemed the most receptive of the group to dealing with the press and the public in a friendly and jovial manner. His early song contributions like "All My Loving" or "I've Just Seen a Face" were generally pop love songs sung to an upbeat tempo. By contrast, Harrison's first contribution to a Beatles album was a song called "Don't Bother Me" on 1964's *With the Beatles*, while "I'm a Loser" and especially "Help!" were admissions on Lennon's part that he was "not who he appeared to be" and that he felt suffocated by the direction his life had taken since the Beatles hit it big.

McCartney certainly proved capable, though, of exploring the dark side of love and romance in a song like 1965's "Yesterday," which Kenneth Womack has called "the Beatles' only thoroughly sad song," while morbidly reflecting on the dark side of the condition of modern humanity in "Eleanor Rigby."[5] In "Yesterday," McCartney writes about an irretrievable past that was infinitely better than either the present or the future that lies ahead. The end of a relationship is thoroughly sad because it is a small reminder of death, carrying as it does the end of one phase of life that prefigures the end of life itself. The start of a new relationship carries with it such joy and excitement precisely because it promises a new life, a rebirth of sorts. This rebirth serves as a reminder of the promise of a future that brings us back to the hopes and aspirations of our childhood and carries with it the possibility of the actual fulfillment of those same hopes and aspirations.

Yet what happens to those lonely people without a relationship, especially the aged and alone? That question becomes the theme of "Eleanor Rigby," which I would argue is a more "thoroughly sad song" than "Yesterday." The singer of "Yesterday" can always start a new relationship, but the lyrics of "Eleanor Rigby" make clear that this possibility does not exist for Father McKenzie, the priest who darns his socks with nobody there and writes a sermon that no one will hear. He is approaching death, old and alone, with even his religious beliefs no guarantor of salvation, at least from the kind of pervasive loneliness McCartney writes about in the song. Eleanor Rigby, the spinster who picks up the rice after a wedding, faces loneliness even in death, with no one to attend her funeral and apparently without even the promise of salvation in the afterlife—"No one was saved." Devin McKinney, who described "Eleanor Rigby" as "at once an impeccably wrought chamber piece and a twisted, miserable thing," argues that this line "refers not to the Devil but to Death," which would fit well with McCartney's experience of death, which even refused to spare his mother when McCartney still needed her.[6] Yet this song also raises the larger question of the ultimate purpose of life, which McCartney himself had begun to struggle with by the mid-1960s.

Similar themes recur in another McCartney song that appears on *Revolver*, which he even titled "For No One," perhaps in reference to the declaration that "no one was saved" in "Eleanor Rigby." "For No One" further explores the mystery behind life's ultimate purpose and the relationships that end so abruptly, whether through physical death, as in the case of McCartney's mother, or simply the death of a relationship (Jane Asher), which in many ways mirrors loss through actual death in the sense of that loss becoming just as permanent. McCartney could be describing the icy stare of a person who no longer reciprocates the love that one partner still feels—or the face of a corpse: "In her eyes you see nothing / No sign of love behind the tears." What right does any lover have to question when a relationship ends by saying, as McCartney does in the song, "A love that should have lasted years!" Should have lasted years according to whom? If a relationship ends, that itself becomes a sign that it actually should not have lasted, unless . . . the love ends because of a premature death caused by illness, accident, or murder (the theme of another McCartney song, "Maxwell's Silver Hammer"). The original title of "For No One" was "Why Did It Die?," a question to which McCartney offers no answer in the song.

McCartney, therefore, despite his frequent association with bright, sunny pop tunes such as "Good Day Sunshine," did not actually shy away from sad or somber topics that represented the darkness that helped give meaning to the light on which he frequently focused. Indeed, not only did McCartney pen a cri de coeur such as "Yesterday" and the sublimely dark "Eleanor Rigby," but also in his personal life, he, like both Lennon and Harrison, found happiness elusive when based solely on material rewards and worldly success. The Beatles' biographer Bob Spitz writes, "Paul would recall how he was 'looking to fill some kind of hole.' He acknowledged feeling 'a little bit of emptiness' in his soul, 'a lack of spiritual fulfillment.'"[7] In 1966, McCartney said the following in an interview with Barry Miles: "Because, you see, we've been in the lucky position of having our child-hood ambitions fulfilled. We've got all the big-house and big car and everything. So that then, you stand on that plank then, having reached the end of space, and you look across the wall, and there's more space! And that's it! You get your car and house and your fame and your World Wide ego-satisfaction, then you just look over the wall and there's a complete different scene there, that it really is, and which is really the scene."[8] This realization led McCartney, who regarded faith in God in a traditional religious sense as spurious, to a further pursuit of personal fulfillment, partially through drugs such as marijuana and LSD but also through his openness to the teachings of the Indian guru Maharishi Mahesh Yogi and the practice of Transcendental Meditation at the height of the Beatles' fame. Only twenty-four years old at the time, McCartney realized that he still had much to learn about a universe that he was only just beginning to perceive in a different way. He told Miles:

> At the back of my brain there's a thing telling me that everything is beautiful and everything is great and that instead of imposing things like: "I don't like that television show" or "No, I don't like the theatre," "No, no. I don't like so-and-so" that I know really that it's all great and that everything's great and that there's no bad ever if I can think of it all as great. . . . I'm only just starting to try and think of things like that, so it still is difficult to communicate with people. But the aim is to just, one day, really just to sit there and not feel any of the hang-ups that people feel towards each other.[9]

Though not religious in the traditional Western sense, this certainly sounds like the beginnings of McCartney's personal religious sensibility. If everything is beautiful, from whence does this universal beauty ultimately derive? One may not choose to call it God, but whether one refers to the source, the universe, or even nature (although with the references to television and theater, McCartney is certainly not confining himself to that here), the origin of that beauty must ultimately derive from something beyond our individual perceptions of it. This is especially the case given how unreliable and inconsistent those perceptions tend to be.

In his own spiritual quest, however, McCartney sought more something he might find useful in his own life rather than some form of ultimate truth or pure escape. McCartney later described his approach to the Beatles' visit to the Maharishi's ashram in Rishikesh in February 1968: "Well, being a little bit pragmatic, I thought in my own mind, I'll give it a month, then If I really like it, I'll come back and organize to go out there for good, but I won't go on this 'I may never come back' thing, I won't burn bridges."[10] While in Rishikesh, McCartney experienced one moment in which he described himself as coming close to a feeling of total bliss: "After one of these sessions, I remember having a great meditation, one of the best I ever had. . . . It appeared to me that I was like a feather over a hot-air pipe, a warm-air pipe. I was just suspended by this hot air, which was something to do with the meditation. And it was a very blissful feeling. . . . And I thought, Well, hell, that's great, I couldn't buy that anywhere. That was the most pleasant, the most relaxed I ever got, for a few minutes, I really felt so light, so floating, so complete."[11]

By 1966, the Beatles had acquired an extraordinary amount of influence over the youth of the 1960s, who saw them as coding powerful spiritual messages into their music and lyrics that reflected not only their artistic preeminence but also their status as secular saints who deserved the level of worship their fans bestowed on them. While the Beatles could never live up to that, it would be wrong to assume that they did not provide their fans with positive messages that carried with them spiritual or religious overtones, including songs written by Paul McCartney. For example, "Good Day Sunshine," inspired by the Lovin' Spoonful's "Daydream," returned listeners of 1966's *Revolver* to the buoyant optimism inspired by new love on a warm spring day from the bleak melancholy of "Eleanor Rigby." More importantly, in "Here, There, and Everywhere," McCartney offered the hope that love would never die and that even in death, it still existed "here, there, and everywhere." McCartney said he wrote "The Fool on the Hill," which appeared on 1968's *Magical Mystery Tour* about "someone like Maharishi," or the idea that someone who appeared foolish in the eyes of the world might possess a wisdom rooted in deeper spiritual truths or teachings. "Divine folly is wiser than the wisdom of man," St. Paul wrote in his letter to the Corinthians. (1 Corinthians 1:25, *New English Bible*).

Nowhere was McCartney's penchant for mining his own wobbly understanding of spirituality for his music more on display than in the Gospel-tinged hymn "Let It Be." Inspired by a dream in which his mother appeared to him uttering the phrase that yielded the title of the song, McCartney took it as a felicitous message related to the ongoing conflicts he was experiencing with the other Beatles over the group's management and finances, which he then extended to a generalized spiritual meaning. The song speaks to the healing that the troubled and downtrodden of the world can find in simple acceptance, a principle common to multiple approaches to religion and spirituality, especially Buddhism. The message also seems at odds with the revolutionary and social change to which the Beatles contributed so heavily during the 1960s.[12]

Cevin Soling has even found something of a metaphysical dimension to McCartney's frequently denigrated "Maxwell's Silver Hammer," which appeared on *Abbey Road*, the last album the Beatles recorded as a group. In the song, one of Maxwell's three murder victims, Joan, is a student of pataphysical science, a concept introduced by the French writer Alfred Jarry (1873–1907), an alcoholic most associated with writing surrealist drama and whose concept of pataphysics involved something called the logic of the absurd. The *Oxford English Dictionary* defines "pataphysics" as "the study of a realm additional to metaphysics."[13] As it applies to the song, McCartney suggests that, even in the most tragic circumstances, there might exist some pataphysical explanation for occurrences, such as the random murders of three individuals by an obviously disturbed psychopath. The lightness and pop sensibility of the music contrasts sharply with the song's contents and reemphasizes the absurdity of these occurrences in what Soling describes as McCartney's "dark masterpiece." He connects the song with McCartney's grief over the equally senseless and inexplicable loss of his mother at such a young age.[14]

McCartney and Death

Ten years after the breakup of the Beatles, McCartney experienced another senseless and profoundly personal loss when John Lennon died from an assassin's bullet on December 8, 1980. Lennon's death affected McCartney deeply and in many ways. The two Liverpudlians had established a closeness as teenagers on the basis of the shared experience of losing their mothers that went beyond the normal ties of friendship, their relationship as bandmates, and even their songwriting partnership. Nor had that closeness completely evaporated, despite the episodes of jealousy and recrimination that accompanied the breakup of the Beatles and the subsequent years in which each strove to carve out their own identities and to emerge from the shadow of the Beatles. As Tim Riley explains, "to prevent runaway rumors and preserve their hard-fought integrity as solo figures, Lennon and McCartney visited far more often and warmly throughout the 1970s than they let on to the press."[15] In addition to losing one of his oldest and closest friends, however, McCartney now faced the prospect of a limitless future in which he would always draw unfavorable comparisons with Lennon, now frozen in time and revered beyond measure, perhaps undeservedly so, something McCartney was in a better position than anyone to recognize. He may also have carried some residual guilt over his role in the quarrels that beset their friendship in the last years of the Beatles and the early years of their breakup, though the fact that they were closer than many people thought in the 1970s suggests that this may not have been as much of a factor in his reaction to Lennon's death as some people think.

McCartney's experience with death of a close loved one had begun far too early, when his mother died when McCartney was only fourteen years old. At the time, he grappled with how to respond to her death in a culture that discouraged any outward displays of emotion from males. This expectation influenced many young men of McCartney's generation, including Lennon, as revealed in his stoic reaction to the news of the death of Stuart Sutcliffe, his close friend and former bandmate. McCartney later bitterly remembered praying during his mother's illness in an attempt to bargain with God to spare her life, recalling, "See, the prayers didn't work! When I really needed them to, as well."[16] This experience caused McCartney to lose whatever faith he had at a young age, depriving him of an important tool with which to handle life's inevitable tragedies.

As devastated as McCartney was by Lennon's death, then, he did not handle it well because he had never really learned how to handle death well, perhaps partly because of his admitted agnosticism when it came to the concepts of God and the afterlife. If McCartney believed that once you're gone, you're gone, for him anyway, this clearly made the loss harder to bear. The harder the loss was to bear, the more difficulty McCartney had in coming to grips with the depth of his emotion, leading to a reaction closer to denial than to authentic grief. Shortly after his mother's death, McCartney callously asked how the family would survive without her income, something for which he always felt remorse. However, his focus on the here and now was probably just a defense mechanism that allowed him to avoid thinking about either his feelings or the loss of his mother on a deeper and more emotional level. Besides, Mark Lewisohn argues that asking about the loss of Mary's income was not an act of frivolity but actually a legitimate concern for a fourteen-year-old to have, given the family's financial exigency.[17] When McCartney was approached by reporters shortly after Lennon died and he replied, "It's a drag," another remark that seemed incongruous with the occasion that elicited it, he likewise did so out of a state of denial of the true extent of his own sorrowful feelings, an intense sense of loss, and perhaps a sense of survivor's guilt. Of course, neither the press at the time nor McCartney's critics since have understood that, preferring to use it as an example of his emotional shallowness.

McCartney regretted this comment as much as, if not more than, the one made after his mother's death. In 1986, McCartney gave an interview to Chris Salewicz of Q magazine and talked about the incident as if it had just happened, still sounding quite defensive about it: "But, anyway, I said, 'It's a dra-a-ag.' If I could've I might've just lengthened that word 'drag' for about a thousand years, to get the full meaning. Hunter Davies was on television that night, giving a very reasoned account of John, and all the puppets sprang right up there. I thought it was well tasteless. Jesus Christ, ready with the answers, aren't we? Aren't we just ready with a summary?"[18] However, the fact that he made these comments following the deaths of his mother and Lennon in the first place illustrates the limitations of his own religious sensibility, which had ill prepared him to deal with death, especially of those taken so young and prematurely, under different but equally tragic and unforeseen circumstances. Lennon's death was obviously sudden, but as a teenager, McCartney had barely known his mother was sick when she went to the hospital, never to return. Furthermore, the loss of his mother was not the only sudden and tragic death that affected McCartney prior to the assassination of John Lennon in 1980. When Stuart Sutcliffe died of a cerebral hemorrhage on April 13, 1962, McCartney had feelings of remorse based on how he had treated Stuart when he was alive and playing alongside him in the band. As someone who always wanted people to like him, McCartney struggled with the ill will Stuart's family and those closest to him harbored for him.

To McCartney's credit, by all accounts, he handled the death of his wife Linda with grace and commitment, allowing himself the full range of emotions that came with it, something he had not succeeded at doing in these earlier instances. The same could be said of McCartney's response to the death of his other former bandmate, George Harrison, who passed away on November 29, 2001. He made a special effort to visit Harrison shortly before he died, taking the Concorde from London to say a special farewell to one of his oldest friends. During the visit, the two held hands and spoke warmly and joyously, no longer at loggerheads over McCartney's instructions to Harrison about how he wanted the guitar played on a particular song or the management and finances of the Beatles. Harrison's equanimity in the face of death impressed McCartney immensely, but he allowed himself to break down and cry after he left Harrison's bedside. Back in London when Harrison died, McCartney spoke to the press quite differently than he had when Lennon died, stating simply, "To me he's just my little baby brother. I loved him dearly."[19]

In the aftermath of his initial response to Lennon's death, McCartney attempted to defend himself, as he has ever since. At the time, he told the press, "I have hidden myself in my work today. But it keeps flashing into my mind. I feel shattered, angry and very sad."[20] His real response, however, came in the song he penned about Lennon's death in 1982, "Here Today." "And I am holding back tears no more," McCartney wrote and sang. Peter Ames Carlin has called the song "a revelation, a clear-eyed description of the most significant friendship in the history of popular music, from the perspective of its sole remaining partner."[21]

The relationship between Lennon and McCartney was also by far the most important friendship in McCartney's life. Many Beatles historians have noted, for example, that the lyrics of the song "Two of Us," from *Let It Be*, while ostensibly about McCartney's relationship with Linda, much more accurately describe his history with Lennon. One wonders how often Lennon might represent the real subject of McCartney's later songs that appear to be written to or about Linda; either way, it is easy to see how the two might become conflated, especially after Linda's death. For example, in "Lonely Road," from 2001's *Driving Rain*, the metaphor of riding down a road juxtaposes well with the trip taken by the two friends or lovers McCartney sang about in "Two of Us." He could even be referring to his mother when he sings that he does not want to get hurt "a second time around," that he does not "want to walk that lonely road again." The song opens with the verse:

> I tried to get over you
> I tried to find something new
> But all I could ever do
> Was fill my time
> With thoughts of you.

McCartney's Evolving Spirituality

Did McCartney's grief over his friend's death make him even angrier at a God in whom he claimed no longer to believe? Alternatively, did it open him up instead to reconsidering his views on religion? In 1991, McCartney composed his most overtly religious piece, a foray into classical music called the *Liverpool Oratorio*, in collaboration with American composer Carl Davis, which was commissioned by the Liverpool Royal Philharmonic Orchestra and performed at Liverpool's Anglican Cathedral, opening to a capacity audience of twenty-five hundred on June 28. McCartney intertwined music inspired by Handel and religious imagery common to the earlier musical forms he sought to imitate. His libretto mostly features scenes from his own life, but in it, McCartney employed lyrics that spoke of God's "eternal love" and "living in God forever." Steve Turner argues in *The Gospel According to the Beatles* that such language merely reflected McCartney's view that in this instance "God" simply meant "Good" and therefore should not be taken seriously as an endorsement of Christianity, despite the references to salvation the piece contained.[22] Perhaps not, but I think it is a mistake to assume that McCartney's religious sensibility had not evolved at all since he roamed the docks of Liverpool in his youth, despite what he might have said in the *The Beatles Anthology* a few years later. McCartney's *Oratorio* was a huge success, drawing a five-minute standing ovation at the premier and garnering mostly positive reviews. Allan Kozinn, writing in the *New York Times*, called it "a richly melodic, lavishly orchestrated piece about the loss and reclamation of innocence, love and faith."[23]

Furthermore, in 1989, McCartney released a live version of the folk song "All My Trials," which groups such as Peter, Paul, and Mary had popularized in conjunction with the social protest movements of the 1960s. In this performance, available on YouTube, McCartney's virtuosity is on full display as he sings a song that features the lyric, "All my trials, Lord, will soon be over." McCartney makes the song his own, appearing to embrace fully the spiritual meaning of the song. This is especially striking since the message seems at odds with both McCartney's generally sunny personality and his life experience. However, McCartney had known severe depression in his life, particularly in the period immediately following the breakup of the Beatles. In this performance, he seems to tap into that feeling and treat the song with the same serious intent expressed by the lyrics. McCartney used the song and music video to call attention to the plight of the poor and homeless affected by Margaret Thatcher's social policies, creating something of a political firestorm in the British press. Interestingly, however, the origins of the song stem from the reassurances a mother gives her children on her deathbed, which might explain why it might have resonated with McCartney and why he treated the material with such lucid sincerity. McCartney's version of the song reached number thirty-five on the UK singles charts.

In examining some of the more traditional pop/rock songs from McCartney's solo career, it becomes clear that he did not always shy away from spiritual messages or quasi-religious themes either, any more than he had as a member of the Beatles, perhaps most blatantly in the title of his 2005 album, *Chaos and Creation in the Backyard*. In the song "Fine Line," he offers the thought that "there is a long way between chaos and creation," but he turns a religious concept related to the origins of the universe into a series of precepts for life related to the importance of the individual choices we make. It is easy to blur the lines between a religious sensibility and a moral sensibility, but the two are directly connected in that the true test of any religion with regard to its service to humanity is how successfully it inculcates a desire to help others and make the world a better place. We have to choose, McCartney tells us, "between recklessness and courage" and weigh every decision because the rest of our life may depend on it and we have so much to lose. In another song from the same album, called "At the Mercy," McCartney further explores the role of contingency in human existence, placing us "at the mercy of a busy day" in one verse and "a busy road" in another. However, these are just metaphors for how the important decisions in life require careful thought because the day-to-day bustle of routine can too easily distract us from the opportunities in front of us. He says that he would "rather run and hide than stay and face the fear inside." Using the religious language of mercy, is he imploring a woman or God to take him on? Is it a woman or God who would like him to become a better man "than the one you know"? Whether intentional or not, the song displays a strong religious sensibility, and one could interpret it either way.

The same could be said of another song from *Chaos and Creation*, titled "Follow Me." The very title of the song evokes Jesus's biblical injunction to his disciples when he said, "Follow me and I will make you fishers of men" (Matthew 4:19, *English Standard Version*). The first verse of the song says:

> You lift up my spirits
> You shine on my soul
> Whenever I'm empty

> You make me feel whole
> I can rely on you
> To guide me through
> Any situation.

Although references to one's soul or sprits appear in any number of rock songs, when they do, they follow a tradition that dates to the early romantic poetry of the High Middle Ages and the tradition of courtly love in which the romantic quest bestows the same ennobling effect as the spiritual quest for a reunion with God. Think the Righteous Brothers' "(You're My) Soul and Inspiration" (1966) or Big Star's "O My Soul" (1973), for example. However, in McCartney's lyric from "Follow Me," the meaning is far more ambiguous because of the obvious religious sensibility of the song, as he addresses the song to one who rescues him from the "shores of sorrow," someone on whom he can count to guide him through "any situation." Clearly, any earthly love on which the singer would place such expectations is answering a need for comfort and guidance beyond that which any mere mortal possesses the capacity to offer. The song ends with the biblical injunction, "Follow me," repeated a number of times.

On his 2020 album, *McCartney III*, McCartney seems ready to face the prospect of death that he found so difficult to confront when he was younger. In his song "Winter Bird / When Winter Comes," McCartney once again uses the sun to evoke the concepts of warmth, divinity, and eternity. It is quite clear when he sings, "We'll fly away to find the sun when winter comes," that he is not speaking of returning to Arizona or the Bahamas. Why else would he sing in the same verse of staying indoors "to warm our toes" and flying away at summer's end? This song is the perfect follow-up to "I'll Follow the Sun" but with a different meaning that is no longer quite so literal. He sings of wanting to plant some trees so some "poor soul" can find shade at some distant point in the future. What a perfect metaphor for the hopes the singer must have that his life's work writing songs will long outlive him and provide comfort to those who listen to his music after he is gone. McCartney sounds serene in this song as he contemplates the winter of his life. In his own life, McCartney, a strict vegetarian, environmentalist, and animal rights activist, has displayed a kind of spiritual approach to life that probably most closely approximates Buddhism. Perhaps it is to these causes that he refers even more than his music when he speaks about planting trees to benefit some poor soul in the future.

Conclusion

Surveying the career of Paul McCartney in the Beatles, Wings, and as a solo artist, did he offer the world a message that was essentially religious or antireligious? As with most either/or questions regarding the Beatles, the answer probably lies somewhere in between. I would argue based on the material and perspective presented in this chapter that the answer was definitely a little of both. He wrote his songs without a specific agenda, but his own religious sensibility, specifically rooted in the desire to choose good over evil and light over darkness, influenced the songs he wrote. He seemed to recognize this himself when interviewed by Barry Miles in the early 1990s. McCartney told Miles, "Looking back on all the Beatles' work, I'm very glad that most of it was positive and has been a positive force. I always find it very fortunate that most of our songs were to do with peace and love, and encourage people to do better and to have a better life. When you come to do these songs in places like the stadium in Santiago where all the dissidents were rounded up, I'm very glad to have these songs because they're such symbols of optimism and hopefulness."[24] Whether such a message is rooted in a specific religious tradition or not, this message has resonated with people all over the world. It carries the message that the true purpose and test of a religion is not found in dogma or definitions of orthodoxy but in the extent to which it encourages people to become better and to make the world a better place. In that sense, the religious sensibility of Paul McCartney shines through his life and work in ways that rival that of any of his bandmates.

NOTES

1. Beatles, *Anthology*, 18.
2. Robinson, *Journey to Beatledom*, 133.
3. Turner, *Gospel*, 39.
4. Ibid., 37.
5. Womack, *Long and Winding Roads*, 113.
6. McKinney, *Magic Circles*, 137.
7. Spitz, *Beatles*, 707.
8. Miles, "Conversation with Paul McCartney."
9. Ibid.
10. Miles, *Paul McCartney*, 409.
11. Ibid., 414.
12. See Campbell, *Beatles and the 1960s*.
13. *Oxford English Dictionary*, 2nd ed., s.v. "pataphysics."
14. Soling, "Hammer of Justice."
15. Riley, *Lennon*, 483.
16. Quoted in Carlin, *Paul McCartney*, 19.
17. Lewisohn, *Tune In*, 101.
18. Salewicz, "Paul McCartney."
19. Quoted in Carlin, *Paul McCartney*, 317.
20. Doyle, *Man on the Run*, 207.
21. Carlin, *Paul McCartney*, 261.
22. Turner, *Gospel*, 175.
23. Kozinn, "Crossover Dream."
24. Miles, *Paul McCartney*, 539.

BIBLIOGRAPHY

Beatles. *The Beatles Anthology*. San Francisco: Chronicle Books, 2000.

Campbell, Kenneth L. *The Beatles and the 1960s: Reception, Revolution, and*

Social Change. London: Bloomsbury, 2022.

Carlin, Peter Ames. *Paul McCartney: A Life*. New York: Touchstone, 2009.

Doyle, Tom. *Man on the Run: Paul McCartney in the 1970s*. New York: Ballantine Books, 2013.

Kozinn, Allan. "A Crossover Dream Comes True in Liverpool: The Philharmonic Plays McCartney's Oratorio; McCartney Classical Work Has Premiere in Liverpool." *New York Times*, June 29, 1991.

Lewisohn, Mark. *Tune In: The Beatles—All These Years*. Vol. 1. New York: Three Rivers, 2013.

McKinney, Devin. *Magic Circles: The Beatles in Dream and History*. Cambridge: Harvard University Press, 2003.

Miles, Barry. "A Conversation with Paul McCartney." *International Times*, November 1966.

———. *Paul McCartney: Many Years from Now*. New York: Henry Holt, 1994.

Riley, Tim. *Lennon: The Man, the Myth, the Music—The Definitive Life*. New York: Hyperion, 2011.

Robinson, Joe. *Journey to Beatledom: The Fabulosity of the Foursquare Golem*. Liverpool: Guido Book, 2020.

Salewicz, Chris. "Paul McCartney: An Innocent Man?" *Q*, October 1986.

Soling, Cevin. "The Hammer of Justice: 'Maxwell's Silver Hammer'—The Beatles' Dark Masterpiece." Paper presented at "Come Together: Fifty Years of *Abbey Road*" conference, Rochester, NY, September 28, 2019.

Spitz, Bob. *The Beatles: The Biography*. Boston: Little, Brown, 2000.

Turner, Steve. *The Gospel According to the Beatles*. Louisville, KY: Westminster John Knox Press, 2006.

Womack, Kenneth. *Long and Winding Roads: The Evolving Artistry of the Beatles*. New York: Bloomsbury, 2007.

CHAPTER 4

John Lennon, Jesus as a Moral Model, and Imagine No Religion

EYAL REGEV

Lennon and Jesus

In May 1968, John Lennon gathered the other three Beatles and announced that he was Jesus Christ reincarnate. Though the revelation had come to Lennon during an LSD trip with his friend Pete Shotton the night before, he was still convinced of its truth when he woke up the following morning. Those assembled, however, weren't so sure: stunned into silence, the Beatles decided to delay comment.[1] Soon Lennon deserted his overt Christ fixation. Yet, this incident demonstrates Lennon's deep empathy for Jesus, as well as his strong religious sensibilities. It shows the other side of Lennon's more familiar antireligious stance.

In this chapter, I discuss Lennon's ideas on religion and unbelief, using his own statements in various interviews as a key to interpreting the religious attitudes conveyed in the lyrics, both with the Beatles and during his early solo career (notably, almost all of Lennon's references to "religion" actually apply to Christianity as he understood it). I intend to show that Lennon's discourse of love and peace stemmed, at least partly, from his recognition of the declining relevance of established religion in society. In some of his songs and public activities, Lennon attempted to *revitalize* certain religious ideals in a new guise. In his later, counterreligious solo tracks—"God," "I Found Out," and "Imagine"—he expressed ideals that purport to replace conventional religious ones. My intention is to demonstrate Lennon's specific interest in Jesus and his awareness of the transformation religion was undergoing in his time. These findings should be studied in light of the concept of secularization in the sociology of religion.

"The Beatles Are More Popular than Jesus" and Secularization

In 1966, Lennon was quoted in an interview with his friend the reporter Maureen Cleave as saying, "Christianity will go. It will vanish and shrink. . . . We're more popular than Jesus now. I don't know which will go first—rock 'n' roll or Christianity. Jesus was alright, but his disciples were thick and ordinary. It's them twisting it that ruins it for me."[2] Not surprisingly, this inflammatory statement raised hackles in the United States: a wave of anti-Beatles demonstrations rolled across the US South; people burned Beatles records in bonfires; radio stations were banned from playing Beatles records. Even the Vatican was sufficiently irked to make a special public comment on the matter. Brian Epstein, the Beatles' manager, expressed his fear that members of the group might be the target of an assassination attempt during the upcoming American tour.[3] Fourteen years later, allegedly enraged by this statement and the "anti-religious" lyrics of "Imagine," Mark David Chapman—a Beatles fan but also a "Jesus freak"—carried out the long-feared deed.[4]

A few months after Lennon's Jesus comment, in his public apology at a Chicago press conference, he explained his statement: "We meant more to kids than Jesus did, or religion at that time. . . . I was just saying it as a fact, and it is true more for England than here. I'm not saying that we're better or greater, or comparing us with Jesus Christ as a person or God as a thing."[5]

Lennon compared the Beatles (and rock music in general) to Christianity, argued for the latter's decrease in popularity and eventual disappearance, and even separated the historical figure of Jesus from the religion that bears his name, on account of the latter's inferiority. All these assertions reflect a process of secularization—that is, a process in which religious creeds, practices, and institutions lose their social significance and individuals or institutions experience a decline in levels of religiosity.[6] But he was not merely announcing this. As a Beatle, he actually had a substantial role in this grand cultural transformation.

Indeed, the furious—some would even say overblown—reactions to Lennon's Jesus statement demonstrate that it was precisely Lennon's portent of secularization that lay at the heart of the controversy. In 1966, the public at large still viewed secularization as a novel phenomenon in both England and the United States; likewise, it was only just beginning to draw scholarly attention.[7] Lennon's statements were arguably the first time that the more conservative segments of his audience had been confronted with this changing reality, and certainly in so bold a manner. Lennon seems to have been keenly aware of the parallels between his stardom and the religion of old: Beatlemania's intense levels of hysteria undeniably mirrored the ecstatic frenzies generally associated with evangelistic revivals. Lennon consciously ushered in a cultural war between institutionalized Christianity and the Beatles, who in turn came to represent something much larger than merely rock and roll music.

Some of Lennon's lyrics and interview statements reveal an awareness of the confrontation between Christianity and the encroaching secularization. At the same time, it is clear that he regarded his art and music as a kind of *reaction* to what he recognized as a momentous religious and cultural change taking place in Western society.

"We're All Jesus": Lennon's Views on Jesus

In interviews granted after the "more popular than Jesus" incident, Lennon consistently articulates an approach that at once combines a deep interest in certain Christian ideas with a rejection of both the church as an institution and several of Christianity's more significant creeds. These interviews may reflect the intellectual backdrop for some of his most famous songs and were the impetus for his cultural-political activism.

To be sure, Lennon believed there was much good in Christianity. In commenting on the benefits of studying with the Maharishi Mahesh Yogi, for example, he conceded that "there's a lot of good in Christianity, but you've got to learn the basics of it, and the basics from the Eastern beliefs, and work them together for yourself."[8] Lennon (as well as the other Beatles and particularly George Harrison) had some interest in Eastern philosophy, Buddhism, Zen, Krishna devotion, and other popular religious ideas of his day.[9] This interest no doubt stemmed from his desire to uncover a spiritual message beyond that laid out in church doctrine.

Lennon attempted to unearth the *original Jesus and his authentic message*—that is, before it was "corrupted" by the later religious establishment. Lennon sought the revitalization of the individual and in particular the desire to be a more "conscious" and moral person. It was reported in 1966 that Lennon "does not feel that one need accept the divinity of Jesus—he, personally, does not—in order to profit from his words." As a result of Lennon's extensive reading on ancient history as well as philosophy, "he contends that man has mishandled Christ's words throughout the centuries." Lennon was quoted as saying, "I believe Jesus was right, Buddha was right, and all of those people like that are right. They're all saying the same thing—and I believe it. I believe what Jesus actually said—the basic things he laid down about love and goodness—and not what people say he said."[10] In other words, Lennon adhered to Christian ethics *without* believing that Jesus was Christ. This is a key aspect of Lennon's general attitude toward religion, later expressed in his song lyrics. This somewhat counterintuitive thinking fits neatly with the phenomena of secularization and the rise of alternative religious forms.

Lennon told Cleave in their conversation that LSD led him to wonder whether Christ might have had similar transcendent experiences that had been reduced to dry dogma by the church. There were times, he said, when he thought he understood the Bible anew. He wondered, for instance, whether, when Jesus said, "The Kingdom of God is within you," he in truth meant that we should be exploring that "within," rather than living obedient lives in return for "pie in the sky" (an expression he later repeated in "I Found Out" and other interviews). Furthermore, wondered Lennon, had Christ been thinking of mystical experiences when he said, "the truth shall make you free"? Was he in fact referring to the dissolution of barriers within one's own ego when he said, "I am in my Father, and ye in me, and I in You"? This sentence recalls the opening verse of "I Am the Walrus" (written a year or so later): "I am he, As you are he, As you are me, And we are all together."[11] Lennon did not hesitate to reassess both Jesus the person and his message in light of the spiritual experiences he had while in a state of altered consciousness.

Sometime between 1969 and 1971, in an interview with Ray Coleman in which Lennon explained his attempts at perfection, he declared, "I'd like to be like Christ." He then went on to describe himself as a Christian communist "in a pure sense, not in the way Russia or Italy think of Christianity or communism."[12] Lennon's admiration of the figure of Jesus coexisted with his belief that the church—and institutionalized religion in general—was in truth the root of the problem, as he stressed in interviews in the early 1970s: "I have nothing against it except that it organizes itself as a business, the

Church. What I do like about it is that Christians talk about being perfect; so was Christ and I was taught that as a child. Christ is the one who most people in the West refer to when they speak of good people.... If I could do what Christ did, be as Christ was, that's what being Christian is all about. I try to live as Christ lived."[13]

In an interview with Steve Turner in July 1971, after recording the album *Imagine*, Lennon reacted spontaneously to a letter from "the Jesus Freaks in America" in which they called on him to come back to Jesus. "I know what the Christian jazz is," he said. "I've had it all my life. This is the Christ bit, you know—'give yourself to Christ.' A: He's dead. B: Prove it to me." The conversation then proceeded to the matter of "looking for gurus," or what Lennon believed lay at the heart of Christians' love for Christ:

> You're looking for the answer that everyone is supposedly looking for. You're looking for some kind of Super Daddy.... I think Jesus was probably a very hip guy. I think a lot of the stuff about magic and miracles is probably a lot of bullshit that was written about years later. I think he was just a very hip guy and you can read his messages. What he really says is "You are here. Be true to yourself. Try to love people. Love your neighbor. Help someone if they're down." They are quite practical statements. It's very aligned to communism, what he says.[14]

In an interview in 1968, Lennon described Jesus as a mere person, albeit one who set a good example for humanity to follow: "We're all Jesus and we're all God.... He's inside all of us and that's what it's all about. As soon as you start realizing that potential in everyone, well, then you can change it [humanity] and the person themselves can change it. That's the whole bit. Jesus wasn't God come down on earth any more than anybody else was. He was just a better example of a good guy."[15]

Lennon also had his own interpretation of the theological concept of the "Kingdom of God," which he associated with meditation. As he explained in an interview in 1967, "It runs alongside Christianity amazingly. Re-read it now, you know, what it's about. The kingdom of heaven within you. It *is* within you."[16]

Lennon's reference to the human's inside, his realization of the human potential, along with his reinterpretation of "the kingdom of heaven *within* you," as well as the lyrics of "Tomorrow Never Knows" (discussed below), all recall the concept of an "inside/outside experience" described in Aldous Huxley's *Doors of Perception* and his claim that "each person is at each moment capable of remembering all that has ever happened to him and of perceiving everything that is happening everywhere in the universe" while high on psychedelic drugs.[17] As already mentioned, Lennon openly confessed that LSD granted him profound insight into Jesus's teachings.[18] In fact, reinterpreting religious traditions on the basis of an altered state of consciousness is common in religious experimentalism; it is an attempt to experience the sacred *without* being committed to it; it is a kind of "religion surrogate."[19]

Lennon, Religion, and the Church

As much as Lennon appreciated certain Christian beliefs, he made no bones about his *rejection of the Christian establishment*, which relates to the British becoming "believers" but not "belongers."[20] He maintained that "Christianity has suffered . . . not only because Christians have distorted Christ's words but because they concern themselves with structures and numbers and fail to listen to their vows"; believers fail to pay attention "to the words of their own prayers." He concluded, "They don't seem to be able to be concerned without having all the scene about, with statues and buildings and things."[21]

He was even more critical in an interview in 1967, when he replied to a question about his feelings on the religious dimension of the "flower-power movement" by saying, "I can understand religion now. I might have come to that conclusion anyway at 25 or 26. But now I understand it—realizing that The Church of England and all those things, they're government. We all rejected that. I'm not against organized religion if it's organized by religious people and not just by politicians disguised. But they've got themselves into the position of any big company—they lose touch. *I've realized religion is personal.* It's 'Do as you would be done by' really."[22] Similarly, when asked in an interview for the BBC in 1969 if he ever went to church, he replied, "No, I don't need to go to church. . . . I respect churches because of the sacredness that's been put on them over the years by people who do believe. [But] I think a lot of bad things have happened in the name of the Church and in the name of Christ and therefore I shy away from church."[23]

Lennon had a distinctive *conception of God*. In his public apology for the "more popular than Jesus" comment, for instance, he explained, "I'm not anti-God, anti-Christ, or anti-Religion. . . . I believe in God but not as an old man in the sky. I believe that what people call God is something in all of us."[24] When asked in 1971 whether he believed in God, Lennon replied that since he "questions everything," he couldn't possibly believe in an "old man in the sky." But on second thought, he added, "I believe in something, definitely. I believe there is a force at work that you can't physically account for."[25]

Lennon gave the best summation of his attitude toward religion in one of his last interviews. Discussing the idea of father figures (such as the psychiatrist Janov and the Maharishi) and the tendency to confuse messages with messengers, he commented, "People always got the image I was an anti-Christ or anti-religion. I'm not. I'm a most religious fellow. I was brought up a Christian and I only now understand some of the things that Christ was saying in those parables. Because people got hooked on the teacher and missed the message."[26] Thus, Lennon appreciated Jesus as a historical figure and a model for moral behavior, but he did not appreciate the church as an institution. Indeed, not only did he deride the church's rituals, but he even rejected the Christian conceptions of God and Christ.

Turning now to Lennon's lyrics, I would like to show that his ideas about Jesus's teachings and the tenuous state of religion in modernity were not the stuff of mere intellectual entertainment, detached from his artistic and cultural activity. On the contrary, interpreting his lyrics and public activity in light of his ideas about religion reveal his attempts, through art, to (1) conceal his religious sensibilities, thus presenting them in a nonreligious guise, (2) express his notion of secularization, and (3) provide an alternative to established religion. In interpreting his lyrics as a religiously inclined discourse, I suggest that Lennon felt, as did Max Weber, not only that art produces values but also that "art takes over the function of a this-worldly salvation.... It provides salvation from the routines of everyday life."[27]

Lennon's Gospel of Love

Lennon, together with the other Beatles, sought above all to advance the message of love as a humanitarian value or, as he defined it in 1972, an "appreciation of other people and allowing them to be. Love is allowing somebody to be themselves."[28]

"The Word," from the Beatles' 1965 album *Rubber Soul*, is probably the earliest example of Lennon's tendency to couch a postreligious message in distinctly religious terms. Here, the Beatles call on their listeners to say the word "love" as a kind of mantra, the key to being free, successful ("Say the word and be like me"), and optimistic. Lennon clearly implies that his message of love accords with the Bible (the "Good Book") but that it is found in other faiths, as well: "Everywhere I go I hear it said, in the good and the bad books that I have read." Love is here portrayed as a kind of divine message, which parallels that of Jesus.[29] Finally, he sings, "Now that I know what I feel must be right, I mean to show everybody the light"—a clear reference to the language of preaching.

Lennon's most famous "sermon" on love is undoubtedly "All You Need Is Love." Written as a hymn (beginning with the chanting of "love, love, love" throughout the first verses), the message is straightforward: "There's nothing you can make that can't be made," that is, as long as you have love. Love is the key to knowledge, understanding, success, and so on. Here, as with "The Word," love is not used in its romantic sense but has an existential meaning: the love of humanity and the universe. Its usage recalls the biblical injunctions to "Love your neighbor" (Lev. 19:18) and "Love your enemies" (Matt. 5:44), along with Paul's gospel of love (1 Cor. 13; cf. 1 John 4:7–12).

The significance of love to one's life is also expressed in another unusual Beatles track, "Tomorrow Never Knows" (*Revolver*, 1966), in which Lennon announces "that love is all and love is everyone." Here love is portrayed as a cosmic entity that transforms individual persons into humanity as a whole. This song was a musically daring, bizarre, hypnotic, and LSD-inspired composition. The words, drawn from Timothy Leary's *The Psychedelic Experience*, were guru-like instructions for achieving a state of altered consciousness.[30] Love, claims Lennon, is nothing less than the essence of life. A somewhat similar mood, referring to "undying love that shines around me like a million suns," is mentioned in one of Lennon's most spiritual and reflective songs, "Across the Universe."

In light of Lennon's special interest in Jesus and his message, I would suggest that his emphasis on the message of existential or humanitarian love not only derived from his involvement with psychedelic drugs and transcendental meditation but was mainly associated with Jesus's gospel, as Lennon understood it.

The Peace Campaign

In an interview in 1969, Lennon said, "I am an artist, and my art is peace."[31] Indeed, Lennon is known for his pacifism, which he viewed as nothing less than a calling. The first musical step in this direction was "Revolution" (later included in the so-called White Album). Recorded in May 1968, the song was Lennon's reaction to the student riots of spring 1968.[32]

With a nod to various revolutionary mottos or activities—"destruction," a change in "the constitution" or "the institution," and, finally, "carrying pictures of Chairman Mao"—Lennon presented himself as someone asked by the revolutionaries to join their cause. He declines to count himself as one of their number: "Don't you know that you can count me out."[33] "All I can tell you is brother you have to wait. . . . You ain't gonna make it with anyone anyhow." He also seeks to diffuse the radicals' passion, repeating three times in the chorus, "Don't you know it's going to be all right."[34]

Lennon also hints at his own alternative: "We'd all love to change your head. . . . Well, you know, you better free your mind instead." The ideal change, it would seem from these lyrics, is not an external one, nor certainly one enacted under threat of violence. Rather, it should come from and remain *within* (which may also be a nod to psychedelics or Eastern meditation). Instead of any political, Marxist, or military attempt to "change the world," people should first try to change their own individual attitudes toward life—a theme that echoes "All You Need Is Love," discussed above.

Lennon's actual peace campaign would begin several months later. Soon after his marriage to Yoko Ono in March 1969, the couple staged their first "bed-in" demonstration for world peace at the Amsterdam Hilton. While lying in bed for seven days wearing white pajamas, Lennon and Ono accepted visits from journalists from around the world who no doubt expected to see the couple doing something other than promoting world peace. Lennon urged others to grow out their hair as a symbol of the peace campaign. As he explained, "We are willing to become the world's clowns if it helps to spread the word for peace." Clearly, the couple's campaign was aimed not so much at politicians as it was at the world's youth, whom they urged to adopt a policy of nonviolence.[35] In the famous Amsterdam press conferences, Lennon expressed this message explicitly, and with surprisingly religious fervor: "All I'm saying is peace. . . . We're not pointing a finger at anybody. . . . The struggle is in the mind. We must bury our own monsters and stop condemning people. We're all Christ and we are all Hitler. *We are trying to make Christ's message contemporary*. We want Christ to win."[36] "Christ" is used in three different contexts in this statement. Does it demonstrate the religious motivation at the heart of the peace campaign or merely disclose Lennon's use of Christian symbolism in the service of promoting "secular" aims? In an interview with Coleman shortly thereafter, Lennon remarked about the peace campaign, "I think I'll win because I believe in what Jesus said."[37] Clearly Lennon's peace campaign was the result of religious sensibilities, if not the conventional Christian ones. Lennon was motivated by what *he* regarded as Jesus's original message of peace and brotherly love, as articulated in the Gospels (e.g., Luke 19:38; John 16:33).

Lennon's musical call for world peace is nowhere more pronounced than in his first solo single, "Give Peace a Chance." The track, which was recorded live in Lennon and Ono's second Montreal bed-in, is a simple repetition of the line, "All we are saying is give peace a chance," dozens of times. In Christmas 1971, immediately after their move to New York, Lennon and Ono released the track "Happy Xmas (War Is Over)," featuring the chorus, "War is over (if you want it)." As Lennon explained it, "If everybody demanded peace instead of another television set, there'd be peace."[38]

There can be no mistaking that Lennon's messages of love and peace are related in some way to his interest in Jesus and in the uncertain role of religion in modern society. In his early solo career, however, Lennon's lyrics were explicitly critical of conventional religious creeds, even going so far as to introduce an alternative belief system. Here, Lennon put forth ideas we have already encountered in his interviews.

"God": Unbelief and Self-Realization

Lennon's most transparent display of unbelief is undoubtedly the song "God," released on his debut solo album, *Plastic Ono Band* (1970). Here, he declared that "God is a concept by which we measure our pain," which, as he explained to Steve Turner, means that "the more pain we're in, the more we need God."[39] He then goes on to list a long series of things he does not believe in, including magic, tarot, Bible, Buddha, Kennedy, Zimmerman (i.e., Bob Dylan), and, most significantly, "Jesus." For the record, Lennon also claimed, "I don't believe in Beatles."[40] As for what he *does* believe in, he sings, "I just believe in me, Yoko, and Me, and that's reality." He then concludes that the dream, of which he was the dream weaver, is over. Now he is reborn.

Lennon's philosophy at that time was, "You are here. Live for today. . . . Why should I follow Jesus? I'll follow Yoko. I'll follow myself." Nonetheless, Lennon's seemingly obsessive need to deny his belief in Jesus and to declare that God is a farce implies that he *did* at one time view religion as truth. Indeed, he confessed to an intensive interest in religion during 1965–66, what he called "the acid days," a period in which his superstar status became the catalyst for a serious reflection on the meaning of life. "Religion was an outlet for my repression," he said, and he even referred to his occupation with religion as "the Godtrip." He also made clear that his current rejection of religion was the result of the "Primal Scream" therapy he was then undergoing with Dr. Arthur Janov.[41] Lennon saw any kind of belief in an external entity as a dependence on fallacies and drew a clear distinction between such beliefs and free will, self-awareness, and social activism.

"I Found Out": Religious Disenchantment

Another counterreligious song from *Plastic Ono Band* is "I Found Out." The track begins with a rejection of the missionaries who knock on Lennon's door. Lennon urges his listeners not to "take nobody's word what you can do," since "I showed you just what I've been through"—a reference, perhaps, to his own religious reflection, which ended, to use Max Weber's term, in disenchantment.[42]

Lennon then moves on to a straightforward attack on Christian belief in the "Second Coming," saying, "There ain't no Jesus gonna come from the sky," followed by a rebuff of Krishna consciousness: both religions "just keep you crazy with nothing to do, keep you occupied with pie in the sky. There ain't no guru who can see through your eyes." Finally, there is a blatant rejection of Christianity and religion in general: "I seen the junkies, I've been through it all, I've seen religions from Jesus to Paul."

The fact that Lennon repeats the line "I found out" throughout the song emphasizes that all his concerted attempts to be converted to Christianity (and other gurus' wisdom) had ended in disappointment, or as he put it, "Now that I found out I know I can cry." Clearly Lennon's search for religious truth was genuine, and his inability to find it painful; nonetheless, he believed it his duty to expose the dubiousness of religious creeds and propaganda to the world.

"Imagine": Religious Utopia Without Religion?

"Imagine" calls on the listener to consider a world devoid of all humanity's flaws: heaven and hell, nationalism ("Imagine there's no countries"), war, religion, possessions, greed, and hunger. It is a call for a new world order, characterized by unity and equality and founded on the complete elimination of the modern social order. In its place, Lennon proposes a principle of mutual responsibility, "a brotherhood of man." "Imagine" accords with Lennon's saying in "Revolution" that people should change their minds first—*this* is the true and essential revolution.

"Imagine" is generally considered an expression of an atheistic worldview, encouraging us as it does to "imagine ... no religion" and "above us only sky."[43] However, given Lennon's concern with religious ideas, demonstrated above, I suggest that even in this seemingly antireligious declaration, Lennon employs deliberate religious idioms. "Imagine no possessions. No need for greed or hunger, a brotherhood of man. Imagine all the people sharing all the world" seems at first glance to mimic the *Communist Manifesto*.[44] Yet, as we have already seen, Lennon associated this approach with the moral message of Jesus. In addition, "Imagine no possessions, ... brotherhood of man" may recall the communal ownership of property in the early Jerusalem church (Acts of the Apostles 2:44–45).

I suggest interpreting "Imagine" not as an antireligious or atheistic song but rather as a model of *alternative* religious thought, one that in truth reinforces certain religious, and particularly Christian, ideas. Imagining no hell or heaven but merely sky accords with the biblical ideal of the End of Days, the creation of New Heaven and New Earth (Revelation 21:1). The disappearance of countries, war, and violence accords with the prophetic ideal of nonviolence ("They shall beat their swords into ploughshares"; "the wolf shall live with the lamb"; Isaiah 2:4, 11:6–9, 65:25). The call to imagine "no religion" can therefore be interpreted as a rejection of the tendency to divide people in the name of religion. Religion may also here refer to religious institutions, specifically the church, which impose restrictions and boundaries on human brotherhood and prevent the world from being "as one."

What is absent in "Imagine," however, is the very essence of religion: God. The belief or expectation that humanity will heal itself, that it can achieve social utopia without divine involvement, is indeed unique, even innovative. It is a religious belief system devoid of God or of any presumption concerning the divine (for a more precise definition, see below).

John Lennon's Religious Sensibilities and Unbelief

Lennon was inspired by Jesus's social message and regarded Jesus as a worthy personal example. At the same time, however, he rejected the conventional belief in Jesus, having determined Christianity (and all religion) to be an illusion or at least unable to deliver on its promises. The religious ideas that Lennon embraced as meaningful were only fragments of the Christian doctrine. His religious preferences were in truth based on his own personal reflections on the New Testament and the history of the Christian faith. Specifically, he rejected the church as a binding religious institution (although, it should be noted, he made clear that this was a personal choice). He also never acknowledged the conventional belief in Christ's divinity, as well as the Christian idea of God, although his refutation of these ideas in his songs implies that he was, in fact, deeply concerned by such Christian conventions.

Whereas Lennon's religious ideas remained consistent throughout the period from 1966 to 1971, he did experience a certain *artistic* transformation. Whereas religion was implicit in his lyrics between 1966 and 1969, in his first two solo albums, released in 1970–71, he turned his attention squarely to unbelief and the relationship between religion and utopia. He displayed dissatisfaction with the traditional concept of God and Christ—and with "mainstream" Western religious thinking in general. It seems, then, that his attraction to Christian ideas and to religious ethics in general and his refutation of the belief in Christ and the supernatural are in fact two sides of the same coin.

In a previous article, I have collected more evidence on Lennon's attitude toward religion and examined it using models from the sociology of religion.[45] I have argued that secularization theories illuminate the background and character of Lennon's complex religious sensibilities, namely, his adoption of major Christian symbols and a religious consciousness, while at the same time rejecting religious institutions and any belief in the supernatural. It is possible to see Lennon's ideas as the result of an overall religious decline, but it should be acknowledged that in Lennon's case, religion gave way to the search for a new form of spirituality. Lennon's attitude toward religion, especially the lyrics of "Imagine," corresponds to the concept of humanistic quasi-religion, which attempts to take the place of conventional religion. It aims to achieve a social utopia without the fallacies of supernatural beliefs and the pitfalls of religious institutions. In this, the case of John Lennon offers an opportunity for reassessing the intersection of individual and societal developments in religion and religious belief.

NOTES

1. Shotton and Schaffner, *John Lennon*, 167–68. See also Hertsgaard, *Day in the Life*, 237–38; Turner, *Gospel*, 17–18. Lennon's exact words to Shotton during the LSD trip were, according to Shotton, "I think I'm Jesus Christ. I'm . . . back again . . . I've got to tell everyone. . . . I've got to let the world know . . . who I am. . . . This is my reason for being here on this earth." Curiously, in 1965, Paul McCartney mentioned that he and Lennon had an idea for a play about Jesus Christ coming back to Earth as an ordinary person (Turner, *Gospel*, 16).

2. Cleave, "How Does a Beatle Live?"; Thomson and Gutman, *Lennon Companion*, 71–75; Cleave, "I Don't Know Which Will Go First"; Turner, *Gospel*, 21–25.

3. Turner, *Gospel*, 20–35; Norman, *John Lennon*, 447–54.

4. Jones, *Let Me Take You Down*, 115–22; Turner, *Gospel*, 27, 36, 192. The connection between this incident and the assassination was also implied by Lennon's first wife (C. Lennon, *John*, 9). Curiously, the Vatican continues to pay attention to Lennon's assertion and recently even offered Lennon a complete absolution. See Pisa and Evans, "Vatican Forgives."

5. Coleman, *Lennon*, 407–8.

6. Wilson, "Secularization and Its Discontents," 149.

7. Cox, *Secular City*; Berger, *Sacred Canopy*; Luckmann, *Invisible Religion*; Kitagawa, *History of Religion*, 19–65.

8. Coleman, *Lennon*, 524.

9. Members of Krishna Consciousness stayed at his Tittenhurst estate in Ascot in 1971 (ibid., 530–31). Lennon's interest in the relationship between Krishna consciousness and Christian theology is documented in the transcript of the meeting of Lennon, Yoko Ono, George Harrison, and the founder of the International Society for Krishna Consciousness, Prabhupada, held in Ascot in September 1969. http://members.tripod.com/~holysm0ke/Ascot.html. Cf. Turner, *Gospel*, 150–52; Wiener, *Come Together*, 101–2.

10. Gross, "John Lennon."

11. Turner, *Gospel*, 125.

12. Coleman, *Lennon*, 525.

13. Ibid., 535.

14. Turner, "John, Yoko"; Turner, *Gospel*, 209–10.

15. Turner, *Gospel*, 11, 212.

16. Nightingale, "What I Believe."

17. Huxley, *Doors of Perception*, 9, 16–17.

18. Lennon used LSD intensively in 1966–68. See C. Lennon, *John*, 241–48, 256, 259–61, 313; Shotton and Schaffner, *John Lennon*, 117–18, 165.

19. Smith, "Do Drugs Have Religious Import?"

20. Davie, *Religion in Britain*.

21. Gross, "John Lennon."

22. Nightingale, "What I Believe" (emphasis added). Similar assertions were repeated in the bed-in for peace in Montreal, 1969. See Cadogan, *Revolutionary Artist*, 72–73.

23. Wigg, "John Lennon and Yoko Ono Interview." Lennon also confessed that the lyrics of his song "Girl" (1965) and his book *In His Own Write* (1964) were in truth a dig at the Roman Catholic Church, in particular the concept of "pain will lead to pleasure." See Wenner, *Lennon Remembers*, 85–86.

24. Coleman, *Lennon*, 408.

25. Ibid., 535.

26. Sheff, *Playboy Interview*.

27. Weber, *Essays in Sociology*, 342.

28. Cadogan, *Revolutionary Artist*, 198.

29. For the modern Protestant association of love with God, see, e.g., Tillich, *Essential Tillich*, 146–85.

30. Hertsgaard, *Day in the Life*, 177–78; Turner, *Gospel*, 124.

31. Coleman, *Lennon*, 531–32, 534.

32. Wiener, *Come Together*, 58–59.

33. In a later version, he added a provocative "in." See Ibid., 61.

34. Coleman, *Lennon*, 543–44; Wenner, *Lennon Remembers*, 110–11.

35. Coleman, *Lennon*, 493–98, 501; Mäkelä, *John Lennon Imagined*, 165–72. On Lennon and Ono's additional, seven-day bed-in in Montreal in May 1969 (Cadogan, *Revolutionary Artist*) and other artistic and political acts for world peace, such as the EP track "War Is Over," see Coleman, *Lennon*, 498–502, 550–51; Wiener, *Come Together*, 129, 159, 199. It is interesting to note Lennon's call to students in Berkeley to avoid a confrontation with the police during the Montreal bed-in (Wiener, *Come Together*, 92–93; Cadogan, *Revolutionary Artist*, 54–55). For Lennon's antiwar views, see Coleman, *Lennon*, 530. For his self-reflection about his role as an artist who promotes a "political" agenda, see Coleman, *Lennon*, 533–34.

36. Coleman, *Lennon*, 498.

37. Ibid., 532.

38. Ibid., 524.

39. Turner, *Gospel*, 210.

40. As he declared in 1970, "I don't believe in the Beatles myth" (Wenner, *Lennon Remembers*, 134).

41. Ali and Blackburn, "John Lennon Interview," 354; on the therapy, see Norman, *John Lennon*, 639–42, 647–52. Lennon put forward a similar notion in his "Serve Yourself" (1980, released on Lennon's *Anthology*),

written as a reaction to Bob Dylan's Christian track "You Got to Serve Somebody" (*Slow Train Coming*, 1979).
42. Weber, "Science as a Vocation."
43. E.g., Wiener, *Come Together*, 161.
44. Jones, *Let Me Take You Down*, 117. Lennon actually acknowledged this interpretation. See Blaney, *John Lennon*, 83.
45. Regev, "Lennon and Jesus."

Bibliography

Ali, Tariq, and Robin Blackburn. "John Lennon Interview." *Red Mole*, January 21, 1971. In *The Beatles Literary Anthology*, edited by Mike Evans, 351–65. London: Plexus, 2004.

Berger, Peter. *The Sacred Canopy. Elements of a Sociological Theory of Religion.* Garden City, NY: Doubleday, 1967.

Blaney, John. *John Lennon: Listen to This Book.* N.p.: Paper Jukebox, 2005.

Cadogan, Patrick. *The Revolutionary Artist: John Lennon's Radical Years.* N.p.: Lulu, 2008.

Cleave, Maureen. "How Does a Beatle Live?" *Evening Standard*, March 4 1966.

———. "I Don't Know Which Will Go First—Rock 'n' Roll or Christianity." *Datebook*, September 1966.

Coleman, Ray. *Lennon. The Definitive Biography.* New York: HarperCollins, 1992.

Cox, Harvey. *The Secular City.* London: SCM, 1965.

Davie, Grace. *Religion in Britain Since 1945: Believing Without Belonging.* Oxford, UK: Blackwell, 1994.

Gross, Leonard. "John Lennon: A Shorn Beatle Tries It on His Own." *Look*, December 13, 1966.

Hertsgaard, Mark. *A Day in the Life: The Music and Artistry of the Beatles.* New York: Macmillan, 1995.

Huxley, Aldous. *"The Doors of Perception" and "Heaven and Hell."* London: Chatto and Windus, 1968.

Jones, Jack. *Let Me Take You Down: Inside the Mind of Mark David Chapman, the Man Who Killed John Lennon.* New York: Villard Books, 1992.

Kitagawa, Joseph M., ed. *The History of Religion: Essays on Problems of Understanding.* Chicago: University of Chicago Press, 1967.

Lennon, Cynthia. *John.* London: Hodder, 2005.

Luckmann, Thomas. *The Invisible Religion: The Problem of Religion in Modern Society.* New York: Macmillan, 1967.

Mäkelä, Janne. *John Lennon Imagined: Cultural History of a Rock Star.* New York: Peter Lang, 2004.

Nightingale, Anne. "What I Believe—by Beatle John." *Daily Sketch*, October 9, 1967.

Norman, Philip. *John Lennon: The Life.* New York: HarperCollins, 2008.

Pisa, Nick, and Martin Evans. "Vatican Forgives the Beatles for 'Bigger than Jesus' Comment." *Telegraph*, April 11, 2010.

Regev, Eyal. "Lennon and Jesus: Secularization and the Transformation of Religion." *Studies in Religion / Sciences Religieuses* 41, no. 4 (2012): 534–63.

Sheff, David. "Playboy Interview with John Lennon and Yoko Ono." *Playboy*, September 1981.

Shotton, Pete, and Nicolas Schaffner. *John Lennon in My Life.* New York: Stein and Day, 1983.

Smith, Huston. "Do Drugs Have Religious Import?" *Journal of Philosophy* 61, no. 18 (1964): 517–30.

Thomson, Elizabeth, and David Gutman, eds. *The Lennon Companion: Twenty-Five Years of Comment.* Updated and exp. ed. Cambridge, MA: Da Capo, 2004.

Tillich, Paul. *The Essential Tillich.* Edited by F. Forrester Church. New York: Macmillan, 1987.

Turner, Steve. *The Gospel According to the Beatles.* Louisville, KY: Westminster John Knox Press, 2006.

———. "John, Yoko, Grapefruit and Jesus." *Beat Instrumental*, September 1971.

Weber, Max. *Essays in Sociology.* Translated and Edited by H. H. Gerth and C.

Wright Mills. New York: Oxford University Press, 1969.
———. "Science as a Vocation." In *From Max Weber: Essays in Sociology*, translated and edited by H. H. Gerth and C. Wright Mills, 129–56. New York: Oxford University Press, 1946.
Wenner, Jann S. *Lennon Remembers: The Full Rolling Stone Interviews from 1970*. New ed. London: Verso, 2000.
Wiener, Jon. *Come Together. John Lennon in His Time*. Urbana: University of Illinois Press, 1991.
Wigg, David. "John Lennon and Yoko Ono Interview: Apple Offices." *Scene and Heard*, BBC Radio-One, May 1969.
Wilson, Bryan. "Secularization and Its Discontents." In *Religion in Sociological Perspective*, 148–77. New York: Oxford University Press, 1982.

CHAPTER 5

George Harrison's Road to India

JOHN COVACH

It is tempting to wonder, but difficult to determine, when George Harrison first took serious note of Indian music and culture. Perhaps his first exposure was in the womb, as his mother listened to Indian music on the radio.[1] He probably heard some Indian music growing up, though it seems not to have made enough of an impression to challenge his passion for Carl Perkins, skiffle, and electric guitars. Harrison recalls that when he was a child, he "had a crystal radio with long and short wave bands," so it's possible he "might have already heard some Indian classical music."[2] There is no doubt, however, that by 1966, Harrison was becoming increasingly engaged with Indian music and spirituality, though as we will see below, some of the figures who would ultimately fascinate Harrison the most were not of much interest to him initially. Already in the fall of 1963, however, during the first months of Beatlemania in Britain, Harrison demonstrated a kind of insight and detachment that resonates sympathetically with Hindu philosophy: "You see your pictures and read articles about George Harrison, Ringo Starr, Paul, and John, but you don't actually think, oh, that's me. There I am in the paper. It's funny. It's just as though it's a different person."[3] This resonates with the *Astavakra Samhita*: "The high-souled person witnesses his own body acting as if it were another's. As such, how can he be disturbed by praise or blame?"[4] It's almost certain that Harrison did not know the *Astavakra Samhita* in 1963—in fact, it's not clear that he ever studied it. But the manner in which the twenty-year-old Harrison viewed himself while in the early throes of national celebrity suggests that he already had intellectual inclinations that might make Indian spirituality a good fit.[5] And as Philip Goldberg would remark, Harrison's "life was about as Vedic as a Westerner's can be."[6]

Harrison's interest in India can be loosely divided into two aspects: the musical and the spiritual—or, more simplistically, sitars and gurus. Though he would work with many Indian musicians during his Beatles years and later, the towering musical influence for Harrison almost from the beginning was Ravi Shankar. With regard to Indian philosophy and spiritual practices, his primary influences were Swami Vivekananda, Paramahansa Yogananda, Maharishi Mahesh Yogi, and A. C. Bhaktivedanta Swami Prabhupada. Because these musical and spiritual influences both come from South Asian culture, there can sometimes be a tendency to assume that they developed in Harrison's music and thought at about the same time.[7] In addition, because of the Beatles' 1968 trip to Rishikesh, it might be assumed that Harrison's interest in meditation was primarily driven by his study with the Maharishi or, because of his very public association with the Hare Krishna movement in the early 1970s, that his later influences were dominated by the bhakti teaching and practices of Prabhupada. A close study of the historical record produces a different picture, however. The musical attraction preceded the spiritual one by approximately a year and a half, though the spiritual aspect ended up being the more enduring. And the influence of Yogananda and Vivekananda remained with Harrison throughout his life. This chapter traces the chronology of both the Indian musical and spiritual influences, while also taking into account Harrison's overall development as a songwriter and the relationship of his songs to the music of John Lennon and Paul McCartney during the Beatles years.

Sources of Engagement: The Musical Dimension

George Harrison's initial engagement with Indian music can be tracked over a roughly two-year period that includes most of 1965 and 1966. Indian music first caught Harrison's attention in the first week of April 1965, during the filming of the band's second feature film, *Help!*[8] One of the scenes included an unlikely (and satiric) Indian musical ensemble performing in a restaurant, but however inauthentic that particular ensemble was, there *was* an authentic sitar on the set. The sound of the sitar, present in this case only as a prop, fascinated Harrison, and not too long after this, he purchased a mediocre instrument from a London shop. In October 1965, the famous sitar lines on "Norwegian Wood" were played on that sitar, which Harrison had barely played since buying it.[9] He recalls, "It was just lying around. I hadn't really figured out what to do with it. . . . I found the notes that played the lick."[10] While the appearance of the sitar on "Norwegian Wood" (released on *Rubber Soul* in December 1965) was indeed a significant moment for what Ravi Shankar would call the "sitar explosion" in Western pop music, it was not the first time fans had heard the instrument on a Beatles album. Sitar is prominently featured in two of the instrumental tracks ("Another Hard Day's Night" and "The Chase") that were included in the film and on the US release of the *Help!* soundtrack in August 1965, though no Beatles actually played on these tracks.[11]

It's also worth noting that in March 1965, about a month before Harrison dabbled with a sitar on the set of *Help!*, the Beatles had met Swami Vishnu-devananda while filming in the Bahamas and were presented with copies of his book *The Complete Illustrated Book of Yoga*.[12] The book offers a comprehensive overview of yoga, including both hatha yoga (employing body postures, or asanas) and the more philosophical aspects of Indian thought. The opening chapter, "Philosophy and Aim of Yoga," quickly turns to the kinds of metaphysical questions that would eventually be central to Harrison: "For spirit or pure consciousness projects the mind and matter, its creative power forms the veiling agent of the consciousness and creates form out of formless spirit, infinite into finite as self-consciousness or individuality."[13] While Harrison subsequently mentioned the book in interviews, it's not clear that it had much impact in 1965; Indian music, not philosophy, was the main focus of his curiosity.[14] This musical interest was further fueled by the enthusiasm for Ravi Shankar's playing that Harrison is reported to have heard from Roger McGuinn and David Crosby when the Beatles were in Los Angeles in August 1965 near the end of their North American tour.[15] Harrison remarked, "Towards the end of the year [1965] I'd kept hearing the name Ravi Shankar, . . . so I went out and bought a record and that was it. I thought it was incredible."[16]

As Harrison was recording "Norwegian Wood" back in London that fall ("towards the end of the year"), he broke a string, prompting a search for a replacement sitar string.[17] Beatles producer George Martin remembered Ayana Angadi, who ran the Asiatic Music Circle in London, and Angadi was only too happy to assist. Harrison quickly became friendly with the Angadi family, attending Circle concerts and becoming more familiar with Indian music as a result. He probably took a few sitar lessons late 1965 and early 1966, and his playing on "Love You To," recorded in April 1966, reflects his progress on the instrument.[18] Angadi knew Ravi Shankar (it was probably his recommendation that caused Harrison to buy the record mentioned above) and arranged a dinner meeting with Harrison in the summer of 1966 in the Angati home. Harrison had already bought a professional-level sitar during a tour stopover in Delhi in early July, and at the dinner, he asked Shankar if he could study with him.[19] Shankar accepted, and two lessons and a concert at Harrison's home in Esher soon followed. According to Shankar, "Initially, I gave him some basic instruction.... We fixed it that he would come to India for a couple of months to learn in more depth."[20] Harrison, accompanied by his wife, Pattie, traveled to India for several weeks to see the sights and study sitar with Shankar during the Beatles' extended vacation in the fall of 1966 following the band's retirement from touring at the end of August.[21] It was during this extended stay in India that the musical aspects of Harrison's engagement with India began to blossom, marking a firm point of arrival for this aspect of his road to India.

Sources of Engagement: The Philosophical and Spiritual Dimension

Harrison's engagement with Indian philosophy and spirituality began to intensify in late 1966, lagging behind the musical one by about eighteen months. While he was in India studying with Shankar and visiting historical locations, Harrison studied books by Swami Vivekananda and Paramahansa Yogananda.[22] Of Vivekanada's works, he was given *Raja Yoga* by Shankar's brother Rajendra, which is partially a book on meditation and yoga broadly and partially a translation of and commentary on Patañjali's *Yoga Sutras*.[23] Vivekananda was a disciple of Ramakrishna, based in Kolkata but also writing and lecturing in the United States and the United Kingdom at the turn of the twentieth century. His lectures at the 1893 Parliament of the World's Religions in Chicago made a tremendous impression on the assembled delegates and went a long way toward bringing Indian philosophical and spiritual ideas to the United States. Visits to England in 1895 and 1896 were also successful. Vivekananda founded the New York Vedanta Society in 1894, with branches in California established soon after. The organizations founded by Vivekananda in the West and in India (the Ramakrishna Mission) went on to be among the primary proponents of Advaita Vedanta.

By the time Harrison read *Raja Yoga*, then, it was already an established classic in Indian spiritual literature in the West.[24] Harrison remarked, "the first yogi I ever read, who really influenced me, was called Vivekananda."[25] In discussing his 1969 song "I Me Mine," for instance, Harrison writes, "Swami Vivekananda says: 'Each soul is potentially divine, the goal is to manifest that divinity.' We have to realize that we are potentially divine and then manifest that divinity."[26] Such an expression of the *tat tvam asi* tenet that is so central to Vedanta is not much different from what Harrison might have encountered if he had read very far into Vishnu-devananda's book in 1965, and while he was clearly attracted to Hindu thought, it is not clear which other elements of Vivekananda's *Raja Yoga* appealed to Harrison in the fall of 1966 and into 1967. Vivekananda begins his book, however, by arguing that religion should be based on experience and not belief: "If there is a God we must see Him, if there is a soul, we must perceive it; otherwise it is better not to believe. It is better to be an outspoken atheist than a hypocrite."[27] He also contends that such experiences are not limited to figures in the distant past: "what once happened can happen always."[28] And further, "Yoga is the science which teaches us how to get these perceptions."[29] Perhaps part of the initial appeal of Vivekananda's writing to Harrison was this commonsense view that seemingly miraculous things can still occur; they can occur to you, he seemed to say, but don't believe it until they do. Harrison, after all, had been using LSD since the spring of 1965 and had his own set of experiences to come to terms with. He recalled, "After I'd had LSD a lingering thought stayed with me, and the thought was 'yogis of the Himalayas.'"[30] It is worth noting in this regard that Harrison would continue to use LSD for several months after his India trip, discontinuing its use only in August 1967 after a disillusioning visit to San Francisco's Haight-Ashbury.[31] Thus, LSD and Indian philosophy both played a role in his life for about a year—something Vivekananda, Yogananda, Mahesh, and Prabhupada would not have condoned.

Harrison also read Yogananda's *Autobiography of a Yogi*. Yogananda had come to the United States in 1920 to lecture at the International Congress of Free Christians and Other Religious Liberals in Boston. Having established the Yagoda Sat-Sanga Society in India in 1917, he soon founded what would eventually be called the Self-Realization Fellowship (SRF) in 1920, establishing a headquarters for that organization in Los Angeles in 1925 and touring the United States extensively during that decade.[32] In the 1930s, he began writing the *Autobiography*, which offered a sometimes-fantastical portrait of Indian gurus and spirituality that clearly inspired Harrison. Published in 1946, the *Autobiography*, like Vivekananda's *Raja Yoga*, quickly became a classic of Indian spiritual literature in the West. Harrison famously included not only Yogananda on the *Sgt. Pepper* album cover but also Yogananda's gurus, Sri Yukteswar, Lahiri Mayasaya, and the elusive Babaji. Ravi Shankar reports that he had already given Harrison Yogananda's book before the Harrisons visited India in late 1966, most likely during one of the sitar lessons during summer of that year.[33] Shankar had met Yogananda in the 1930s and performed at the SRF Hollywood Temple in the 1950s, and so he was well aware of Yogananda's teaching before he met Harrison.[34] Harrison would later remark, "The moment I looked at that picture of Yogananda on the front of the book, his eyes went right through me and zapped me, and to this day I have been under the spell of Yogananda. It's a fantastic great truth."[35]

Yogananda's book provided an insider's view of Indian religious culture to the West that was novel in the late 1940s, and while many people have appreciated it on those grounds, many others have also been charmed by the many accounts of miraculous occurrences—a saint with two bodies, another who levitates, a mystical amulet that appears and disappears, and much more. Philip Goldberg has calculated that the book contains 132 miraculous occurrences, taking up roughly 44 percent of the book, though he points out that the title page contains the biblical epigraph, "Except ye see signs and wonders, ye will not believe" (John 4:48).[36] As Harrison might have understood it, Vivekananda claimed that miracles are possible—indeed Patañjali devotes most of an entire chapter to yogic powers—and Yogananda chronicled dozens of such occurrences, though perhaps in some cases simply to illustrative ends. While such tales must have captured Harrison's imagination, he might also have been drawn to the heart of Yogananda's book, which is the chapter on Kriya yoga. Yogananda writes, "A yogi who faithfully practices the technique is gradually freed from karma or the lawful chain of cause-effect equilibriums."[37] Yogananda's discussion of the Kriya technique of meditation is sober and intellectual, citing both the Bible and Patañjali while making constant appeals to science and logic. The chapter provides no precise instruction on meditation, however, and Harrison would have been left with some questions about how to actually practice Kriya.

As 1967 began, Pattie Harrison—who was also enthusiastic about Indian music and philosophy—learned of the Maharishi Mahesh Yogi and his technique of Transcendental Meditation (TM), which she began to practice in February.[38] By that time, Mahesh had already been teaching his approach to meditation in India, Europe, and the United States for more than ten years.[39] When it turned out that Mahesh was going to be giving a talk in London in August of that year (and just days after the events in San Francisco that caused Harrison to swear off LSD), she told her husband, he told the other Beatles, and everybody (except Ringo) ended up at Mahesh's lecture.[40] Vivekananda and Yogananda had been tremendously influential for Harrison, but they were historical figures. Mahesh, by contrast, was a living teacher he could learn from in person, somewhat as he had studied with Shankar; the opportunity to develop his meditation abilities must have seemed to come at just the right time. He remarked, "I was actually after a mantra. I had got to the point where I thought I would like to meditate."[41] The band was enthusiastic about Mahesh after his lecture and immediately traveled to Wales for what was supposed to be a ten-day retreat in Bangor. The sudden death of the Beatles' manager, Brian Epstein, in London forced the group to cut short their stay with Mahesh.[42]

In early 1968, however, the four Beatles, their wives, and other rock stars and celebrities went to Rishikesh, India, for an extended stay with the guru. Harrison meditated extensively during this period, causing John Lennon to remark, "the way George is going, he will be flying on a magic carpet by the time he is 40."[43] According to Harrison, "I went on a meditation course, where the object was to meditate deeper and deeper and deeper for longer periods of time. The goal is really to plug into the divine energy and to raise your state of consciousness and tune in to subtler states of consciousness."[44] Aside from meditation activities, the Beatles, their entourage, and the other students at the ashram also attended lectures by Mahesh, and some of what they heard was probably familiar to Harrison from his reading of Vivekananda and Yogananda.[45] Of course, the trip ended with a scandal involving charges that Mahesh had tried to take advantage of one or more of the young women in attendance, though Harrison later apologized to Mahesh about this incident.[46] Lennon and Harrison were the last two Beatles to leave Rishikesh, and they were gone by early April 1968.

During the summer of 1967, just weeks before Mahesh's lecture in London, the Beatles had traveled together to Greece to vacation and investigate buying an island retreat. Earlier in the year, Harrison had purchased a recording by A. C. Bhaktivedanta Prabhupada that featured the Hare Krishna chant (the maha-mantra). Lennon and Harrison had enjoyed the chanting so much that they reportedly chanted for hours one night on a boat trip during the Greek excursion.[47] Prabhupada had come to the United States in 1965 and founded the International Society for Krishna Consciousness (ISKCON) in New York, often referred to as the "Hare Krishna movement."[48] ISKCON devotees were typically young Americans known for their traditional Indian attire, shaved heads, and chanting of mantras in the bhakti manner, often to the accompaniment of drums and cymbals. In late 1968 and about eight months after the break with Mahesh, Harrison became friendly with a group of Americans who had established the London branch of ISKCON earlier that year. He embraced their musical and devotional practice of chanting while also providing significant financial support to the organization.[49] While ISKCON's public face was dominated by images of fervent chanting, Prabhupada's literary output—books, pamphlets, translations, and commentaries—is staggering in its volume.

Harrison soon developed a close personal relationship with Prabhupada, and their discussions were at times markedly theological. A widely circulated recording of Harrison, Lennon, Yoko Ono, and Prabhupada debating spiritual matters from September 1969 suggests that these could often be intensely critical discussions.[50] While Yogananda's writing stressed the primary importance of meditation, his approach also contained a strong devotional component. But Prabhupada's approach to spirituality was markedly more devotional than Mahesh's teaching or Vivekananda's writing (at least as it appeared in *Raja Yoga*). While Harrison enthusiastically took up chanting, he continued to meditate as well. He did, at least early on, have some reservations about Prabhupada's claims about the primacy of Krishna—claims that ran counter to the "one goal, many paths" attitude he would have absorbed in Yogananda's and Vivekananda's writing and heard from Mahesh.[51]

It is worth noting that Harrison was exposed to the ideas of Yogananda, Mahesh, and Prabhupada well before he took serious note of any of them. In January 1964, the sculptor David Wynne tried to tell Harrison about Mahesh, but Harrison seemed uninterested.[52] When the Beatles visited Elvis Presley in Los Angeles during the summer of 1965 (the same visit that produced the encounter with Crosby, McGuinn, and Fonda), Larry Geller attempted to interest Harrison in Yogananda's writing. Geller was a member of Presley's inner circle and had been an SRF member since 1960. Once again, however, Harrison could not be drawn in.[53] Finally, George had known Prabhupada's chanting and philosophy in 1967 though only became interested In ISKCON in late 1968. He had indeed chanted the maha-mantra with Lennon for hours in the summer of 1967, but the two were tripping on LSD at the time, and not long after, he became a devotee of Mahesh.[54]

The Songs

If there is one George Harrison song that seems to capture the influence of Indian music and philosophy, that song is probably "Within You Without You." This track combines the three key elements drawn from India: (1) the use of Indian instruments, (2) the use of Indian philosophy in the lyrics, and

(3) the use of musical features drawn from Indian music (such as drones and distinctive rhythmic patterns). As it turns out, there are few Harrison songs recorded with the Beatles aside from "Within You Without You" that include all three elements, and if one is strict about it, there are no others. There are many Harrison songs, by contrast, that employ one or two of these elements, as well as a small group of songs written by both Lennon and McCartney that use these elements. During Harrison's time of maximum engagement with these three elements—roughly from "Love You To" of 1966 to "The Inner Light" of 1968—his music also focuses on elements that have little or nothing to do with the Indian influence.[55]

As noted above, Harrison plays sitar on "Norwegian Wood," a song written primarily by John Lennon.[56] Aside from the use of sitar, however, there are no other features drawn from Indian music or ideas from Indian philosophy in the lyrics. Appearing alongside "Norwegian Wood" on *Rubber Soul* is Harrison's "If I Needed Someone." This latter track uses no Indian instruments or philosophical ideas, but it does employ a drone in the verse sections, created by the voicings on electric twelve-string guitar, capoed at the seventh fret, and McCartney's use of a repeated A note in the bass.[57] The bridge uses standard pop harmony, abandoning the drone, while the lyrics throughout hint at a kind of grouchy nonchalance that Harrison had employed earlier in "Don't Bother Me" and would turn to again, perhaps with more anger than nonchalance, in "Think for Yourself." Similar drones can be heard in Lennon's "Rain" and "Tomorrow Never Knows," recorded within a little more than a week of each other in April 1966.[58] There are no Indian instruments in "Rain," and though the lyrics are philosophical, there is no particular influence of Indian ideas. "Tomorrow Never Knows," by contrast, features tambura and sitar, with lyrics drawn indirectly from the *Tibetan Book of the Dead* (the direct source being Timothy Leary's *The Psychedelic Experience*).[59] Like Lennon's "Tomorrow Never Knows," Harrison's "Love You To" also appears on *Revolver*. Sitar is featured prominently on this Harrison track, with tabla providing Indian rhythmic patterns and tambura sounding a drone. The lyrics, however, are more of the kind of angry complaining found on "Don't Bother Me," "If I Needed Someone," and "Think for Yourself." Harrison's "Taxman" also appears on this album, with lyrics that turn his angry complaints to humorous effect. And while "Taxman" is a riff-driven rock track, the guitar solo on that track does indeed seem to emulate the sitar, but in this case, the solo is played by Paul McCartney.

When "Within You Without You" appeared on *Sgt. Pepper's Lonely Hearts Club Band*, it was the first Harrison song to employ all three elements of

Indian influence, though strictly speaking, the first Beatles track to do this is "Tomorrow Nevers Knows." The instrumentation includes sitar, tabla, tambura, swarmandal (also included on "Strawberry Fields"), and dilruba; a drone and Indian rhythm organization are employed; and the lyrics articulate the classic Advaita (nondual) Vedanta notion of "tat tvam asi"—the unity of Self and World, Self and God.[60] In Advaita, the Sanskrit phrase "tat tvam asi" is one of the four Mahāvākyas, or principal sayings drawn from the *Upanishads*; "tat tvam asi" occurs in the *Chandogya Upanishad* as a father instructs his son, who is just back from years of study, on the truth by which all other truths are known. The phrase translates as "thou art that," and the father uses it to point to a wide variety of things in the world, repeatedly coming back to the idea that no matter what it is, it's you.[61] Harrison's lyrics engage this idea by suggesting that whatever is outside you (without you) is also within you: any other understanding is caused by "a wall of illusion," and in the end, "we're all one." Indian instrumentation appears on Lennon's "Lucy in the Sky with Diamonds" and McCartney's "Getting Better," though only as an accompanimental tambura drone. The band also began work on Harrison's "Only a Northern Song" during the *Sgt. Pepper* sessions, and this track was meant to be Harrison's contribution to the album (but was rejected). The lyrics poke fun at songwriting and royalties, much as "Taxman" jokes about taxes and as "Piggies" (begun in 1966) lampoons the wealthy establishment. These three songs, together with "Savoy Truffle," form a clutch of Harrison songs that show no significant Indian influence. Another song recorded in the summer of 1967, "It's All Too Much," does feature a drone in the bass throughout and lyrics that seem to endorse a philosophy consistent with Indian philosophy. Both this track and the finished version of "Only a Northern Song" include musical collages at the end, much like Lennon's "All You Need Is Love." "Blue Jay Way" employs no Indian instrumentation or lyrical content, though it features a prominent drone.

The last of Harrison's "Indian" songs, "The Inner Light," comes closest to "Within You Without You" in its use of all three elements. The track employs harmonium, flute, sarod, pakava, shenai, tabla, tablatarang, and vocals and uses a drone and Indian rhythmic patterns and meter.[62] The lyrics, though consistent with Indian philosophy, are drawn almost verbatim not from an Indian source but from the Chinese *Tao Te Ching*.[63] The practice of taking lyrics directly from an extant source is a feature of Lennon's "Tomorrow Never Knows" and "Being for the Benefit of Mr. Kite," as well as McCartney's later "Golden Slumbers." "The Inner Light," then, participates in a second context within the Beatles catalog, one that is even broader if we loosen that context to include the external textual paraphrases and inspirations that prompt the Lennon songs "Cry Baby Cry" and "Happiness Is a Warm Gun," as well as Harrison's "While My Guitar Gently Weeps" and "Savoy Truffle."[64] If "The Inner Light" is counted as the last of Harrison's three primarily Indian songs with regard to musical features, it is worth noting that it was recorded in early 1968 (at about the same time as the Indian tracks on Harrison's *Wonderwall Music*) and thus *before* the Beatles went to Rishikesh. On a similar note, "Love You To" was recorded before Harrison met Shankar or began studying Indian philosophy, and "Within You Without You" was recorded before Harrison met Mahesh; both were recorded while Harrison was still using LSD.

By the time the Beatles were recording *The Beatles* (the White Album) in mid-1968, Harrison had abandoned the sitar, and aside from lyrics, the Indian musical influence was mostly absent. "Sour Milk Sea" was inspired by Indian sources, but Lennon refused to include it on that album, forcing Harrison to produce the song for Jackie Lomax. Indian influence continued in Harrison's lyrics: "Long Long Long" is clearly a prayer, "Something" could be interpreted as a love song to God, and "I Me Mine" was mentioned above. Among the many Harrison songs rejected by the Beatles that ultimately appeared on *All Things Must Pass*, there are numerous examples of lyrics clearly engaging Indian spirituality, establishing the pattern for Harrison's subsequent work: the Indian music was gone, but the Indian ideas remained. From 1968 onward, Harrison's activity in promoting Indian musical practices instead took the form of supporting the work of others: in 1969–70, he produced two singles and an album for Radha-Krsna Temple, including the singles "Hare Krishna Mantra" and "Govinda," both of which charted in the United Kingdom (and elsewhere), and he promoted the music and career of Ravi Shankar, including funding a documentary film.

In conclusion, Harrison was not a theologian, and it would be unfair to expect him to have reconciled certain significant differences between his spiritual influences. Still, these influences can be viewed productively according to Vivekananda's "four yogas" scheme, which divides into jnana yoga (based on knowledge), raja yoga (based on meditation), bhakti yoga (based on devotion), and karma yoga (based on service and duty).[65] Vivekanada's raja yoga blends meditation with jnana, Yogananda's Kriya yoga blends meditation with bhakti, Mahesh's TM is principally raja yoga, and Prabhupada's approach is primarily bhakti. Though bhakti is sometimes thought to dominate Harrison's thinking after 1969, his approach after the Beatles instead blended these elements, much as Vivekananda discusses in his writing. All four influences remained in Harrison's life and music. He would remain close to ISKCON members for the rest of his life. In Harrison's 1991 apology to Mahesh, he reportedly told the guru that he loved him.[66] Harrison kept copies of Yogananda's book in his house to give to friends, wrote a song devoted to him ("Dear One"), and supported SRF financially.[67] Harrison mentions these various forms of yoga in his opening dedication ("Words from Apple") to Prabhupada's Krishna book, which Harrison funded. Though Harrison does not use Vivekananda's precise scheme, he closely paraphrases Vivekananda's words from *Raja Yoga*, bringing together the alpha and omega of the philosophical influences on his road to India: "If there's a God, I want to see him. It's pointless to believe in something without proof," closing with, "I also request that you make an appointment to meet your God now, through the self-liberating process of YOGA (UNION) and GIVE PEACE A CHANCE."[68]

NOTES

1. Joshua Greene notes that George's mother enjoyed the weekly broadcasts of Radio India: "Every Sunday she tuned in to the mystical sounds evoked by sitars and tablas, hoping that the exotic music would bring peace to the baby in her womb" (*Here Comes the Sun*, 2).

2. Beatles, *Anthology*, 196.

3. This interview for the BBC documentary *The Mersey Sound* is reprinted in Kahn, *George Harrison*, 7.

4. Nityaswarupananada, *Astavakra Samhita*, 39.

5. Greene interprets Harrison's openness to Indian spirituality in the context of the pressures of celebrity (*Here Comes the Sun*, 37).

6. Goldberg, *American Veda*, 17.

7. In Susan Shumsky's recent study of the influence of India on the Beatles, for instance, she interprets the lyrics in Harrison's "Love You To"—a song written in early 1966 and prominently featuring Indian music and the sitar especially—in terms of Indian philosophy. But as we shall see shortly, Harrison would not study that philosophy in any depth until many months later, making it unlikely that the song is influenced by Indian thought to the extent that Shumsky claims, though it is certainly possible to view it as having a certain resonance with these ideas. See Shumsky, *Inner Light*.

8. Lewisohn, *Complete Beatles Chronicle*, 187.

9. Lewisohn, *Complete Beatles Recording Sessions*, 63, 65.

10. Beatles, *Anthology*, 196. See also Craske, *Indian Sun*, 291–94, for discussion of "Norwegian Wood," as well as Farrell, *Indian Music*, 171–72. As noted by Craske (*Indian Sun*, 292), Farrell suspects Harrison used a guitar pick to play the sitar on this track. Farrell writes, "The soft attack of the notes suggests that Harrison may have been using a guitar plectrum rather than the wire *mizrāb* customarily used to pluck the strings of the sitar" (*Indian Music*, 172).

11. Peter Lavezzoli also notes these two pieces on the US soundtrack album, noting that even if fans skipped over those tracks, an introduction to "Help!" included a prominent sitar flourish. Growing up with this album in the 1960s, I had no idea that introduction was not part of the song. Lavezzoli, *Dawn of Indian Music*, 174. For an exploration of earlier instances of "raga rock," see Bellman, "Indian Resonances."

12. Vishnu-devananda, *Complete Illustrated Book of Yoga*; Lewisohn, *Complete Beatles Chronicle*, 185.

13. Vishnu-devananda, *Complete Illustrated Book of Yoga*, 6.

14. According to Lavezzoli, "After setting the book aside for a couple of years, Harrison would pick it up again when he developed a genuine interest in yoga" (*Dawn of Indian Music*, 173).

15. Lavezzoli reports an incident of McGuinn, Crosby, Harrison, and Lennon discussing Shankar's music that occurred on August 25 during a party at a house the Beatles were renting during their Los Angeles stay. His account follows McGuinn's recollection of that event, though Crosby admits that he still does not know if he was "really the one who turned him on to Ravi." See ibid., 153, 165, 169. This was the same party at which Peter Fonda is reported to have unnerved John Lennon by claiming that he knew what it was like to be dead.

16. Beatles, *Anthology*, 196.

17. See Craske, *Indian Sun*, 293, for a fuller account of this episode.

18. Craske cites an unpublished memoir by Patricia Angadi stating that her husband, Ayana, referred Harrison to a student of Shankar's student Motiram for lessons, though no precise name is provided (*Indian Sun*, 292). Anil Bhagwat was hired to play tabla on "Love You To"—an arrangement facilitated by Angadi (Lewisohn, *Complete Beatles Recording Sessions*, 72).

19. Beatles, *Anthology*, 222.

20. Shankar, *Raga Mala*, 190.

21. There are many accounts of this sequence of events. Craske's account seems the most reliable, and he places the dinner party on July 16 or 17, the first lesson on July 23, and the second on July 24 or 25 (*Indian Sun*, 312–15). Compare with Lavezzoli, *Dawn of Indian Music*, 176–77. For a firsthand account of these events, see Boyd, *Wonderful Tonight*, 86–89; and Shankar, *Raga Mala*, 189–96. Shankar places the first meeting in June.

22. See Craske, *Indian Sun*, 318; Greene, *Here Comes the Sun*, 68–72; Shankar, *Raga Mala*, 193.

23. Vivekananda, *Raja Yoga*; Shankar, *Raga Mala*, 193.

24. For a detailed discussion of Vivekananda's role in the transmission of Indian philosophy to the West, as well as an outline of his life and work, see Michelis, *History of Modern Yoga*, esp. chapters 3–5; and Harris, *Guru to the World*. For a study of Vivekananda's interpretation of the *Yoga Sutras* in a broad historical context, see White, *Yoga Sutras of Patañjali*; and Bryant, *Yoga Sūtras of Patañjali*. And for a biography of Vivekananda, see Nikhilananda, *Vivekananda*.

25. Kahn, *George Harrison*, 343. These remarks were made during a 1987 interview with Anthony DeCurtis for *Rolling Stone*.

26. Harrison, *I Me Mine*, 156. Harrison quotes this passage at greater length in Shankar, *Raga Mala*, 195, though this quotation differs slightly from Vivekananda's published version. These lines appear in Vivekananda's commentary at II, 25, but are also used to introduce the preface of the book. See Vivekananda, *Raja Yoga*, 4, 245–46.

27. Vivekananda, *Raja Yoga*, 15. See also Thomson, *George Harrison*, 120; and Greene, *Here Comes the Sun*, 69.

28. Vivekananda, *Raja Yoga*, 14.

29. Ibid., 15.

30. Beatles, *Anthology*, 233.

31. For a vivid account of Harrison's first and last LSD experience, see Boyd, *Wonderful Tonight*, 100–106; as well as Beatles, *Anthology*, 177–80, 259. See also C. Lennon, *John*, 181–86.

32. Florio and Leeman, *Awake*; Goldberg, *Life of Yogananda*; Newman, *Finding God Through Yoga*. Newman reports that from 1920 to 1935 in the United States, Yogananda used the name Yogada Sat-Sanga for his organization, adopting Self-Realization Fellowship in 1935 (*Finding God Through Yoga*, 121). Newman's book also offers several insightful comparisons of SRF and the Vedanta Society, as well as of Yogananda and Vivekananda.

33. Craske, *Indian Sun*, 318.

34. Ibid., 187. Shankar's home in Encinitas was near the SRF center there; he mentions his close relationship with Brother Mitrananda in Encinitas, as well as his friendship with then–SRF president Shri Daya Mata. See Shankar, *Rag Mala*, 145–47.

35. Shankar, *Raga Mala*, 195.

36. Goldberg, *Yogananda*, 266–67.

37. Yogananda, *Autobiography*, 13th ed., 263. This sentence in the first edition of the book differs slightly: "A yogi who faithfully follows his technique is gradually freed from karma or the universal chain of causation" (Yogananda, *Autobiography*, 1st ed., 231). The topic of editorial changes and the debates surrounding them are beyond the scope of the current chapter.

38. Boyd, *Wonderful Tonight*, 96.

39. See Mason, *Maharishi Mahesh Yogi*.

40. Boyd, *Wonderful Tonight*, 96–100. See also Beatles, *Anthology*, 260, for Harrison's slightly different account.

41. Beatles, *Anthology*, 260.

42. Boyd, *Wonderful Tonight*, 106–7.

43. Badman, *Beatles Off the Record*, 340; Badman gives the date of these remarks as February 18, 1968. Susan Shumsky reports that Lennon and Harrison were meditating eight hours a day (*Maharishi and Me*, 162). Pattie Boyd (Harrison) reports that her longest meditation session in Rishikesh was seven hours, "from five in the afternoon until midnight" (*Wonderful Tonight*, 116).

44. Badman, *Off the Record*, 341. Badman gives the date of these remarks as February 19, 1968.

45. See Maharishi, *Science of Being*, for a sense of the likely content of these lectures. See also Mason, *Beatles, Drugs, Mysticism and India*, for partial transcriptions of tapes of Maharishi's lectures recorded at the ashram during this time.

46. For an almost day-to-day account of the Beatles' time at Rishikesh, including the many versions of the scandal, see Mason, *Beatles, Drugs, Mysticism and India*. For a summary of George Harrison's visit with and apology to the Maharishi in September 1991, as reported by eyewitness Deepak Chopra, see Shumsky, *Maharishi and Me*, 218–19.

47. Beatles, *Anthology*, 258.

48. Greene's *Swami in a Strange Land* provides a comprehensive biography of Prabhupada and ISKCON.

49. Greene, *Swami in a Strange Land*, 190.

50. For partial transcriptions of this conversation, see Kahn, *George Harrison*, 128–35; and Prabhupāda, *Chant and Be Happy*, 39–46.

51. Greene, *Here Comes the Sun*, 168–69; Prabhupāda, *Chant and Be Happy*, 44–45.

52. Turner, *Gospel*, 139. Turner interviewed Wynne for his book, and this information may be drawn from that session. Wynne has also stated that while he visited the Beatles in Paris at that time to work on a sculpture of the group, he introduced Harrison to Mahesh later. See Wynne, "My Bizarre Life."

53. This account is provided in Greene, *Here Comes the Sun*, 57–58, and is based on Green's own interview. Geller's account of this meeting can be found in Geller, Spector, and Romanowski, *If I Can Dream*, 122. Harrison remarked, "I spent most of the party trying to suss out from his gang if anyone had any reefers" (Beatles, *Anthology*, 191). Harrison seemed mostly surprised to learn that Presley was involved in SRF. For Geller's account of Presley's involvement in SRF and Kriya yoga, see Geller, Spector, and Romanowski, *Elvis's Own Story*, 132–35.

54. Beatles, *Anthology*, 258.

55. See Covach, "George Harrison, Songwriter," for a comprehensive overview of Harrison's songwriting during his Beatles years. See also Reck, "Beatles Orientalis," for a detailed account of the specific elements of Indian music employed in some of the Beatles' tracks.

56. Throughout this discussion, authorship of songs will be attributed to Lennon, McCartney, and Harrison. Lennon and McCartney frequently did not write as a team; rather, one would have a song, and the other would help out. Harrison's songs are mostly written solo.

57. The use of a capo to affect guitar voicings is a common technique in folk music.

58. While "Rain" was recorded at about the same time as the tracks on *Revolver*, it was released as a single before the album in June 1966. Work on "Tomorrow Never Knows" preceded "Rain" by ten days. See Lewisohn, *Complete Beatles Recording Sessions*, 70, 75.

59. Leary, Metzger, and Alpert, *Psychedelic Experience*.

60. The Indian musicians performing on this track were unknown for more than fifty years until Mike Smith was able to identify them. See University of Liverpool, "Unrecognised Indian Musicians to Perform."

61. Advaita interpretations of this *Upanishad* tend to begin with the commentary of Adi Shankaracharya (ca. 700 CE). See Gambhirananda, *Chandogya Upanishad*, 306–502; and Jagadananda, *Vakyavritti*.

62. Everett, *Beatles as Musicians*, 153.

63. The text was suggested to Harrison by the Cambridge scholar Juan Mascaró. At the time that he was in contact with Harrison, Mascaró had translated both selections from the *Upanishads* (1965) and the full *Bhagavad Gita* (1962); these ubiquitous Penguin paperback versions might even have been

on Harrison's bookshelf. See Harrison, *I Me Mine*, 116–17.

64. Harrison's use of the *I Ching* to prompt the lyrics for "While My Guitar Gently Weeps," as well as the use of a candy box for the lyrics of "Savoy Truffle," is discussed in Harrison, *I Me Mine*, 118–21, 126–28. The *I Ching* was the third book Harrison had with him in India during his extended stay in 1966.

65. For a detailed discussion of Vivekananda's four yogas, see Michelis, *Modern Yoga*, 123–25.

66. Shumsky, *Maharishi and Me*, 218.

67. Florio and Leeman, *Awake*, 176.

68. Prabhupada, *Krsna*, ii.

BIBLIOGRAPHY

Badman, Keith. *The Beatles Off the Record*. New York: Omnibus, 2008.

Beatles. *The Beatles Anthology*. San Francisco: Chronicle Books, 2000.

Bellman, Jonathan. "Indian Resonances in the British Invasion, 1965–1968." *Journal of Musicology* 15, no. 1 (1997): 116–36.

Boyd, Pattie. *Wonderful Tonight: George Harrison, Eric Clapton, and Me*. New York: Three Rivers, 2007.

Bryant, Edwin F., ed. *The Yoga Sūtras of Patañjali*. New York: North Point, 2009.

Covach, John. "George Harrison, Songwriter." In *The Beatles Through a Glass Onion: Reconsidering the White Album*, edited by Mark Osteen, 177–96. Ann Arbor: University of Michigan Press, 2019.

Craske, Oliver. *Indian Sun: The Life and Music of Ravi Shankar*. New York: Hachette Books, 2020.

Everett, Walter. *The Beatles as Musicians: "Revolver" through the "Anthology."* New York: Oxford University Press, 1999.

Farrell, Gerry. *Indian Music and the West*. Oxford: Oxford University Press, 1997.

Florio, Paula di, and Lisa Leeman. *Awake: The Life of Yogananda*. Los Angeles: Self-Realization Fellowship, 2015.

Gambhirananda, Swami, trans. *Chandogya Upanishad with Commentary by Shankaracharya*. Kolkata: Advaita Ashrma, 1983.

Geller, Larry, Joel Spector, and Patricia Romanowski. *If I Can Dream: Elvis's Own Story*. New York: Simon and Schuster, 1989.

Goldberg, Philip. *American Veda*. New York: Three Rivers Press, 2010.

——. *The Life of Yogananda*. Carlsbad, CA: Hay House, 2018.

Greene, Joshua M. *Here Comes the Sun: The Spiritual and Musical Journey of George Harrison*. Hoboken, NJ: Wiley, 2006.

——. *Swami in a Strange Land: How Krishna Came to the West*. San Rafael, CA: Mandala, 2017.

Harris, Ruth. *Guru to the World: The Life and Legacy of Vivekananda*. Cambridge: Harvard University Press, 2002.

Harrison, George. *I Me Mine*. Ext. ed. Guildford, UK: Genesis, 2017.

Jagadananda, Swami, trans. *Vakyavritti of Sri Sankacharya*. Mylapor/Madras: Sri Ramakrishna Math, 1973.

Kahn, Ashley, ed. *George Harrison on George Harrison: Interviews and Encounters*. Chicago: Chicago Review Press, 2020.

Lavezzoli, Peter. *The Dawn of Indian Music in the West*. New York: Continuum, 2007.

Leary, Timothy, Ralph Metzger, and Richard Alpert. *The Psychedelic Experience: A Manual Based on the Tibetan Book of the Dead*. New York: Citadel, 1964.

Lennon, Cynthia. *John*. New York: Three Rivers, 2005.

Lewisohn, Mark. *The Complete Beatles Chronicle: The Definitive Day-by-Day Guide to the Beatles' Career*. Chicago: Chicago Review Press, 2010.

——. *The Complete Beatles Recording Sessions: The Official Story of the Abbey Road Years, 1962–1970*. London: Hamlyn, 1988.

Maharishi Mahesh Yogi. *The Science of Being and Art of Living*. New York: Signet, 1968.

Mason, Paul. *The Beatles, Drugs, Mysticism and India*. Truro, UK: Premanand, 2017.

——. *Maharishi Mahesh Yogi: The Biography of the Man Who Gave Transcendental Meditation to the World*. Rev. ed. Truro, UK: Premanand, 2020.

Michelis, Elizabeth de. *A History of Modern Yoga*. New York: Continuum, 2004.

Newman, David J. *Finding God Through Yoga: Paramahansa Yogananda and Modern American Religion in a Global Age*. Chapel Hill: University of North Carolina Press, 2019.

Nikhilananda, Swami. *Vivekananda: A Biography*. New York: Ramakrishna-Vivekananda Center of New York, 1953.

Nityaswarupananada, Swami, trans. *Astavakra Samhita*. Kolkata: Advaita Ashrama, 2019.

Prabhupāda, A. C. Bhaktivedanta Swami. *Chant and Be Happy: The Power of Mantra Meditation*. Los Angeles: Bhaktivedanta Book Trust, 1982.

——. *Krsna: The Supreme Personality of the Godhead*. London: Bhaktivedanta Book Trust, 1970.

Reck, David R. "Beatles Orientalis: Influences from Asia in a Popular Song Tradition." *Asian Music* 16, no. 1 (1985): 83–149.

Shankar, Ravi. *Raga Mala: The Autobiography of Ravi Shankar*. New York: Welcome Rain, 1999.

Shumsky, Susan. *The Inner Light: How India Influenced the Beatles*. New York: Permuted, 2022.

——. *Maharishi and Me: Seeking Enlightenment with the Beatles' Guru*. New York: Skyhorse, 2018.

Thomson, Graeme. *George Harrison: Behind the Locked Door*. London: Omnibus, 2013.

Turner, Steve. *The Gospel According to the Beatles*. Louisville, KY: Westminster John Knox Press, 2006.

University of Liverpool. "Unrecognized Indian Musicians to Perform After Being Tracked Down by Liverpool Academic." June 6, 2017. https://news.liverpool.ac.uk/2017/06/06/unrecognised-sgt-peppers-indian-musicians-perform-tracked-liverpool-academic/.

Vishnu-devananda, Swami. *The Complete Illustrated Book of Yoga*. New York: Julian, 1960.

Vivekananda, Swami. *Raja Yoga, or Conquering the Internal Nature*. 1896. 3rd ed. Kolkata: Advaita Ashrama, 2017.

White, David Gordon. *The Yoga Sutras of Patañjali*. Princeton: Princeton University Press, 2014.

Wynne, David. "My Bizarre Life with the Beatles, by the Sculptor Who Immortalized Good, Great, and Even Gorillas." *Daily Mail*, June 26, 2010.

Yogananda, Paramahansa. *Autobiography of a Yogi*. 1st ed. 1946. Repr., New York: MJF Books, 2015.

——. *Autobiography of a Yogi*. 13th ed. Los Angeles: Self-Realization Fellowship, 1998.

CHAPTER 6

Don't Pass Me By

To Hell and Back with Ringo Starr

MICHAEL MCGOWAN

"I Honestly Don't Know . . ."

In late October 1964, Ringo Starr said in an interview that he and his bandmates were not "anti-Christ" but rather "anti-Christian."[1] The next year, Starr described himself using the same term John Lennon had used for the Beatles—"agnostic"—because, Ringo said, "I honestly don't know if there's anything up there or down there."[2] When the Beatles were in an exploratory phase of their musical, intellectual, and religious/spiritual development, the world's historic wisdom traditions held no privileged position in their thinking about matters of ultimate concern. Reflecting on the negligible influence of those institutions, Starr said in 1965, "Religion just doesn't do anything for me, really."[3]

But Ringo's story is fascinating precisely because he *did* change his mind, because his views were *evolutionary*.[4] This chapter discusses Starr's religious journey, a story that begins with significant medical issues as a child, paternal abandonment, and relationship problems. He and the other Beatles went from obscurity to worldwide stardom during Beatlemania, but when the band stopped touring and Lennon's and McCartney's songwriting interests became more sophisticated, Starr's vital role in the band began to diminish. His life changed again when the Beatles broke up, after which he spent two decades battling alcohol and drug addictions. Fortunately, Ringo found his way out, so a large part of this chapter will discuss his post-Beatles recovery efforts, in which Starr found belief in a "higher power" essential to stop drinking. Only through belief in and submission to God could Starr make his way out of his darkest period. What sort of beliefs and practices made possible the journey from Starr's agnosticism to his overt postrecovery proclamation, "God saved my life"? This chapter answers that question. I conclude by suggesting that Starr's willingness to share his story and post-Beatles art stands as evidence of the depth of his conversion and enduring commitment.

It Don't Come Easy

Ringo Starr was born "Richard Starkey" in 1940. He has discussed his upbringing by saying, "I had a great childhood," but there is at least some evidence to the contrary.[5] While it is true that he lived in a supportive environment in the Dingle, one of Liverpool's working-class communities in which neighbors chipped in to help with each other's children, little Richy Starkey grew up without his biological father around. When Richy was only three years old, marital tensions mounted between his mother, Elsie, and her husband, Richard Sr., who abandoned Elsie and their young son in 1943.[6] Fortunately, the impact of the absence of Richy's biological father was partially mitigated by Elsie's overwhelming love for her son and her supportive second husband, Harry, whose generosity and soft-spoken demeanor made him great stepdad material.[7] Elsie and Harry may have affected Richy's religious sensibilities at a young age. Reflecting on those times years later, he said, "I feel I had spiritual moments as a young kid. And I feel I had spiritual moments as a teenager."[8]

But growing up in Liverpool brought its own set of challenges. Liverpool's male youth culture was prone to creating and resolving conflicts through gang violence. "Every gang had a leader," writes Mark Lewisohn, "and Richy Starkey was never it." His physical appearance did not intimidate others; Richy was "smaller, leaner, weaker than the strapping toughs he did his best to buddy up with." In this precarious situation, Richy was a target even if he didn't seek out trouble himself. "I didn't knife anyone or kill anybody," he says, "but I got beaten up a few times—mainly by the people [I was] with, because it's that terrible craziness, that gang situation, where, if you're not fighting an outsider, you get crazy and start fighting amongst yourselves, like mad dogs."[9]

School, too, was difficult for Richy, who "always did something that annoyed people" and had serious health issues while growing up.[10] In the summer of 1947, Starkey was rushed to the Royal Liverpool Children's Hospital due to appendicitis, but attending physicians realized that his appendix had already burst and caused peritonitis. Richy was "barely conscious as he was wheeled into the operating room" and didn't get better for ten weeks. "Three times, doctors told Elsie he'd not survive the night."[11] Starkey recovered, but a few years later, in 1954, he was hospitalized again, this time with tuberculosis. And this time, Starkey's initial ten-week stint at Myrtle Street Children's Hospital was followed by a two-year stay in Heswall Children's Hospital. Any chance Richy might have had at a normal childhood with a regular education was gone. Fortunately for Starkey (and the world), at Heswall he was introduced to the drums, and it was "love at first strike."[12]

There were also problems with women, and sometimes these conflicts had a religious dimension to them. In one of his early relationships, with Geraldine ("Gerry") McGovern, the Protestant/Catholic split became insurmountable. This was because "religion was still a divisive issue between their respective families and it remained to be seen how this would be settled." Nevertheless, it wasn't the religious difference that caused division in their relationship but rather his first love, the drums: "of one thing Richy was quietly (or not-so-quietly) certain: if Gerry thought he was going to give up his drums for her, she was mistaken."[13] Richy decided when he was only eighteen years old that drumming would be his life's work.[14]

Ten years after his introduction to the drums in Heswall, Richy Starkey had adopted the stage name "Ringo Starr" and joined the Beatles, and Beatlemania had swept through Britain and the United States. In 1964, he and the other Beatles began to believe the hype that was written about them. "I went absolutely mad," Ringo says. "My head was just so swollen. I thought I was a God, a living God." In response to his self-adulation, he says, "the other three looked at me and said, 'Excuse me, *I* am the God.'"[15] These four Liverpudlians who, just two years earlier, were anonymous to the world now had to wrestle with the implications of celebrity and their vanishing independence. Naturally, due to swift and unrelenting changes in their lives, the Fab Four weren't quite sure what to believe about their lives and religion's place in it. So, toward the end of the year, they reasonably described themselves as "agnostic."

Don't Pass Me By

As Lennon and McCartney began crafting more sophisticated and introspective songs, Starr thought he would give songwriting a shot. But drumming and songwriting are two different animals, and the Beatles separated themselves from the herd by the latter. One of Starr's only contributions to the Beatles' catalog, "Don't Pass Me By," was, in fact, passed by for years. Although McCartney said the song had "a beautiful melody," he also said, "there's never enough time to fit Ringo's song on an album."[16] Rather than Starr taking umbrage at his first song being absent from album after album, sitting on the shelf for five years, he understood that what he brought to the Beatles was different than what Lennon and McCartney brought. "Out of four people," he said, "you wouldn't expect them all to be creative, would you? Fifty percent is enough." To have even *one* great songwriter in a group is remarkable, not to mention two: "Think of all the groups, good groups, who can't write anything at all."[17] Not only was he limited by his bandmates' extraordinary output, but also something *inside* Ringo limited him. Of his songwriting abilities, Ringo said in 1967, "I try. I have a guitar and a piano and play a few chords." But unfortunately, no matter what or how hard he tried, "no great tune comes out."[18] So, Starr used their studio time differently than the others. During the *Sgt. Pepper* sessions, for example, he learned to play chess. At other times, he would read the newspaper, chat with friends and staff, or "just sit there for hours waiting for the others to turn up.... [He] was often virtually ignored.... There was often no need for Ringo to be there at all."[19] Toward the end of their career, after touring had ceased, Starr's role was just above that of a studio musician.[20] Of course, Ringo was willing to do whatever the others wanted him to do because he loved to play.

Starr's "Don't Pass Me By" is not a terribly complicated song, musically or lyrically. But the lyrics reveal something of note about its writer. The song is narrated by a man who expects his beloved to arrive at his home. When she does not show, the narrator assumes it's because something is wrong with *him*: "Does it mean you don't love me anymore?" The narrator understands the absence of the girl as something done *to him*, in response to which he pleads that she not pass him by and make him cry or make him blue. It is not until the third verse that the listener discovers the reason for her absence, a car crash that made the woman a few hours late, upset, and anxious (on a British reading of the phrase "lost your hair").[21] When reflecting on the content of the lyrics, Hunter Davies wished Lennon or McCartney had made more suggestions that would have imbued Starr's song with a more sublime meaning and less silliness, as the original orchestral arrangement may have added. Deploring the lyrical triviality, Davies said, "It's a country and western number with a mean fiddle, a perfect sing-along tune, but oh, the words.

'You were in a car crash / and you lost your hair.' Couldn't Paul or John have saved him from such bathos?"[22]

In response to critiques from Davies and others, it would be tempting to pass Ringo Starr by as overly simple, unreflective, and, because he was never much of a songwriter, less worthy of our consideration than the other three Beatles. This would be a profound mistake. Of the four Beatles, Starr is the one whose life journey situated him in a very structured program of faith that promotes belief in and total surrender to God, so his path there is worth considering.

Beneath the surface, the lyrics of "Don't Pass Me By" reflect an individual's attempt to make sense of and cope with life's disappointments by any means necessary and *on one's own*, not as a member of a supportive community. And so *The Beatles*, the band's 1968 eponymous White Album, was the song's natural home insofar as the category of "album" returned to a pre–*Sgt. Pepper* collection of singles by band members acting as individuals with no organizing motif.

Perhaps Starr was tuned into something the other Beatles were not. If Peter Jackson's *Get Back* docuseries confirmed for us anything about Ringo, it's that he showed up when others did not. Toward the end, it seems as if the union of the Beatles meant more to Ringo Starr than to the others. McCartney was interested in maintaining the Beatles' status as cutting-edge artists (while privately working on a solo project). Lennon and Harrison were readying themselves for their solo careers as well. The band splintered along creative lines, and Ringo rationalized it all this way: "The break-up came because everyone had ideas of what *he* wanted to do, whereas everyone used to have ideas of what *we* would do, as a group. We weren't really fulfilling John's musical ambitions or Paul's or George's or my own, in the end, because it was separate."[23] In other words, the group was not functioning as a group. What Starr loved most was the *band*, playing as a *band*. He says, "I've always been 'the band guy.' I never wanted to be, like, 'Okay it's *me*.' . . . I listen to *them*, and I give *them* room. . . . This is how I am and how I've been. I only wanted to play."[24] Years later, he revealed what the Beatles meant to him by saying that joining the band "was the best move [he] ever made. . . . The light was shining on them."[25] He appreciated not only their music making but also their friendship. "Four guys looked out for each other, loved each other, and played well together."[26] This is precisely why Ringo was *not* primarily interested in being a solo artist. When he visited Elvis Presley and saw his entourage, it was "one of the saddest moments" because they were not mutually enriching relationships. Elvis's so-called friends were just "doing his bidding." That's not how

Starr was wired. He loved being in a band: "I've had friends around. I think that's very important."[27]

The breakup of the Beatles hit Ringo especially hard. He understood the reasons for it, but "dealing with the emotional consequences" of the band's dissolution was "quite another" matter. Starr says, "I sat in the garden for a while wondering what the hell to do with my life. . . . After you've said it's over and go home, you think, Oh God—that's it, then. Now what do you do? It was quite a dramatic period for me—or traumatic, really."[28] What were his options? He could have joined another band but decided against it because of the experience he had with the Beatles: "because I was bigger than any band I could have joined." Bandmates worried about Starr, especially Lennon, who did not want Ringo to end up playing Northern England nightclubs, a fate unworthy of the former Beatle's fame.[29] Instead of running full speed ahead with anything, Starr says, "I was hiding because of all those pressures." The situation made him feel "absolutely lost."[30]

Beneath the Waves

It would be inappropriate for me or anyone with inadequate training and experience to offer conclusions on the precise causes and conditions that pushed a person toward an addiction. There may be a straight line from the breakup of the Beatles to Ringo's subsequent two decades of substance abuse, or it may go deeper, further back into his childhood. I do not know. However, by his own admission, we do know that he managed the stress of his Beatles years with a little help from the bottle: "In my case, early on, the pressures were just there. You'd have a drink and later on, it got to be cocaine or whatever."[31] His struggles with substance abuse intensified after the breakup, and he referred to alcohol as his "medication."[32] He also found himself between the others, often acting as a mediator: "They were fighting for position more than I was. Also, I was a people pleaser who always wanted things to be cool and happy even when they weren't."[33] Many people with addiction issues attempt to numb their pain in order to cope with hidden and/or unimaginable suffering. This was the case with some of Ringo's closest friends of the period, not all of whom made it out alive. Other writers have suggested that it was the breakup of the Beatles that did Starr in, like Peter Doggett in *You Never Give Me Your Money: The Beatles After the Breakup*, in which he argues that Starr "found it so difficult to survive outside the group that he lost himself in alcohol and cocaine."[34]

Like the rest of the Beatles, Ringo had a history with mind-altering substances.[35] He drank as a child, even to the point of getting blackout drunk,[36] and he participated in Hamburg's hedonistic sex, drugs (pills), and rock and roll.[37] It was Starr who first smoked marijuana on Bob Dylan's suggestion, according to the man who introduced the Beatles to Dylan, Al Aronowitz.[38] (Coincidentally, Aronowitz also described the Beatles as religious figures in the *Saturday Evening Post*.) But it was after the breakup that Starr's alcohol and drug use became unmanageable. "I was mad for 20 years," says Ringo, and now "some of those years are absolutely gone."[39]

During the 1970s, Starr's public and private life bifurcated: the funny and lovable drummer was replaced with an addict whose duplicity was apparent to the people around him. Geoff Emerick, the Beatles' sound engineer and producer, says, "Ringo was uptight all the time, or perhaps it was just an act to keep me at a distance. The problem was that I never knew if I was talking to the actual person underneath the veneer or not." According to Doggett, "for Starkey perhaps more than the other Beatles, the gulf between his lovable public image and his authentic self would grow increasingly difficult to bridge."[40] The public image of a respectable former Beatle was maintained by professional choices Ringo made, like to record the "No No Song" for his album *Goodnight Vienna*, in which the narrator refuses marijuana, cocaine, and alcohol when, in point of fact, the singer himself often did not refuse. Starr's alcohol and drug use concerned Lennon, who knew about substance abuse from firsthand experience. "Lennon had lamented to his friends," writes Doggett, that Starr's "career had been in free fall since the mid-1970s, mirroring his decline into acute alcoholism." Lennon's "relationship with Starkey was closer and less complicated than his dealings with Harrison or McCartney, not least because Starkey represented no artistic or financial threat. Lennon offered Starkey unconditional love and acceptance."[41]

The women in Ringo's life were also impacted by his substance abuse. His mother, Elsie, now in her eighties "and still living in Liverpool, worried about their son, who was a continent away and seemingly adrift."[42] His drug and alcohol addiction also impacted his marriage to the actress Barbara Bach, who "fell into the trap" because of him, he admits: She "used to go to bed at 10 at night and get up at 8 in the morning. Till we met. Then her career went the same way as mine. . . . Working two days a year is not having a career."[43] Eventually, Bach began the attempt to turn their lives around. "Every couple of months she'd try and straighten us out," Ringo says, "but then we'd fall right back into the trap."[44]

To call Starr's drinking "excessive" is an understatement. There were times when he consumed sixteen bottles of wine a day. He would, of course, later admit, "I had a serious drinking problem," which impacted not only his personal but also his professional life: "I didn't work or do anything. I wouldn't go out, because you'd have to be in the car for 40 minutes without a drink."[45] He and others would make great plans; they would "sit around for nights on end and talk about what [they] were going to do"—but, of course, those plans fell apart: "I'd get so bleedin' drunk, I couldn't move. The result of being drunk was that nothing happened." Even when he did go out for social events, Ringo's addiction was a source of derision. After arriving drunk to a comedy show in Los Angeles, Starr began heckling Dave Letterman onstage, after which Letterman, who "had a reputation for eviscerating hecklers," shot back, "Oh, that makes sense. . . . You ruined your career, and now you've come here to ruin mine."[46] Reflecting on their time under the influence and how it interfered with their lives, years later Starr would remember, "in the old days the bar is as far as we would have gone, at nine in the morning and right through the day."[47] As with all untreated addictions, "it got progressively worse." Starr said, "The blackouts got worse, and I didn't know where I'd been, what I'd done. I knew I had the problem for years. But it plays tricks with your head. Very cunning and baffling is alcohol."[48]

"It Was My Moment"

Eventually, Ringo Starr hit rock bottom. After a devastating night and subsequent blackout, he says, "I 'came to' the next day and had done a lot of damage. I was about to lose the love of my life, Barbara, and everything else. And it was my moment." Bach refused to live like that anymore: "We went into rehab because we needed desperately a change," she says. "I got used to living at the bottom. But you get to a point where you realize, 'This isn't living.'" Starr and Bach checked into the Sierra Tucson rehab clinic in Arizona for five weeks, which led to a transformation in Starr's heart and mind. Often, it takes a major event such as a "rock bottom" to give alcoholics the willingness to consider other ways of living. Starr and Bach write, "we needed something big like addiction to come into our lives and knock us down and make us realize that a total change was necessary."[49] To people in recovery, the rock-bottom moment is seen as almost sacred, the moment of clarity that enables a total life change: "It's brilliant that we both found ourselves in the gutter," Ringo says, "and we both are now climbing the ladder to daylight."[50] In what follows, I discuss the steps that Starr took to address his addiction, paying particular attention to the first three steps and the idea of "God" in recovery programs.

Like the Beatles' music itself, the first three steps of Alcoholics Anonymous (AA) bring light into dark places. These steps are prerequisites that enable the addict's transition from hiding, shame, and dishonesty to openness, grace, and honesty. The first step is a simple admission that one's problem is out of one's control and that life has become unmanageable. The addict just has to tell the truth. "I'm here to get help because I know I'm sick," says Starr of his stint in Arizona.[51] This first step waves the white flag of surrender and recognizes the futility of white-knuckling efforts to overcome one's powerlessness over one's addiction. Starr and Bach wrote the foreword to a book by Joan and Derek Taylor (the Beatles' press officer) called *Getting Sober . . . And Loving It!*, in which they describe alcoholism as a deadly serious issue that requires admission of the problem before it can be addressed: "the *only* way to deal with it is first to admit you have it and then decide to go after recovery."[52] If the first step identifies the problem, the second step identifies the solution: people in recovery "came to believe that a Power greater than [them]selves could restore [them] to sanity."[53] Some participants in recovery programs call it their "higher power," while others use the word "God." But belief in God's existence does not necessarily a transformation make, so the addict must then entreat this God for help. Step 3, therefore, requires alcoholics to make an important decision. Those who have done so say, "[We] made a decision to turn our will and our lives over to the care of God *as we understood Him*."[54]

Before discussing steps 4–12, let us consider in a brief excursus this idea of a "God as we understood Him" by highlighting the fascinating difference between the religion of recovery programs and the world's major religious traditions. Whereas members of most wisdom traditions spill much ink and devote considerable time working on intellectual problems in the faith, Twelve Step recovery programs bypass the systematic and intellectual explication of their God and instead encourage the addict to choose whatever higher power works for them. This radically subjective form of faith is, one might say, a manifestation of the 1960s "spiritual awakening" in which the Beatles participated in a "shift in religious imagination" from modernity to postmodernity, away from absolute answers and toward "increased personal autonomy in religion."[55] People became free to craft an understanding of God from multiple influences rather than any single authority. Starr's recovery program is less concerned with *which* deity a person recognizes and more that they *do in fact* recognize a power greater than themselves. The central problem to be overcome, recovery programs suggest, is one's ego, or pride, our tendency to say of ourselves, "I'm the Greatest . . . In this world, in the next world and in any world!"[56]

What is more, accepting God "as we understood him" permits various religious hybridizations, like the merging of Ringo's Protestant Christian background with everything since, including India and the Maharishi, who, he says, "gave me something nobody can take away from me." He notes, however, "there's lots of others who have said good things; it's like filling up the ocean with good pebbles."[57] These "pebbles" are the various tidbits of wisdom that Starr and others have picked up over the years and merged into one spirituality that is uniquely suited to them and their quandary (i.e., their need for God to solve their addiction problem). Taking information in from different and at times contradictory sources, these things Ringo has heard from various people, he says, are "my own well that's filling up slowly but surely with a lot of concepts I take on board."[58] And if multiple voices are too overwhelming, alcoholics can, by dint of their own autonomous decision, strip away any concept that doesn't help: "People are frightened of the word 'God,'" says Ringo, but they can "keep it simple. God is love."[59]

What is more, the AA "fellowship"—another religiously significant term—addresses reticent agnostics and atheists in its literature. AA's primary text, known colloquially as the *Big Book*, asks those who don't believe in God to consider the outcomes of their attempts to use reason and faith thus far. It suggests to agnostics and atheists that they have placed their faith in something already without even realizing it. Faith, the AA program says, is inevitable. Or, as the American novelist David Foster Wallace put it, "Everybody worships."[60] The important choice is *what* to worship. As the *Big Book* says, "Had we not variously worshipped people, sentiment, things, money, and ourselves? . . . It was impossible to say we had no capacity for faith, or love, or worship. In one form or another we had been living by faith and little else."[61] Twelve Step fellowships codify this idea in a slogan that sums up the problem with the addict's mind, explaining why addicts cannot rely on reason to get them out of their problem: "My best thinking got me here."

For Starr and other alcoholics, the concept of "God" becomes appealing because of how radically *practical* it is after the destruction caused by alcohol. For many of them, belief in God was their only option left. "When we saw others solve their problems by a simple reliance upon the Spirit of the Universe," the *Big Book* says, "we had to stop doubting the power of God. Our ideas did not work. But the God idea did."[62] Essentially, that *it works* is all Ringo needed to know. "God is in my life," he said in a panel discussion about meditation and religion, and "I have no problem saying 'God.' That's how your life changes."[63]

Presumably this is why Starr also participated in a June 2007 interview with Peter Rodger for a documentary that asked famous people—believers and atheists alike—one simple question: "What is God?" Released in 2009 as *God: The Almighty Question* (or elsewhere as *Oh My God*), this movie gave Starr a chance to discuss his own understanding of who and what God is. In the interview, he says, "God is love . . . Pure love." He continues, "Love is an incredible power. . . . The reaction to it is so great, even to crazy violent people. . . . If you give out love they stop for a minute because everybody notices when it's love coming your way."[64] Belief in a higher power helped bring perspective to life by managing hard times without retreating back to the bottle. In this interview, Ringo remembered the wise counsel of the Vietnamese Zen monk Thích Nhất Hạnh, who urges followers to let go of desire. Starr agrees and tries to put these principles into action in his life: "When you get to the traffic light, it's no use getting crazy. Love the red light, and when it changes, drive on. . . . It's no good being angry at yourself, 'cause then you're twice as angry. I like to keep that in my life also."[65] People in recovery programs repeat this idea to themselves every time they pray the "Serenity Prayer," in which they ask God to grant them "the serenity to accept the things [they] cannot change, courage to change the things [they] can, and the wisdom to know the difference."[66]

Belief in a power greater than oneself does not by definition imply that the power is *super*natural in any way. Some alcoholics identify their higher power with their (all human, all broken, all healing) recovery group. However, when Ringo made up his mind to believe in and submit to a God, he went all in. Now, he endorses a metaphysical dualism according to which the spirit and body are separate ontological realities, each equally real and each equally deserving of our attention. Metaphysical dualism permits Starr to expand on the problem confronting humanity. When asked if he believed body and spirit are separate, he said, "I do. And the spirit does not cause the madness. It's not the sort of power-hungry situation many humans go into. That's the *human condition*."[67] If body and spirit exist on differing planes of existence, the spirit can exist without the body. So, when asked if he believed in an afterlife when we die, Starr said, "Personally, I believe I go somewhere."[68]

In the first three steps, Ringo came a long way toward admitting the problem and, after all else failed, recognized his need to believe in and submit to God to regain control of his life, but he was not finished. Steps 4 through 7 remove the barriers between an individual seeking to recover and the higher power they hope can restore them to sanity. These steps are intended to cleanse the alcoholic of their impurities. In step 4, the alcoholic takes stock of their life by listing what they have done well and poorly in their life or, using the language of the program, make "a searching and fearless moral inventory of [them]selves." In step 5, the addict shares what they have learned by revealing their moral inventory with a person they trust. Alcoholics "admitted to God, to ourselves, and to another human being the exact nature of our wrongs." This adds yet one more radical element to recovery programs: in addition to having a radically practical approach to recovery and a radically subjective concept of God, recovery programs are radically antiauthoritarian: the step 5 confession is not given to a guru, monk, priest, or rector but rather to a fellow addict, one's "sponsor," usually a recovering alcoholic who has completed the Twelve Steps. This, of course, means that the program is nonjudgmental and radically inclusive by design, immune from the "holier than thou" attitude that attends some religious communities. No one is there to condemn; their "leaders are but trusted servants" who "do not govern," and "the only requirement for A.A. membership is a desire to stop drinking."[69]

As Starr and Bach wrote in their foreword to *Getting Sober*, "Addiction is a disease, not a moral failing," and in recovery, "you can *identify* with other people and realize that you are not alone."[70] All over the world, "there are people who are happy to share with you their own experience, strength, and hope."[71] When they went into treatment in Tucson, Starr and Bach weren't treated as the former Beatle and Bond girl; rather, they write, "we were treated like everybody else."[72] The dedeification of Ringo Starr was, in his view, a "wonderful" thing. The anonymity of the fellowship functions as an equalizer. Everyone is treated the same, because everyone is equally unable to get better on their own. They all need a little help. And the supportive environment makes the next steps easier. "The strength of getting sober and loving it," Starr and Bach write, "lies in the power to identify with others; no matter where they come from or what they've experienced, if they're compulsive users of whatever, there is so much in common it's amazing. It's just great to be able to see so clearly."[73] Confessing one's moral failures is possible because the one to whom one confesses is in no better moral position than the confessor is. Once the confession has taken place, the alcoholic must prepare themselves for redemption, becoming "entirely ready to have God remove all these defects of character." And then comes the moment of submission, wherein the alcoholic "humbly asked Him to remove [their] shortcomings."

Steps 8 and 9 enabled Starr to repair the relationships his addiction has damaged. Step 8 asks the addict to make "a list of all persons [they] had harmed, and become willing to make amends to them all." Step 9 acts on that list by making "direct amends to such people wherever possible, except when to do so would injure them or others." Naturally, Starr's amends would include the people with whom he was violent while drunk (e.g., Bach) but also those hurt by his addiction in other ways. One of the interesting features of recovery programs is their full confidence in the objective power and value of forgiveness and reconciliation.

This also means that no one religion can lay exclusive claim to the moral law; recovery programs tap into those same moral intuitions. In Ringo's interview for *God: The Almighty Question*, he says religions are made up of people, but "this is not God. It's what the religion says. It's what the people in that religion say." Tragically, what they really want is power: "I think everyone wants their religion to be universe-wide, and they're not."[74] Instead, the alcoholic recognizes that their relationship with their higher power is unique, which enables them not just to "believe" but to "know" that God exists.[75] If steps 2–7 wipe the vertical slate clean in relation to God, steps 8–9 attempt to wipe the horizontal slate clean by repairing the relationships that were harmed while an addict was under the influence.

Finally, the last three steps are intended to create the conditions under which the recovering alcoholic can maintain their sobriety long term by habitually aligning themselves with the moral law and the Lawgiver in perpetuity, and Starr puts these steps into practice as well. In step 10, addicts "continued to take personal inventory and when [they] were wrong promptly admitted it." In step 11, "[We] sought through prayer and meditation to improve our conscious contact with God *as we understood Him*, praying only for knowledge of His will for us and the power to carry that out." For Ringo, it's a daily practice. "I am not religious," he says, but "I'm trying my best, on a daily basis, to have a spiritual life."[76] The addict also learns to "practice an attitude of gratitude," thanking their higher power for victories large and small, one day at a time. And those days add up: "I haven't had a cigarette in thirty years. Thank You, Lord!"[77] Steps 10–12 are the plan for perpetual growth, and when they speak of "prayer," this is not simply a metaphorical mind-set; it's a practice that Starr takes seriously. When asked whether prayer is identical to Transcendental Meditation, the practice given to the Beatles by the Maharishi in India, he says, "No. I [actually do] get on my knees and pray. I pray to God. My God in heaven. . . . I do it on my knees; it's like *respect*."[78]

No One Will Hear?

Although Ringo's songwriting credits for the Beatles are meager, his small additions to other Beatles songs are profound. Fans know that "A Hard Day's

Night" and "Tomorrow Never Knows" are Starr's malapropisms borrowed by the others in service to their own songs. One of his lesser-known contributions, however, is found in "Eleanor Rigby." According to some reports, Starr added the line about Father McKenzie "writing the words of a sermon that no one will hear."[79] Given his mid-1960s agnosticism and the period's burgeoning incredulity toward metanarratives, lines like this are not surprising. These words offered a searing indictment of traditional religions with hierarchical authority structures to address seekers in an emerging postmodern era.

But the Twelve Steps are also evangelistic in a way. Although recovery is based on attraction and not promotion, Starr's program has taught him that he needs to "carry the message" to others to help stay sober. In step 12, alcoholics recognize from whence they have come and seek to help others as they struggle against substance abuse. They accept, as part of their new life's mission, to help others outrun their demons: "Having had a spiritual awakening as the result of these steps, we tried to carry this message to alcoholics, and to practice these principles in all our affairs." Starr has done this by speaking openly, honestly, and without reservation about his struggles with alcohol and drugs. He has granted major interviews with television shows like *Good Morning America* and publications like *People* and *Rolling Stone*.[80] He has also teamed up with other recovering addicts—like the Eagles guitarist Joe Walsh—to share his experience with the newly sober.[81] He shares his unique view of the world in books like *Photograph* and *Another Day in the Life*. His art has become his new passion. Of course, he still writes and records music, but his avenues of expression have expanded dramatically since his time in recovery. Ringo Starr even paints.[82] Each is an avenue within which Starr promotes the values that run contrary to the addictive mind, namely, peace and love.

There is a paradox here: one carries the message to others and benefits from sharing one's story with another person, but one should only do so when the other person is able to hear it. A decision must precede involvement. In the foreword to *Getting Sober*, Starr and Bach write, "You are simply being asked to take care of yourself and let other people look after themselves. *It's self-help, in treatment*."[83] Either by design or by coincidence, in recovery programs, the efforts one makes to ensure one's own sobriety are, in fact, efforts that help others. Self-interest *does* serve others' interests; a clean conscience brings inner peace and enables outer love. As Ringo says in *God: The Almighty Question*, "You feel incredible when you give love back.... When you're doing something with love, all of this is behind you. It'll all support you. That's how the world works."[84]

Looking toward the future, Starr has reason to be hopeful about the next generation of musicians because, he says, "a lot of new artists are sober people. The part of it where musicians felt it was their right to get crazy has changed."[85] As recently as the early 2020s, Starr was still touring with his All-Starr Band. He knows that his act is unique and that the concertgoers aren't expecting much: "I'm not Pavarotti. People know who I am, and I'm giving them my best shot on my songs. And when the other guys are doing their numbers, I get back on the kit, and we play. It's fabulous."[86] He still loves playing more than anything (except his sobriety): "There's a magic moment where the band and the audience are just *on*, and that's a lot of peace and love."[87]

NOTES

1. Shepherd, "Interview with the Beatles."
2. Turner, *Gospel*, 40.
3. Ibid., 37.
4. Biographical details in this chapter come from the following texts: Lewisohn, *Tune In*; M. Starr, *Ringo*; R. Starr, *Another Day*; R. Starr, *Photograph*; R. Starr and Bach, foreword to *Getting Sober*; Harry, *Ringo Starr Encyclopedia*; Clayson, *Ringo Starr*; and Dougherty and Balfour, "Ringo on the Rebound."
5. M. Starr, *Ringo*, 19.
6. R. Starr, *Photograph*, 3; M. Starr, *Ringo*, 12.
7. Lewisohn, *Tune In*, 70.
8. Rodger, *God*.
9. R. Starr, *Photograph*, 21; Lewisohn, *Tune In*, 87.
10. Lewisohn, *Tune In*, 69.
11. Ibid., 45; R. Starr, *Photograph*, 12, 16, 17.
12. There are several competing narratives that explain Starr's introduction to the drums. This one is found in Lewisohn, *Tune In*, 70–71. See also R. Starr, *Photograph*, 17, 25.
13. Lewisohn, *Tune In*, 212.
14. Ibid., 186; R. Starr, *Photograph*, 44.
15. Hibbert, "Who the Hell."
16. Turner, *Beatles*, 83.
17. M. Starr, *Ringo*, 176–77.
18. Turner, *Beatles*, 83.
19. M. Starr, *Ringo*, 195–97.
20. Now, for the sake of clarity, it is worth mentioning that Starr was indisputably a good drummer. Without his precision and stability, the others would have no canvas on which to paint their sonic masterpieces. What is more, he was innovative in his own way, even pioneering some techniques that other drummers have gone on to emulate. For example, he lays cloths on top of the snare and toms for what he calls a "deeper" sound without reverb (R. Starr, *Drumming*, episode 5). Additionally, the industry's great drummers from the past seven decades recognize his skill, and they speak warmly and generously about his influence on their own drumming. See M. Starr, *Ringo*, 340–45, for statements by Phil Collins, Max Weinberg, Kenny Aronoff, and John Densmore.
21. Of course, an American reading of "lost your hair" might suggest a sort of Flannery O'Connor–ish grotesque scalping.
22. Davies, *Beatles Lyrics*, 287.
23. Doggett, *You Never Give Me Your Money*, chapter 3.
24. R. Starr, *Drumming*, episode 3 (emphasis added).
25. Ibid.
26. R. Starr, *Drumming*, episode 8.
27. Grant, "Joe Walsh, Ringo Starr."
28. Doggett, *You Never Give Me Your Money*, chapter 3.
29. M. Starr, *Ringo*, 209.
30. Dougherty and Balfour, "Ringo on the Rebound."
31. Grant, "Joe Walsh, Ringo Starr."
32. Warren, "Ringo Starr at 70."
33. Wild and Seliger, "Ringo, Confident and Sober."
34. Doggett, *You Never Give Me Your Money*, introduction.
35. For an overview of the Beatles' drug use, see Goodden, *Riding So High*.

36. Clayson, *Ringo Starr*, 24; R. Starr, *Photograph*, 28. See also Lewisohn, *Tune In*, 93, 138, 170, 185.
37. Lewisohn, *Tune In*, 380.
38. M. Starr, *Ringo*, 133.
39. Bertodano, "Ringo Starr."
40. Doggett, *You Never Give Me Your Money*, chapter 3.
41. Doggett, prologue.
42. M. Starr, *Ringo*, 288.
43. Dougherty and Balfour, "Ringo on the Rebound."
44. Ibid.
45. Ibid.
46. Knoedelseder, *I'm Dying Up Here*, 106–7.
47. Starr and Bach, foreword to *Getting Sober*, x.
48. Dougherty and Balfour, "Ringo on the Rebound."
49. Starr and Bach, foreword to *Getting Sober*, ix.
50. Harry, *Ringo Starr Encyclopedia*, 315.
51. Dougherty and Balfour, "Ringo on the Rebound."
52. Starr and Bach, foreword to *Getting Sober*, ix (emphasis added).
53. Wilson, *Big Book of Alcoholics Anonymous*, 49. The remaining steps in the following few paragraphs come from this edition unless otherwise noted.
54. Ibid., 49–50 (emphasis in original).
55. Ellwood, *Sixties Spiritual Awakening*, 327.
56. Starr, "I'm the Greatest."
57. Rodger, *God*.
58. Ibid.
59. Ibid.
60. Wallace, *This Is Water*.
61. Wilson, *Alcoholics Anonymous*, 54.
62. Ibid., 45–46.
63. While promoting his book *Photograph*, Starr participated in a panel discussion with Backstory Events, "Ringo Starr."
64. Tragically, the son of Starr's interviewer would, a few years later, murder six people near the University of California's campus in Santa Barbara.
65. Rodger, *God*.
66. Wilson, *Alcoholics Anonymous*, 350.
67. Rodger, *God* (emphasis added).
68. Ibid.
69. Wilson, *Alcoholics Anonymous*, 562.
70. Starr and Bach, foreword to *Getting Sober*, ix.
71. Ibid, ix.
72. Ibid, x.
73. Ibid, x.
74. Rodger, *God*.
75. Ibid.
76. Ibid.
77. R. Starr, *Drumming*, episode 4.
78. Rodger, *God*.
79. Campbell, *Continuing Story of Eleanor Rigby*, 3.
80. Harry, *Ringo Starr Encyclopedia*, 314–15.
81. Grant, "Joe Walsh, Ringo Starr."
82. Starr, *Painting Is My Madness, Too*.
83. Starr and Bach, foreword to *Getting Sober*, ix (emphasis in original).
84. Rodger, *God*.
85. Grant, "Joe Walsh, Ringo Starr"
86. M. Starr, *Ringo*, 313.
87. R. Starr, *Drumming*, episode 9.

BIBLIOGRAPHY

Backstory Events. "Ringo Starr on His Relationship with George Harrison and God." YouTube, December 19, 2019. https://youtu.be/PZTVPVJaw0Q.

Bertodano, Helena. "Ringo Starr on Not Looking Back." *Times*, April 11, 2015.

Campbell, Colin. *The Continuing Story of Eleanor Rigby: Analyzing the Lyric of a Popular Beatles Song*. Market Harborough, UK: Troubadour, 2018.

Clayson, Alan. *Ringo Starr: A Life*. London: Sanctuary, 2005.

Davies, Hunter. *The Beatles Lyrics: The Stories Behind the Music, Including the Handwritten Drafts of More than 100 Classic Beatles Songs*. New York: Little, Brown, 2014.

Doggett, Peter. *You Never Give Me Your Money: The Beatles After the Breakup*. New York: HarperOne, 2009. ebook.

Dougherty, Steve, and Victoria Balfour. "Ringo on the Rebound." *People*, August 28, 1989.

Ellwood, Robert S. *The Sixties Spiritual Awakening: American Religion Moving from Modern to Postmodern*. New Brunswick: Rutgers University Press, 1994.

Goodden, Joe. *Riding So High: The Beatles and Drugs*. Wales: Pepper & Pearl, 2017.

Grant, Sarah. "Joe Walsh, Ringo Starr and the Mission to End America's Addiction Crisis." *Rolling Stone*, March 16, 2019.

Harry, Bill. *The Ringo Starr Encyclopedia*. London: Virgin Books, 2004.

Hibbert, Tom. "Who the Hell Does Ringo Starr Think He Is?" *Q*, June 1992.

Knoedelseder, William. *I'm Dying Up Here: Heartbreak and High Times in Stand-Up Comedy's Golden Era*. New York: PublicAffairs, 2009.

Lewisohn, Mark. *Tune In: The Beatles—All These Years*. Vol. 1. New York: Crown Archetype, 2013.

Rodger, Peter, dir. *Oh My God*. Later retitled *God: The Almighty Question*. Los Angeles: Syzygy Productions, 2009. Film.

Shepherd, Jean. "Interview with the Beatles: A Candid Conversation with England's Mop-Topped Millionaire Minstrels." *Playboy*, February 1965.

Starr, Michael Seth. *Ringo: With a Little Help*. Milwaukee: Backbeat Books, 2015.

Starr, Ringo. *Another Day in the Life*. Guildford, UK: Genesis, 2019.

———. *Drumming and Creative Collaboration*. Online class. MasterClass, 2021.

———. "I'm the Greatest." On *Ringo*. Apple, 1973.

———. *Painting Is My Madness, Too: The Art of Ringo Starr*. Plymouth Meeting, PA: ArtCelebs, 2020.

———. *Photograph*. Guildford, UK: Genesis, 2015.

Starr, Ringo, and Barbara Bach. Foreword to *Getting Sober . . . and Loving It! Hope and Help from Recovering Alcoholics*, edited by Joan and Derek Taylor, ix–xi. London: Vermillion, 1992.

Turner, Steve. *The Beatles: The Stories Behind the Songs, 1967–1970*. London: Carleton Books, 2009.

———. *The Gospel According to the Beatles*. Louisville, KY: Westminster John Knox Press, 2006.

———. *A Hard Day's Write: The Stories Behind Every Song*. New York: MJF Books, 2005.

Wallace, David Foster. *This Is Water: Some Thoughts, Delivered on a Significant Occasion, about Living a Compassionate Life*. New York: Little, Brown, 2009.

Warren, Jane. "Ringo Starr at 70: I've Beaten Drink, Drugs, and Depression." *Express*, July 9, 2010.

Wild, David, and Mark Seliger. "Ringo, Confident and Sober: The Former Beatles Releases His Best Album in Nearly Two Decades." *Rolling Stone*, July 23, 1992.

Wilson, Bill. *The Big Book of Alcoholics Anonymous (Including Twelve Steps and Twelve Traditions), Special 2013 Edition*. New York: Alcoholics Anonymous World Service, 2013.

PART 3

THE BEATLES AND RELIGIOUS EXPERIENCE

CHAPTER 7

Songs of Self-Emptying in the Beatles

SCOTT FREER

Songs of self-emptying both unite and divide the three songwriters of the Beatles. In the Christian tradition, *kenosis* refers to the self-emptying of Jesus and the way toward salvation. In the context of the countercultural sixties, the Beatles drew on interfaith, as well as psychological and ethical, notions of kenosis as a means of experiencing the divine or secular manifestations of ego death. Through a comparative study of the lyrics of McCartney, Harrison, and Lennon, it is possible to measure various refashioned invocations of self-emptying that span a wide secular-religious spectrum and that enabled each member of the band to arrive at divergent points of faith and spirituality.[1]

When Christ is exalted through a humbling to the human as a powerless slave, kenosis expresses one idea of self-emptying: "Let the same mind be in you that was in Christ Jesus, who, though he was in the form of God, did not regard equality with God as something to be exploited, but emptied himself, taking the form of a slave, being born in human likeness" (Philippians 2:5–8, NRSV). Christ's action demonstrates God's true nature and is opposite to a grasping selfish attitude, and so kenosis in this respect bears theological and ethical meaning.[2] Kenosis, through Christ's suffering, is also the staging of humanity's atonement and can also mean an openness to the pain of others.

According to David T. Williams, "the passage must be read as a basis not for Christology, but for the Christian life."³ The Lukan account of Mary's Annunciation focuses on her acceptance of the divine will: "Behold the maidservant of the Lord! Let it be to me according to your word" (Luke 1:38). And, with Jesus as the hypostasis of divine Word and human Son, kenosis is judged to have occurred at the moment of the child's conception.⁴ The Annunciation is testimony to Mary's receptiveness to the Word of God, a staging for Christ's incarnation and the salvation of self-emptying love. An important aspect of Christian theology, kenosis shares affinities with Catholicism, Hinduism, and Buddhism. For example, in Nāgārjuna's *Mūlamadhyamakakārikā* (a foundational text in Buddhist philosophy, 150 CE), understanding the emptiness of phenomena is a means of realizing the "nirvana" of nonself.⁵ For inclusivists, "kenosis" and "sunyata" are mutually compatible terms through the disentangling of human egoism, resulting in psychological liberation.⁶

In the context of the countercultural sixties that drew on the comparative religious symbolism of death and rebirth, healing the wound of the ego via kenosis was perceived to be realizable through experimentations in psychedelic drugs, psychotherapy, mysticism, meditation, and mind expansion. For example, Timothy Leary's advocacy of psychedelic drugs was predicated on the ego death of Eastern mysticism. According to Morgan Shipley, the emancipatory value of psychedelic substances, in transcending "ordinary consciousness," resided in the sacramental capacity to exceed habitual thinking, and in this sense, "psychedelic mysticism" highlighted "a return to religious sentiment."⁷ Furthermore, "psychedelic Buddhism" with its "imperatives of compassion" enabled many devotees in the postwar United States to "reimagine and re-engage complex dialogues between self and other."⁸ In this respect, interfaith kenosis, in bypassing the social controlling mechanism of the ego, resembles the Christian effect of humility and love that "flows from a free disposition" and unseats the self.⁹ In effect, self-emptying, as a transcendental experience that spanned the secular-religious spectrum in the sixties, was a pivotal means of overcoming entrenched ideological binaries and breaching damaging mind-sets and appears similar to kenosis. To quote Lennon, "Until you/we change our heads—there's no chance. Tell me of one successful revolution."¹⁰ In the 1968 song "Revolution," Lennon touches on the perennial Gordian knot: "change the head to change society or change society to change the head."¹¹ But while the 1969 "Bed-ins for Peace" with Yoko Ono resonate with Christian doctrines of love and "sin" in their countering of the systematic destruction of people, the emptying of the self was not for Lennon a preparation of the soul to be led by divine direction.

This said, interfaith kenosis was the bridge that enabled the Beatles to move from their orthodox religious upbringings to an eclectic mix of spirituality by the end of the sixties. McCartney and Harrison were baptized as Roman Catholics (and raised denominationally), Starr attended an evangelical Anglican church, and Lennon was "brought up Christian."[12] By February 1965, they declared themselves to be agnostic:

McCartney: We probably seem antireligious because of the fact that none of us believe in God.

Lennon: If you say you don't believe in God, everybody assumes you're antireligious, and you probably think that's what we mean by that. We're not quite sure *what* we are, but I know that we're more agnostic than atheistic.[13]

Following the Beatles' 1966 US tour and their visit to Rishikesh in North India to study meditation with the Maharishi Mahesh Yogi, the four became interested in Eastern philosophy.[14] With the breakup of the band, Lennon and Harrison embraced opposing spiritual paths: Harrison became a devotee of Hinduism and Hare Krishna, and this is epitomized in the 1970 single "My Sweet Lord," with Lennon's rejection of organized religion expressed in his 1971 single "Imagine."

However, the spiritual destination is rarely as telling as the spiritual journey of discovery itself, and so to mark Lennon out as an atheist as opposed to the theism of Harrison ignores the religious import of Lennon's own quest of self-emptying. In an interview with David Sheff (three months before his death), Lennon said, "People always got the image I was anti-Christ or antireligion. I'm not at all. I'm a most religious fellow. . . . I'm certainly not an atheist. There is more that we still could know."[15] Out of the four, Lennon's so-called antireligious position is more indicative of the subtle shades of spirituality that characterize a postreligiosity witnessed in the poetics of literary modernists.[16] A theological view of kenosis is one of self-humbling to serve God and others. But kenosis in secular forms that serve a personal end can lead to a kind of self-referential solipsism (as in the case of Lennon) or passive resignation toward the world when self-exhausted. Pope Pius XII in *Sempiternus Rex Christus* (1951) condemned a particular liberal interpretation of kenosis as the emptying of "the Word in Christ," or a losing of Godness. In this sense, Harrison was respectful to the Christian doctrine of kenosis, echoing Julian of Norwich's impersonal and receptive love, and servitude, toward a metaphysical God. Lennon's various experimentations with ego death (e.g., via LSD and meditation), on the other hand, exemplify desacralized kenosis. Self-emptying was largely a means of healing childhood trauma and of finding a liminal space freed from the regulating conformity of the ego.[17] In simple terms, Harrison sought the inscrutable divine Other, and Lennon sought temporary liberations of the self that in turn led to humanist reassessments of Christ's parables. So, Lennon was Gnostic, and Harrison, a theist. And in comparison, McCartney was the spiritually nonstriving earthed realist.

Paul McCartney ("Let It Be")

As Rob Sheffield has stated, there is "no scrap of religiosity discernible in" Paul McCartney.[18] McCartney's no-nonsense attitude toward divine possibilities is captured thus: "This is life. We're born, we die."[19] And this is evident in nonconfessional lyrics that intimate a homely individual untroubled by the big life-death questions. The impersonal lyricist, McCartney, "like a novelist," writes "third-party songs."[20] Whereas Lennon is often the visionary Romantic, McCartney is earthed, not floating as a lonely cloud or looking for the numinous in nature. McCartney rarely gives voice to the existential angst that accompanies the search for a godhead, despite some songs expressing longing for something beyond the given or the here and now, for example, "The Long and Winding Road"—"Let me know the way." McCartney's lyrical input pertains instead to contemporaneous British New Wave cinema, with its focus on real locations and people. For example, "She's Leaving Home" is a domestic drama, a condensation of the intergenerational tensions played out in sixties films, such as *A Taste of Honey* (1961) and *A Kind of Loving* (1962). It is no coincidence that Richard Lester's *A Hard Day's Night* (1964)—note the scene in which estranged working-class Ringo walks down a river of *disjecta membra* and encounters canny cockney kids—is rooted in cinema verité. McCartney's best songs bear the minutiae of realism.

The spliced lyrics of "A Day in the Life" (1967) exemplify the contrasting preoccupations of the Lennon-McCartney double act. As Tim Riley sees it, "Paul's complementary section is the day in the life of a modern everyman who sets forth each morning unaware of the tragedy around him. . . . Lennon's agonized empathy surrounds Paul's blissful ignorance."[21] McCartney occupies the waking world, assuming the persona of the commuter: "Woke up, fell out of bed." Lennon, on the other hand, is desirous to slip into a semiconscious dreamy world. "Penny Lane," accompanying "Strawberry Fields Forever" on the 1967 double A-side single, is further evidence of McCartney's contained realism, with an enchanting view of interconnected suburban life: "Penny Lane is in my ears and in my eyes / There beneath the blue suburban skies." Everything points to McCartney being content when immersed in an immediate living reality. "Fixing a Hole" is generally perceived as a coded LSD-DIY song, but the opening lines suggest a resistance toward mind expansion: "I'm fixing a hole where the rain gets in / And stops my mind from wandering." One of McCartney's few contentious songs, "Eleanor Rigby," resonates with William Blake's "The Garden of Love," in viewing organized religion as a joyless and soulless place: "Father McKenzie / Writing the words of a sermon that no one will hear / No one comes near." The unheard sermon indicates that religion does not speak to McCartney, nor does it prompt alternate insights.

It is only in the single "Let It Be" (1970), a counterpoint to the breast-feeding, making "ends meet" "Lady Madonna" (1968), that a religious figure is invoked to express a collective sense of grace. The song itself was inspired by a spiritual happening—Paul dreamt of his mother during a restless night. There are literal sources for the song's spiritual meaning: Mary (who was Roman Catholic) was Paul's mother's name, and the idiomatic sense of "let it be" is one of letting things run a natural course.[22] However, Paul also invokes a Catholic honoring of the Virgin Mary, alluding to Luke 1:38. And in turn, the song points to an established interpretation of the Annunciation as one of self-emptying, with Mary (favorably likened to a lowly servant) passively accepting the commission of God, that is imitative of her son's.

> When I find myself in times of trouble, Mother Mary comes to me
> Speaking words of wisdom, let it be.

With the emphasis on the feminine symbolism of Mariology and the association with passivity, Paul sustains the Beatles' countering of a Western emphasis on active overcoming.

> And when the broken-hearted people living in the world agree
> There will be an answer, let it be.
> For though they may be parted, there is still a chance that they will see.

Curiously, McCartney eschews the lines in "Mary's Song of Praise" (from Luke 1:52–53) that have inspired Latin American Liberation Mariology:

> He has put down the mighty from *their* thrones,
> And exalted *the* lowly.
> He has filled *the* hungry with good things,
> And *the* rich He has sent away empty.

The Catholic notion of self-surrendering (to give up control for someone else) bears Buddhist overtones, too, for Mary is a symbol of surrender and peace rather than mental strife. Paul also adapts Catholic iconography to underscore a social ethos that is one of world harmony via kenotic love (rather than personal struggle), and this chimes with the communitarian idealism of Lennon and Harrison.

George Harrison ("Within You")

Whereas Paul is the realist, George is the "realist theist" for whom kenosis is the method of experiencing the divine that orthodox faith had not yet achieved: "Christianity as I was taught it was a demand that I should believe in Jesus and in God but they didn't actually show me any way of experiencing God or Jesus."[23] In a revealing interview with Tony Barrow (*KRLA Beat*, November 4, 1967), before departing for India, Harrison likens meditation to a tabula rasa effect, while for John, it is similar to sleeping:

George: When your mind is a complete blank it's beyond all previous experience. That level is timeless, spaceless. You can be there for five minutes or much longer. You don't actually know how long when you come out of it and back to the everyday, the gross level of thinking.
John: It's like sleeping. You don't know you've been sleeping until you're awake again. It seems as though no time has gone at all.

The way to God, for Harrison, was the discovery of a kind of emptying of the Christian Logos (John 1). In an interview with Barry Miles from the *International Times* (May 1967), he speaks about the significance of the "Hare Krishna" chant: "They get hung up on the meaning of the word rather than the sound of the word. 'In the beginning is the Word.'"[24] To reach the divine, Harrison had to be divested of the conceptual burden of language or signifiers of some external reality.

As Laurence Coupe sees it, "My Sweet Lord" (1970) is the apotheosis or affirmation of Harrison's devout religious beliefs. "If one is in any doubt about Harrison's embrace of theism, one should listen to that. It is a song to God—a hymn—and it is brimming with devotion":[25]

> I really wanna know You
> I'd like to go with You
> I wanna show You, Lord
> That it won't take long, my Lord
> (Hallelujah)

Harrison's interest in Eastern kenosis was first explicitly signaled on the *Sgt. Pepper's Lonely Hearts Club* album (1967) through the song "Within You Without You":

> We were talking about the space between us all
> And the people who hide themselves behind a wall of illusion
> Never glimpse the truth
> Then it's far too late
> When they pass away

Harrison alludes to Hindu philosophy, in particular, the concept of "maya," which means in Sanskrit "illusion" or "magic." Perhaps for this reason, the song "sits outside the *Pepper* fantasy in its own self-contained musical temple."[26] For Ian MacDonald, while Harrison is "seeing the world metaphysical perspective of Indian philosophy," it is also a countercultural protest of the inner self against materialism.[27] In a similar vein, "It's All Too Much"—from the 1969 album *Yellow Submarine*—is a rejection of external reality: "And the more I go inside, the more there is to see." And again "The Inner Light," on the B-side to the 1968 "Lady Madonna" single, propounds a belief in self-emptying at the expense of the outdoors:

> Without going out of my door
> I can know all things of earth
> Without looking out of my window
> I could know the ways of heaven
> The farther one travels
> The less one knows

Dissimilar to McCartney, Harrison is unenthused by the sensory experiences of the material world. "All Things Must Pass," from Harrison's 1970 solo album, underscores his view of the impermanence of the physical world, taking its premise from Timothy Leary's *Psychedelic Prayers after the Tao Te Ching* (1966):

> Everything comes to pass
> in its time, dynamic
> and unauthored, proceeding
> despite expectations.
> Take what happens
> naturally, go on:
> no one knows how or why,
> it lasts forever.

Lao Tzu's teachings are aimed at "self-effacement," and accordingly, identifying with external reality clouds the psyche: "When you close your eyes you go inside, you no longer see the external world and begin to feel one with all."[28] And the idea to "take what happens naturally" echoes the acommittal kenosis of "Let It Be." In many respects, Harrison's lyrics substantiate the view that the Beatles toward the end of the sixties were showing signs of world-weariness.[29] During Harrison's solo career, bookended by the albums *All Things Must Pass* and *Brainwashed*, world-weariness turns into a dualistic vision, one that resonates with Swami Prabhupada's teachings of body and soul dualism and the words of Ezekiel, in that humanity's distorted perception of life constitutes "a heap of broken images." Ultimately Harrison, unlike Lennon, is less enamored by spiritual openings of the everyday and less inspired by the calls of nature (as in McCartney's "Blackbird," 1968).

John Lennon ("I Was the Dream Weaver / But Now I'm Reborn")

With regard to self-emptying, the lyrics of Lennon are the most expansive, spanning a complex agnostic spectrum. Lennon's experimentation in drugs, meditation, and therapy is indicative of a person searching for religious substitutes and a shifting spirituality. Lennon's affinity with Harrison resides in a world-weariness, but it is a thematic preoccupation often accompanied with confessional exorcisms of pain, from "Help!" (1965) to "Cold Turkey" (1969)—personal records of an individual exhausted by an orgiastic life of excess. "Nowhere Man," released on *Rubber Soul* (1965), is perhaps Lennon's first statement of "ennui"—an emptied self that amounts to spiritual deadness, the kind of living death that marks T. S. Eliot's Dantesque vision of living hell in "The Love Song of J. Alfred Prufrock" (1915) and "The Burial of the Dead" (1922).[30] Lennon's lyrics draw on a long literary tradition, hence the ability to express subtle gradations of self-emptying (from LSD psychedelic depression to Hinduism and Zen self-liberation). For Lennon, the spiritual emphasis is "The Kingdom of Heaven is within you," and according to Eyal Regev, he voiced an "individualistic religious sensibility."[31] And as Lennon said in his interview with Tony Barrow (1967), this relates "directly to meditation."[32] Lennon, too, was comfortable with a syncretic view of religion: "Everything you read about, all the religions, are all the same basically. It's just a matter of people opening their minds up."[33] For Lennon, drugs, meditation, and religion are equivalent as means to mind expansion and inner searching without recourse to a metaphysical absolute. In this respect, Lennon's lyrics of paralysis and reverie are comparable to the preconversion poetry of T. S. Eliot in occupying positions of doubt and unbelief: searching for religious substitutes to counter the modern malaise, while aware of the dislocation between the inner and outer self.

Lennon's sleep songs are often expressive of a kenosis that is akin to the dream-possessed imagination of the Romantic poets who were also drug (opium) impregnated. Dreams constitute an escapism to unknown realms, and the imagination can exist in a double state, between sleep and waking. Samuel Taylor Coleridge's "Christabel" exemplifies the borderline state: "With open eyes (ah woe is me!) / Asleep, and dreaming fearfully, / Fearfully dreaming, yet, I wis, / Dreaming that alone."[34] Coleridge, too, was influenced by Orientalist learning, and his dream of Kubla Khan is often read as a nonsensical eruption of the unconscious mind brought on by drugs. For Percy Bysshe Shelley and John Keats, too, dreams were seen as a direct opening of the imaginative realm or the realm of the gods and an antidote to a tangled emotional life.[35] MacDonald likens "I'm Only Sleeping" (from *Revolver*, 1966) to the permanent psychedelic reverie of Oblomov, who is emptied of the mundane world, and this is an intriguing counterpoint to the spiritual ennui of "Nowhere Man."[36] These solipsistic sentiments are shared by Harrison, yet Lennon is never completely cut off from the passing world: "Keeping an eye on the world going by my window." Lennon's drug-induced rejections of the fast-paced material world recall the Romantics' indulgence in narcotics as a means of transcending the familiar. In "She Said She Said," another "acidy song" from *Revolver* and inspired by Peter Fonda's comments during an LSD trip in August 1965 about a near-death experience, Lennon conveys a cautionary tale of the dangers of self-emptying via drug experimentation with the refrain, "I know what it's like to be dead." Lennon's retort, "'Cause you're making me feel like I've never been born" subverts the symbolism of spiritual rebirthing that frames Timothy Leary's LSD therapy. Lennon is aware that psychedelic reverie can both approximate the modern acedia of the "Nowhere Man" and unhinge a fragile grip on living reality.

Romantic borderline kenosis can also be identified in Lennon's songs of surrealism that express the creative potential of the unconscious mind to explore other realities. *In His Own Write* (1964) and *A Spaniard in the Works* (1965), published before *Sgt. Pepper's Lonely Hearts Club Band* (1967), reveal Lennon's leanings toward a tradition of surrealism, experimental literature, nonsense poetry, automatic writing, and free association. As I have argued elsewhere, surrealist artists, such as René Magritte, belong to a modernist postreligious context that is dependent on neither a metaphysical absolute or a secular renunciation of the sacred.[37] This is revealed through an uncanny sublime aesthetic that sustains a tensive dynamic between the visible and the invisible, the known and the unknown. Such a surrealist perspective, in which dreams are also unconscious reality, accords with Lennon's agnostic position in the midsixties. "Lucy in the Sky with Diamonds" (1967), one of "Lennon's dreamier songs" and sometimes likened to "Kubla Khan," took its inspiration from Lewis Carroll's *Alice in Wonderland* books through the use of irrational juxtapositions of images.[38] As Riley notes, Lennon immerses himself in the joy of language through which there is "a sense of discovery."[39] It is a calling for self-transcendence via surrealistic mind expansion:

> Picture yourself in a boat on a river
> With tangerine trees and marmalade skies
> Somebody calls you, you answer quite slowly
> A girl with kaleidoscope eyes.

There are echoes of John Keats's ballad "La Belle Dame dans Merci," with regard to an alluring femme fatale dream. But for Lennon, sleep is not a deadly end but an awakening—or what Keats called "negative capability" (an ego death in itself): "I mean *Negative Capability*, that is when man is capable of being in uncertainties, Mysteries, doubts, without any irritable reaching after fact & reason."[40] For Keats, negative capability, as a kind of self-emptying, is about poetic feeling that leads to other forms of identification and empathy through the experience of uncertainty.[41] For Lennon, the openness to "being in uncertainties" marks out "Strawberry Fields Forever," another LSD-induced somnambulistic song, which too opens with an inviting welcome:

Let me take you down
'Cause I'm going to Strawberry Fields
Nothing is real
And nothing to get hung about
Strawberry Fields forever

The line "living is easy with eyes closed" signifies a nonreceptive mind to an unreality in which uncertainties, mysteries, and reflective doubt prevail:

Always, no, sometimes think it's me
But you know I know when it's a dream
I think, er, no, I mean, er, yes
But it's all wrong
That is, I think I disagree

Lennon's linguistic playfulness, wrestling with the paradoxes of oppositions and the acknowledgment of self-doubt, is an articulation of the elusive realms.

"Tomorrow Never Knows" (the final track to *Revolver*) appears to be the centerpiece of Lennon's romance for self-emptying, and with its Indian-inspired backing of tambura and sitar drone (as well as the dispensing of chord changes), the song bears an affinity to Harrison's Eastern spiritual questing. As Shipley puts it, the song "upholds that the ego death experienced under the influence of psychoactive substance unburdens the psychedelic voyager from instrumental thinking."[42] It takes it cue from *The Psychedelic Experience: A Manual Based on the Tibetan Book of the Dead* (1964), which advocates the therapeutic potential of psychedelic drugs. The song's "willful transcendence of death ... links up fully with *Revolver*'s earlier songs" and the death-in-life theme running through the Beatles' catalog.[43] At this stage, Lennon has seemingly found the solution to the existential void that prompted his cry for help; for ego death or depersonalization is the means of being spiritually reborn. For Harrison, the song is about meditation and transcending the modes of "waking, sleeping, and dreaming." But it is curious that Harrison saw Lennon as missing the point: "But to have experienced what the lyrics in that song are actually about? I don't know if he fully understood it."[44] Harrison's criticism is probably just, because the lyrics are mainly derivative and Lennon's self-emptying posturing lacks conviction. Lennon had at the time been looking for a copy of *The Portable Nietzsche*, and *Thus Spoke Zarathustra* is a satirical deconstruction of the cross-religious tropes of benighted spiritual gurus.[45] The outro echoes the opening line of T. S. Eliot's *East Coker* (1940)—"In my beginning is my end"—but Lennon breaks the circularity of spiritual journey: "Or play the game 'Existence' to the end / Of the beginning."[46] Frequently, Lennon's anarchic wordplay or free association appears no more than jesting—as in "Glass Onion" (from the White Album, 1968). The refrain "looking through a glass onion" is a surrealist allusion to "[seeing] Through a glass, darkly" (1 Corinthians 13:12), suggesting an obscure or imperfect vision. Lennon is self-deprecating with regard to the perceived idea of his Zen-guru status.

The "cosmic" ballad "Across the Universe" is probably the ultimate expression of Lennon's preoccupation with ego death, using free-floating imagery and music to convey also the experience of meditation. The song has been criticized for "its vague pretensions and listless melody [that] are rather too obviously the products of acid grandiosity rendered gentle by sheer exhaustion."[47] According to Jon Weiner, "John hoped meditation would do what LSD hadn't, bring him closer to truth and reality. Meditation also promised to provide some relief from his depression." For Weiner, the line "Nothing's gonna change my world" could be a personal admittance to "fatalism and pessimism" brought on by the experience of meditation.[48] In the first verse, Lennon's paradoxical fusing of opposites and the familiar trope of drifting and "endless rain" convey a totality of organic oneness:

> Words are flowing out
> Like endless rain into a paper cup
> They slither while they pass
> They slip away across the universe
> Pools of sorrow, waves of joy
> Are drifting through my open mind
> Possessing and caressing me

Rather than assuming the role of the privileged prophet-poet, Lennon is gently beckoned by an invisible voice: "They call me, . . . inciting and inviting me." MacDonald calls the song a "plaintively babyish incantation."[49] Yet Lennon, in the words of Shipley, is remapping a world bound by ego and presenting a "psychedelic topography" that dissolves the hostile and reified dichotomies of "you" and "we" and "self" and "nature."[50] Lennon is implying that the nonself, through "limitless undying love," can be integrated into the divine logos of the universe. The otherworldliness may appear a passive rejection of this-worldly turmoil, with the chorus line "Nothing's gonna change my world" smacking of resigned defeatism (or defiant passivity). But the song first appeared, with Lennon's permission, on the ironically titled compilation charity album *No One's Gonna Change Our World* (1969). Rather than world-weary exhaustion, the song is another timely reminder that to exceed bitter rivalries (whether on a micro or macro level), a therapeutic way of self-preservation is the means of reconnecting with collective love. This is underscored by the repeating Sanskrit fragment, "Jai guru deva" (paraphrased as "Hail to the divine guru"), and perhaps here, Lennon comes closest to the kenotic Krishna love of Harrison's songs by echoing the communal and private utterances of inner peace. Yet, Lennon's interest in comparative religion dissolves into lyrical fragments, foreshadowing the line in "God," "I don't believe in mantra." This is a prime example of what T. E. Hulme regarded as "spilt religion" (pouring treacle onto fine food), with reference to Romanticism's tendency to humanize Christianity and to praise, instead, the infinite creative capacity of human nature.[51] In other words, Lennon's refashioned kenosis does not resort to religious dogma.

The iconoclastic song "God," from Lennon's first post-Beatles solo studio album, *John Lennon/Plastic Ono Band* (1970), in which he "rejects political, religious and cultural false consciousness," is often seen as the telos of Lennon's spiritual questing.[52] For Coupe, Lennon comes close to a "purely secular atheism."[53] For Weiner, "John undertakes a deliberate shattering of the illusions of the Sixties, starting with the Beatles as the representation of a genuine community."[54] And in declaring disbelief and stating, "I just believe in me / Yoko and me," Lennon is aligning himself with the "Me Generation."[55] The litany of "I don't believe" blasphemies gives the impression that Lennon is a churlish debunker of sixties idealism. But this is also an exorcism of the raw psyche, this time brought on by Arthur Janov's primal scream therapy in 1970. As Lennon recalled, "You're born into pain. . . . And I think that the bigger the pain, the more gods we need," and this resonates with the infamous opening line of "God": "God is a concept by which we measure our pain."[56] Lennon was able to unblock the feelings of childhood trauma through spontaneous screaming. It is perhaps natural to surmise that "God" is an atheist statement, for Lennon remarked during the "Red Mole" interview (January 1971), "This therapy forced me to have done with all the *God* shit."[57] "God" is expressive of a psychological purging; nonetheless, the confession constitutes a vein of spiritual self-emptying, showing that religious and secular understandings of pain, suffering, and sorrow coexisted in Lennon's mind: "When I felt it [the pain], it's like I was crucified."[58] Again, Lennon intuitively draws on borderless notions of kenosis this time to be released from Oedipal associations with his parents and divinity. Lennon's discovery of an authentic self is modeled on symbolic patterns of death and rebirth that underpin Timothy

Leary's LSD therapy, as in *Psychedelic Prayers: And Other Meditation* (1966)—with *Tao Te Ching* as the spiritual source, as well as Janov's holistic primal therapy. "God" is not an end but rather one more stage in Lennon's spiritual questing (without an end), one more "rediscovery of the self!"[59] Lennon remains the open-minded agnostic—rejecting radical ideologies of the sixties and religious establishments that insist on dogma rather the freedom of self-discovery. For the self is also a deceptive illusion, and Lennon expresses this by drawing on the liberating voices of Leary and Janov: "I was the dream weaver / But now I'm reborn." He also recalls the playful intertextuality of "The Glass Onion": "I was the Walrus / But now I'm John." Here, stripped of manufactured masks, false substitutes, and parental figures, Lennon may seem to have arrived at the authentic self (a goal in his self-emptying quest).

Songs of self-emptying both unite and divide the three main songwriters of the Beatles by revealing varied poetic and subjective engagements with kenosis. Only for Harrison did self-emptying constitute a religious means toward divine salvation, which manifested itself via musical equivalences—for example, *Brainwashed* (2002). And the same, with regard to self-expression of belief and skepticism, can probably be said of Lennon and McCartney. The latter's headlining set at Glastonbury 2022, at the age of eighty, exhibited a varied back catalog with tracks taken from the oeuvre of Wings and from his recent solo albums. Yet at the heart of McCartney's vast body of work, there generally exists a quiet, enchanting realism—unbedevilled by overreaching egotism. The touchstone of Lennon's lyricism, though, is not self-effacing quietism. The only vestige of belief in "God" is an apolitical romance between Yoko and him. The cosmic spectacle of "Across the Universe" also affirms self-centered amorality: "Nothing's gonna change my world." For the theologically minded, human equivalents are incomparable to the kenosis of the Word (Philippians 2:6–11), in which the Exalted slave is given the Divine Name and when every bending knee and tongue acknowledges that he is Lord (Isaiah 45:23 and Romans 14:11). Nonetheless, given the postsecular emphasis on the falsity of the secular-religious binary, the Beatles' lyrics of self-emptying remain a key aesthetic for better understanding the myriad ways in which popular culture intersects doctrinal and nondoctrinal forms of kenosis.

NOTES

1. For Ringo Starr's story of self-emptying, see chapter 6 in this volume.
2. Hawthorn, *Oxford Companion*, 591.
3. Williams, *Kenosis of God*, 42.
4. Bill Myers (deacon of the Leicester Catholic Church), email message to author, March 30, 2021.
5. Jones, "Emptiness, Kenōsis, History, and Dialogue." For Langdell, Christian kenosis also bears affinities with Buddhist

meditation and breaking down the dualism between "me" and "you," "us" and "them" (*Kenosis*, 9).

6. Tsui, "Seeing Christian Kenosis."
7. Shipley, *Psychedelic Mysticism*, 2; Shipley, "Hippies and the Mystic Way."
8. Shipley, "Critique of Culture."
9. Byrne, "Letter to the Philippians."
10. Plantoff, "John Lennon," 266.
11. I am grateful for Professor Phil Shaw for this thought.
12. Sheff, Lennon, and Ono, *All We Are Saying*, 141. "Aunt Mimi sent John to an Anglican Sunday school at Peter's Church in Woolton, where he sang in the choir." Comfort, *Beatles, God, and the Bible*, 28.
13. Frontani, *Beatles*, 99.
14. According to Hamelman, the "Indian influence" had been with the four Beatles, as postwar coming-of-age subjects of the British Empire, before 1965, starting on the set of the *Help!* movie ("Leaving the West Behind").
15. Sheff, Lennon, and Ono, *All We Are Saying*, 149.
16. See Freer, *Modernist Mythopoeia*.
17. Shipley, *Psychedelic Mysticism*, 150: "Liberation to a state between death and rebirth—what Leary, Alpert, and Metzner describe as a liminal space freed from the regulating conformity of the ego."
18. Sheffield, *Dreaming the Beatles*, 244.
19. Comfort, *Beatles, God, and the Bible*, 137.
20. Sheff, Lennon, and Ono, *All We Are Saying*, 224.
21. Riley, *Tell Me Why*, 227.
22. This also connects Paul's spirituality with at least one central idea in Taoism: *wu wei*. This is the act of letting things be, leaving them alone, waiting for time to clear things up, or aligning one's energies with the direction that larger forces are moving. *Wu wei* results in works without working, action without strain, persuasion without argument, and eloquence without flourish. As stated in verse 15 of the *Tao Te Ching*, "Do you have the patience to wait till your mud settles and the water is clear? Can you remain unmoving till the right action arises by itself? The Master doesn't seek fulfillment. Not seeking, not expecting, she is present, and can welcome all things" (in Novak, *World's Wisdom*, 151).

23. Interview with Tony Barrow, *KRLA Beat*, November 4, 1967.
24. In Kahn, *George Harrison*, 62.
25. Coupe, *Beat Sound, Beat Vision*, 159.
26. Riley, *Tell Me Why*, 220–21.
27. MacDonald, *Revolution in the Head*, 243.
28. Lao Tzu, *Tao Te Ching*, viii. See also Lao Tzu, *Tao Te Ching: Adapted for the Contemporary Reader*, 21.
29. See Collins, *Beatles and the Sixties*, xiv.
30. See Freer, "Man Enough for Damnation."
31. See Regev, "Lennon and Jesus."
32. Barrow interview.
33. Barrow interview.
34. Coleridge, "Christabel" (lines 292–95), 195.
35. Lindop, "Romantic Poetry," 36. (I am grateful for Dr. Felicity James for supplying this article.)
36. MacDonald, *Revolution in the Head*, 201–2.
37. Freer, "Magritte."
38. MacDonald, *Revolution in the Head*, 240.
39. Riley, *Tell Me Why*, 215–16.
40. Keats, "Letter to George and Tom Keats," 109.
41. I am grateful for Felicity James's reflections on John Keats in an email to the author, February 3, 2021.
42. Shipley, "Mystical Rock and Visionary Sounds," 134.
43. Luminoso, "Tomorrow Never Knows," 115.
44. Beatles, *Anthology*, 210.
45. See Sheffield, *Dreaming the Beatles*, 117–18.
46. Eliot, *Four Quartets*, 15.
47. MacDonald, *Revolution in the Head*, 277.
48. Weiner, *Come Together*, 54.
49. MacDonald, *Revolution in the Head*, 277.
50. Shipley, "Hippies and the Mystic Way," 234–35.
51. Hulme, "Romanticism and Classicism," 118.
52. Weiner, *Come Together*, 6.
53. Coupe, *Beat Sound, Beat Vision*, 157.
54. Weiner, *Come Together*, 6.
55. Ibid., 6.

56. Wenner, *Lennon Remembers*, 26.

57. Ali and Blackburn, "John Lennon Interview," 354. This comment may be reflective of Janov's view that "religious ideation" is a means of controlling the unconscious pain (*New Primal Scream*, 230).

58. Wenner, *Lennon Remembers*, 26.

59. Sheff, Lennon, and Ono, *All We Are Saying*, 23. In Ali and Blackburn's *Red Mole* interview (1971), Lennon likens therapy to LSD trips ("John Lennon Interview," 354).

BIBLIOGRAPHY

Ali, Tariq, and Robin Blackburn. "John Lennon Interview." *Red Mole*, January 21, 1971. In *The Beatles Literary Anthology*, edited by Mike Evans, 351–65. London: Plexus, 2004.

Beatles. *The Beatles Anthology*. San Francisco: Chronicle Books, 2000.

Byrne, Brendan, SJ. "The Letter to the Philippians." In *The New Jerome Biblical Commentary*, edited by Raymond E. Brown, Joseph A. Fitzmyer, and Roland E. Murphy, 791–97. London: Geoffrey Chapman, 2000.

Coleridge, Samuel Taylor. "Christabel." In *The Complete Poems*, edited by William Keach, 187–205. London: Penguin, 2004.

Collins, Marcus. *The Beatles and the Sixties*. Cambridge: Cambridge University Press, 2020.

Comfort, Ray. *The Beatles, God, and the Bible*. Washington, DC: WND Books, 2012.

Coupe, Laurence. *Beat Sound, Beat Vision: The Beat Spirit and Popular Song*. Manchester: Manchester University Press, 2010.

Eliot, T. S. *Four Quartets*. London: Faber and Faber, 1944.

Freer, Scott. "Magritte: The Uncanny Sublime." *Literature and Theology* 27, no. 3 (September 2013): 330–44.

———. "'Man Enough for Damnation': Ennui and Acedia in T. S. Eliot's Poetry." In *Religion and Myth in T. S. Eliot's Poetry*, edited by Scott Freer and Michael Bell, 77–98. Cambridge, UK: Cambridge Scholars, 2016.

———. *Modernist Mythopoeia: The Twilight of the Gods*. Basingstoke, UK: Palgrave, 2015.

Frontani, Michael R. *The Beatles: Image and the Media*. Jackson: University Press of Mississippi, 2007.

Hamelman, Steve. "Leaving the West Behind: The Beatles and India." In *The Beatles in Context*, edited by Kenneth Womack, 278–88. Cambridge: Cambridge University Press, 2020.

Hawthorn, Gerald F. *The Oxford Companion to the Bible*. Edited by Bruce M. Metzger and Michael D. Coogan. Oxford: Oxford University Press, 1993.

Hulme, T. E. "Romanticism and Classicism." In *Speculations: Essays on Humanism and the Philosophy of Art*, 111–40. London: Routledge and Kegan Paul, 1987.

Janov, Arthur. *The New Primal Scream: Primal Therapy Twenty Years On*. London: Abacus, 1995.

Jones, Charles B. "Emptiness, Kenōsis, History, and Dialogue: The Christian Response to Masao Abe's Notion of 'Dynamic Śūnyatā' in the Early Years of the Abe-Cobb Buddhist-Christian Dialogue." *Buddhist-Christian Studies* 24 (2004): 117–33.

Kahn, Ashley, ed. *George Harrison on George Harrison: Interviews and Encounters*. Chicago: Chicago Review Press, 2020.

Keats, John. "Letter to George and Tom Keats, December 21, 1817." In *Keats's Poetry and Prose*, edited by Jeffrey N. Cox, 108–9. New York: Norton, 2009.

Langdell, Tim. *Kenosis: Christian Self-Emptying Meditation*. Oxford, UK: StillCenter, 2020.

Lao Tzu. *Tao Te Ching*. New York: Penguin, 2000.

———. *Tao Te Ching: Adapted for the Contemporary Reader*. Translated by James Harris. Independently published, 2020.

Leary, Timothy. *Psychedelic Prayers: And Other Meditation*. Berkeley, CA: Ronin, 1997.

Lindop, Grevel. "Romantic Poetry and the Idea of the Dream." *Keats-Shelley Review* 18, no. 1 (2004): 20–37.

Luminoso, Vacio. "'Tomorrow Never Knows' and the Coherence of the Impossible." In *Reading the Beatles: Cultural Studies, Literary Criticism, and the Fab Four*, edited by Kenneth Womack and

Todd F. Davis, 111–28. Albany: SUNY Press, 2006.

MacDonald, Ian. *Revolution in the Head: The Beatles' Records and the Sixties*. 3rd ed. Chicago: Chicago Review Press, 2007.

Novak, Philip, ed. *The World's Wisdom: Sacred Texts of the World's Religions*. New York: HarperOne, 1994.

Plantoff, John. "John Lennon, 'Revolution,' and the Politics of Musical Reception." *Journal of Musicology* 22, no. 2 (Spring 2005): 241–67.

Pope Pius XII. *Sempiternus Rex Christus*. 1951. New Advent. https://www.newadvent.org/library/docs_pi12sr.htm.

Regev, Eyal. "Lennon and Jesus: Secularization and the Transformation of Religion." *Studies in Religion* 41, no. 4 (2012): 534–63.

Riley, Tim. *Tell Me Why: A Beatles Commentary*. London: Bodley Head, 1988.

Sheff, David, John Lennon, and Yoko Ono. *All We Are Saying: The Last Major Interview with John Lennon and Yoko Ono*. Edited by G. Barry Golson. London: Pan Macmillan, 2020.

Sheffield, Rob. *Dreaming the Beatles: The Love Story of One Band and the Whole World*. New York: First Dey Street Books, 2018.

Shipley, Morgan. "'A Critique of Culture': Alan Watts, Psychedelic Buddhism, and Religious Play in Postwar America." *Self and Society* 45, nos. 3–4 (2017): 233–43.

———. "Hippies and the Mystic Way: Dropping Out, Unitive Experiences, and Communal Utopianism." *Utopian Studies* 24, no. 2 (2013): 232–63.

———. "Mystical Rock and Visionary Sounds." In *Finding God in the Devil's Music: Critical Essays on Rock and Religion*, edited by Alex DiBlasi and Robert McParland, 134–50. Jefferson, NC: MacFarland, 2019.

———. *Psychedelic Mysticism: Transforming Consciousness, Religious Experiences, and Voluntary Peasants in Postwar America*. Lanham, MD: Lexington Books, 2015.

Tsui, Teresa Kuo-Yu. "Seeing Christian Kenosis in the Light of Buddhist Sunyata: An Attempt at Inter-faith Hermeneutics." *Asia Journal of Theology* 21, no. 2 (2007): 357–71.

Weiner, Jon. *Come Together: John Lennon in His Time*. London: Faber and Faber, 2000.

Wenner, Jann. *Lennon Remembers: The Rolling Stone Interviews*. London: Penguin Books, 1980.

Williams, David T. *Kenosis of God: The Self-Limitation of God: Father, Son, and Holy Spirit*. New York: iUniverse, 2009.

CHAPTER 8
Yeah, Yeah, Yeah

Beatlemania and the Cult of Dionysus—
The Resurrection of a New Consciousness

SEAN MACLEOD

In *The Birth of Tragedy*, the German philosopher Friedrich Nietzsche proposed that modern Western culture had become anemic due to its one-sided, rationalistic view of the world. Such rationalism, resulting from the Socratic/Platonic tradition, associated with the Apollonian element of beautiful dreaming, intellect, and "identification of the individual," disconnects humanity from life and all its horrific and absurd messiness. Dionysus (or Bacchus), the god of revelry and intoxication, of ecstatic dance and song, is, on the other hand, concerned with irrational exuberance and with a "deintellectualization" of the self.[1] Dionysus, the polar opposite of Apollo, symbolizes a return to a primordial unity and the reconciliation of humanity with itself and the "innermost depths of the world."

As Nietzsche had called for the reawakening of the Dionysian in Western society, this essay argues that the Beatles and the 1960s in general were a moment in Western culture that experienced a reaffirmation of the Dionysian and a reintegration of the Apollonian and Dionysian duality necessary for a healthy social organism. The musicologist Ruth Padel observes that tragedy, the beginning of Western theater, of which rock and roll as a live performance was part, was written for Dionysus's festival and that "drink, drugs, ecstatic loss of self in illusion of every kind (especially drink and madness)" and "violent dance, crowds, theatrical spectacle and violence" were as much a part of 1960s culture as they were of the ancient, pre-Socratic Greek cult of Dionysus. "As a summary of Sixties rock," writes Padel, "Dionysus couldn't be bettered. . . . In the Sixties, popular culture made him the figurehead for the male rock god."[2]

Beatlemania and the Cultural Zeitgeist

"It is impossible to exaggerate Beatlemania because it was itself an exaggeration," wrote Hunter Davies in his 1968 biography of the Beatles.[3] Beatlemania was the result of a youth culture, of rock and roll, and of a diversion from the pessimism of war and nihilism; it was the product of consumerism and a distraction from its emptiness; it was a release of sexual emotions and feelings, a mask for the psychosis of modern life and the beginnings of a social expression, as well as the coming together of a group of people who felt these things and collectively experienced them through the Beatles. Beatlemania was above all a mirror of both Britain's and the United States' changing attitudes and values, a release of the pressures that past traditions had confined them to. Uncontrollable, frenzied, and beyond any proper intelligent explanation, Beatlemania was, above all, a Dionysian emotional and irrational response to something of a nonmaterial, almost supersensible, nature.

The Beatles were important on many levels, but spiritually they brought something hopeful after the horrors of two world wars; in Britain, they brought relief to the endless political scandals that defined postwar politics, heightened by the Profumo scandal, while in the United States, they brought a similar hope and youthful energy following the death of President John F. Kennedy. In this sense, Beatlemania was a remedy, a cure, and a resurrection. The journalist Ross Langager suggests:

> The Beatles were consistently constructed as symbolic avatars for the social and cultural shifts of their time and place, even while they were still in the midst of that time and place. Their 1964 descent on America came mere weeks after the young, hopeful King-Arthur-Proxy-in-Chief was gunned down by shadowy forces in a sunny plaza in Dallas. Their giddy pop songs were derived from the ghettoized music of the same Black America that was marching for its civil rights across the South, and their shaggy haircuts and dismissive wit spoke to an impetuous

rejection of fossilized mores and codes whose breakdown was the fuel for Swinging London. Their very being seemed to presage a burst of mass enlightenment, a collective epiphany for the messy cannibalistic social and cultural superstructure of the Western democracies that never quite came.[4]

The Beatles triggered a mania so intense that it was unlike any mass popularity the world had seen before, setting the standard for the pop star that has remained ever since and opened the floodgates for a host of other talented British groups, like the Rolling Stones, into the United States, while also reestablishing the British Empire as a modern force. "The pundits," said one commentator, "decided the Beatles were of social significance, symbolizing all the frustrations and ambitions of the new emergent, shadow of the bomb, classless, unmaterialistic, unphoney teenagers."[5] The Beatles would also exert a profound effect on the United States' new archenemy, Russia, and for many people, they played a significant role in the fall of communism. "For millions of [Russian] kids," writes Leslie Woodhead, it was dangerous but irresistible to trade "Lenin for Lennon."[6]

While many people were impressed with the Beatles, there was a portion that was horrified by them and their cultural influence. Paul Johnson, a journalist for the *New Statesman*, saw the Beatles as an "electorally valuable property" but ultimately thought them the epitome of a declining culture: "the growing public approval of anti-culture is itself, I think, a reflection of the new cult of youth, . . . a collective groveling to gods who are themselves blind and empty."[7] Johnson bemoaned the lack of interest by the sixties youth in cultural heroes, like Wagner, Proust, and El Greco, but these figures, some of whom lived over four hundred years before, could not be a reflection of the 1960s social, political, and cultural thoughts and feelings and, from that point of view, were irrelevant. The Beatles, on the other hand, perfectly reflected the soul of the new society, at least as it was experienced by those who were growing up in it. It was not the past-present-future linear consciousness of Apollonian rationalism that concerned the postwar generation but the Dionysian loss of self in the oneness of life, in the "NOW."[8]

Gods of Epiphany

In some cults, Dionysus arrives from the East as an Asiatic foreigner; in others, he arrives from Ethiopia in the South. He is a "god of epiphany," "the god that comes," and his "foreignness" as an arriving outsider-god may be inherent and essential to his cults. Thus, the Beatles "arriving" in the United States in 1964 and "returning" to Britain, following the media hype of their US tour, can be seen as an expression of the Dionysian myth of the god of epiphany. The Beatles arrived in both Britain and the United States at a time of great social, political, and emotional upheaval, healing and transforming both nations, but it was society itself that went through its own grieving process, followed by a deep social and spiritual transformation. The Beatles (and the 1960s in general) were more so a vehicle through which this process could happen.

With the coming of rock and roll's "messiah," Elvis Presley, a fuse was lit that prepared the way for greater cultural forces to emerge, but with the death of Kennedy, a vacuum was created to allow for such cultural forces to penetrate deeper into US (and British) society. So horrific was Kennedy's assassination that the country went into mourning for the entire winter of 1963–64. The media propaganda surrounding Kennedy's assassination created in the minds of the American people a strong sense of paranoia, not to mention the claims that Kennedy's assassin was a supposed communist, thus making the Cold War more justifiable, as well as making the threat of nuclear devastation more probable. With the earlier possibility of a nuclear war having just been diverted by the Cuban Missile Crisis, the assassination of Kennedy tore open the wound again, leaving people in a frozen state of fear regarding their future. Vietnam was also looming on the horizon, another "communist threat" that would need to be dealt with.

If the Beatles had arrived on the scene at the end of 1963, as opposed to the spring of 1964, things may have been entirely different. Not only did Kennedy's death leave a vacuum to be filled, a need for something to distract the nation from its loss, but also it demanded that something, preferably non-American, something more traditional and stable, something possibly English (considering the growing Anglo-American relations), to give guidance to a relatively "new" country momentarily losing its way, as well as something unusual and novel and unlike anything that the country had experienced before. The Beatles, in the form of haircuts, accents, clothes, and their unique fusion of rock and roll, Motown, and homegrown music hall, arrived in a United States still reeling from the trauma of the assassination of its president. The musicologist Paul Gambaccini has suggested as much, saying that a great trauma requires a great positivity to heal it.[9] It is also significant that Kennedy was murdered in the winter of 1963, the season of death and completion, while the Beatles brought, like Dionysus, the god of spring and regeneration, a rejuvenating element, when they arrived in the spring of 1964.

The evangelist Billy Graham suggested that the Beatles were simply a passing phase: "all are symptoms of the uncertainty of the times and the confusion about us."[10] He was right in some respects, although he misunderstood the group's real cultural significance. In many ways, Beatlemania was a necessary "religion," which wiped away the hypocrisy of the old order. "I only joined," said their public relations officer, Derek Taylor, "because I wanted to be transported from the world I had always known."[11] Taylor expressed what many young people of the time felt. They wanted to be transported from the emptiness of modern life, and the Beatles allowed them that escape.

The arrival of the Beatles in the United States marks the moment when the postwar baby boomers claimed their time. William Deeds, a British cabinet minister during the early sixties under Prime Minister Harold MacMillan, said of the Beatles, "They herald a cultural movement among the young which may become part of the history of our time. . . . The young are rejecting some of the sloppy standards of their elders, by which far too much of our output has been governed in recent years. . . . They have discerned dimly that in a world of automation, declining craftsmanship and increased leisure, something of this kind is essential to restore the human instinct to excel at something and the human faculty of discrimination."[12] Pete Townshend of the Who hit the nail on the head when, the year after the Beatles' descent on the United States, he exclaimed to *Melody Maker*, "the big social revolution that has taken place in the last five years is that youth, and not age, has become important."[13] The Beatles themselves were fully aware of their role as youth's ambassadors. "Youth," they pronounced, "is on our side, and it's youth that matters right now."[14] In the words of their friend the actor Victor Spinetti, they were "the young speaking to the young."[15]

The adolescent attraction toward music and intoxication, often through alcohol, is significant in the development of the teenager and is closely linked to the cult of Dionysus, the "youthful god" and the god of intoxication and rapture. The myth and symbolism surrounding alcohol (particularly wine) is too great to deal with here, but transcended consciousness seems to be strongly connected with the consumption of wine. In Christian symbolism, Jesus Christ identifies himself as the "true vine" and as the transformed, resurrected god (John 15:1–17). In this capacity, Christ can be closely identified with the myth of Dionysus, the god of wine, which encompasses life, death, and rebirth. The trance induction central to the Dionysian cult involved not only chemo-gnosis—that is, transformation, usually of consciousness, through chemical substances or alteration of biochemical substances in the human being—but also an "invocation of spirit." In the Dionysian cult, this would be through communal dancing to music, while characteristic movements (such as the backward head flick found in all trance-inducing cults, such as Afro-American voodoo) were also part of the transforming effect. Interestingly, it was the famous head shake of the Beatles, equivalent to Elvis's pelvic thrust, that would have the girls screaming in frenzy.

The Beatles, through music and dance, intoxicated their audience, as their appearance on *The Ed Sullivan Show* indicated, with seventy-three million Americans enraptured for those fifteen minutes while the Beatles performed. It is in song and in dance, wrote Nietzsche, that "man expresses his sense of belonging to a higher community. . . . There now sounds out from within man something supernatural. . . . Man is no longer an artist, he has become a work of art: all nature's artistic power reveals itself here."[16] The Beatles, through their Dionysian energy, transcended the individuating, separating nature of Western society and brought it back into harmony with itself—even if only momentarily.

Dionysus, also called Eleutherios—"the liberator"—through wine, music, and ecstatic dance frees his followers from self-conscious fear and care and subverts the oppressive restraints of the powerful. Those who partake of his mysteries are possessed and empowered by the god himself. He is represented by city religions as the protector of those who do not belong to conventional society, such as women, slaves, outlaws, and "foreigners," those who have not had "access to the implied rewards."[17] All were equal in a cult that inverted people's roles. The Dionysian rite removed inhibitions and social constraints, liberating the individual to return to a natural state. The myth and rituals of Dionysus can be interpreted as a reconciling of the Apollonian individualization of humanity (through its separation from the Cosmic Soul) with the primordial unity (the "common soul of mankind").[18]

The Beatles were entirely democratic, as their accents and look, as well as their appreciation of other artists, including Black artists and girl groups, certainly indicated. They were, as Bob Stanley observed, "cultural omnivores. . . . The Beatles, through their appetite for cultural newness and apparent fearlessness, seemed to speak a future language."[19] And it was because of these "north-Western gods" that "pop became respectable—indeed desirable—across all social barriers."[20] Seeing the Beatles, remembered the comedienne Whoopie Goldberg, was a "revelation."[21] They opened the door for individual freedom despite class, race, or sex. "The Beatles had songs for heartbreaks, troubles, loners, miscommunications, friendship and more. There were relatable and realistic themes in the lyrics containing a broader scope than their musical predecessors. The music spoke to the audience as if it were written for each individual on a personal level, which further bonded fans together as a community. At times, the music was playful, lively and full of high energy, while also being soft, soulful and reflective."[22] All who wanted to be were welcome into the world of the Beatles, just as the group of social outcasts were all welcome to the Dionysian rites.

The Beatles and the "Mad Women" of Dionysus

As well as being representatives of the new youth culture, the Beatles also encouraged the release of sexual tensions and explorations that had been suppressed during the postwar Anglo-American culture and, without doubt, as a response to changing attitudes toward women after the war. The music journalist Alison Taich expresses such a change in social attitudes: "When the Beatles hit, females responded to their work with unpredicted emotional outbursts. At the time, sex was seen as taboo and full of consequences if performed out of wedlock. Due to the Beatles' comfortable and sensitive aura, sex became approachable and enjoyable as opposed to horrifying and full of penalties. Pent up energy and hormones surfaced in the form of rebellion and global lust and challenged the notion that women were to remain pure and domestic. The change in opinion and comfort levels furthered the gap between the old-fashioned, conservative ideology from the new progressive thinking."[23] The Beatles unleashed dormant sexual urges that manifested themselves like a Dionysian rite. Girls seemed to behave like maenads, the priestesses who oversaw these rites. In Greek mythology, the maenads—"mad women" or "raving ones," often portrayed with supernatural associations—were inspired by Dionysus into a state of ecstatic frenzy through a combination of dancing and intoxication. Dionysus, a catalyst of wild energy, was the link between new, raw, sappy growth (in vines or young men) and crowd ecstasy and violence; he maddened his worshipers, the maenads, who tore up live animals and expressed their suddenly abnormal consciousness in hallucinating and wild dance.

In January 1964, a month before the Beatles first stepped foot on US soil, *Life* reported, "A Beatle who ventures out unguarded into the streets runs the very real peril of being dismembered or crushed to death by his fans," to which Taich adds, "When the Beatles officially arrived in the United States, a mere two months after the assassination of John F. Kennedy, thousands of fans, specifically young females, *enthusiastically* greeted them by storming the Kennedy Airport in New York. Sure, there had been fan frenzies for musicians and celebrities in the past, but nothing to the extent of Beatlemania."[24] Girls' act of pulling at the Beatles, pulling their clothes, or pulling their own hair seemed to reflect the activities at Dionysian rites, in which the maenads would pull apart the flesh of the resurrected Dionysus. The fact that the Beatles often barely got away with their lives when they were surrounded or pursued by hormonal teenage girls seemed also to parallel the activities of these "raving ones," while Beatles' concerts were a direct manifestation of the Dionysian rite, as Pedal keenly observes: "An unearthly howl went up from thousands of possessed teenagers. Girls began pulling their hair out, ... pupils dilating, shaking uncontrollably. ... Clinical Dionysian mass hysteria was breaking out everywhere."[25]

The plays that dealt with myths of Dionysus show how essential violence was to him, as someone is always torn to pieces. "The gods of music and theatre," suggests Pedal, "are the two gods of violent dismembering."[26] (It is significant to note that the Beatles were constantly surrounded by violence and tragic death, including the untimely deaths of Lennon's and McCartney's mothers, the tragic deaths of Stuart Sutcliff and Brian Epstein, numerous death threats against the band, and most obviously Lennon's violent assassination.) The philologist Walter Otto, in trying to comprehend the Dionysian, suggests that "the rapture and terror of life are so profound because they are intoxicated with death" and that the more intense a participant's libido or life drives are, "the worse one can fall towards motionless death and decay." A participant in rites of Dionysus, or equally so in a Beatles concert, may find an asylum from the "traditional life-death power struggle."[27]

The frenzy of Beatlemania was in a sense a dying and a rebirth, an orgy of ecstasy, in which young girls, particularly, would emerge, brought on by the social frenzy of Beatles concerts, as women, losing their innocence with their first experience of "sex." One fan, Elizabeth Hess, recounted her experiences with feminism in relation to the Beatles: "I was 12," she wrote, "just beginning to understand that sex was power: my first feminist epiphany. As the Sixties tore on, the crowd of girls, now women, was still moving together, marching against the war in Vietnam."[28]

The Beatles, having a strong feminine quality to them, were both safe and dangerous at the same time. At live shows, girls could find a socially acceptable environment to allow their newly discovered sexuality to unravel, often in the form of hysterical communal screaming, which, at times, led to uncontrolled body functions and loss of consciousness. The girls could also form their own Beatles-focused social groups, in which one girl may like Paul, another John and a third Ringo, thus allowing the girls to have the same fantasies, or shared fantasies, without encroaching on the fantasies of the other. They could join their fantasies together, as two girls of the same group could imagine that they were each married to a Beatle, touring together and possibly living together, as that was how the Beatles were perceived, especially in their films *A Hard Day's Night* and *Help!* This would be typical, as Padel suggests, of pop music's ability to transpose the teenage mind into the theater of Dionysus, in which these myths are played out. "Like Greek myth, a pop song is about relationships staged in the teenage mind rather than in the theatre of Dionysus.... The whole project is focused on an intensely teenage search for identity through music. And the currency of its lyrics is relationship."[29]

As well as filling a void left in the sociopolitical environment of the United States and Europe during the early sixties, the Beatles also represented the changing attitudes in personal affairs. Hunter Davies presents the effects of Beatlemania in the United States through the eyes of one typical American teenage girl named Sandi Stewart, an ordinary Beatles fan, fifteen years old, growing up in New Hampshire. "I became obsessed about John," says Stewart, and "I dreamt about him all the time. We'd compare dreams at school. Tell each other what we did with our favourite Beatle.... When absolutely nothing else was good, I'd go to my room and have the Beatles, especially my darling John. They all furnished something I desperately needed. The sort of rich community I lived in in New Hampshire gave me nothing. I didn't like school and I didn't like home. They gave me something to live for when everything was black and depressing."[30]

The English poet Philip Larkin would express such an idea when he wrote in his poem "Annus Mirabilis," "Sexual intercourse began / In nineteen sixty-three / (which was rather late for me)— / Between the end of the Chatterley ban / And the Beatles' first LP."[31] Of course, sexual intercourse had been around forever, but Larkin is referring to its sudden awakening in the human psyche as something very personal and emotional, not just a Darwinian matter of function and duty, which society had turned it into. The Beatles (and the birth control pill), Larkin is suggesting, were the catalyst for a whole generation awaking their sexual impulses, as well as their inner emotional life, independent of societal duties, concerns, repressions, and taboos. The Beatles wiped these all away and freed the postwar baby boomers from such social constraints. Dustin Garlitz, in his essay on Nietzsche, points out that the Dionysian spirit "involves the scenario where a worshiper (a common mortal) is brought about by intoxicating methods to heightened inner awareness."[32] Likewise, the Beatles were an awakening for girls like Sandi Stewart, girls who were becoming aware of themselves, of their sexuality, and of the "insipid" world in which they lived.

In a more simplistic way, this idea corresponds to the philosopher Bertrand Russell and his interpretation of the Dionysian/Bacchic ritual undertaken by the initiates on their journey to self-knowledge. Russell writes, "In intoxication, physical or spiritual, the initiate recovers an intensity of feeling which prudence had destroyed; he finds the world full of delight and beauty, and his imagination is suddenly liberated from the prison of everyday preoccupations. The Bacchic ritual produced what was called 'enthusiasm,' which means etymologically having the god enter the worshipper, who believed that he became one with the god."[33]

It would be inaccurate, however, to see the effect the Beatles had on teenage girls of the 1960s in only sexual terms. The Beatles were, in many respects, as Yoko Ono mentioned in one of the final interviews she and Lennon gave, in 1980, also a representation of the "feminine side of society."[34] The Beatles gave purpose and meaning to this new generation of lost souls. The sexual aspects of Beatlemania were not just something of a crude erotic nature but something life-affirming, an expression of the life force and of an element of the human being that was suppressed, damaged, and unhealthily distorted by a prudish, overly unfeeling and cold society, a society controlled by intellect and reason, a society afraid of the emotional power of the feminine, what Russell suggests as the "intensity of feeling which prudence had destroyed." In the culture of the 1960s, the Beatles seemed to bring a sense of enlightenment, a sense of realizing new things that were beyond the scope of comprehension to the society as it had been before their arrival—a new consciousness, a new awakening similar, in some ways, to what other prominent religious figures had brought with them at various times throughout history.

Androgyny and the New Adam

Dionysus is an androgynous god. The Beatles' admiration for the US girl groups of the late 1950s and early 1960s has generally been taken by musicologists, like Barbara Bradby, to imply an "androgynous" positioning on their part, while cultural critics such as Simon Firth and Angela McRobbie suggest that the Beatles epitomized an interesting process of "feminization" that rock underwent in the late 1950s and early 1960s.[35] According to Firth and McRobbie, the music of the Beatles "articulated simultaneously the conventions of feminine and masculine sexuality, and the Beatles' own image was ambiguous, neither boys-together aggressiveness nor boy-next-door pathos."[36] After the Beatles' first performance on *The Ed Sullivan Show*, girls as well as boys began to form their own groups, such as the Bootles and the Pleasure Seekers. The girls began to occupy a space that was not open to them before.

Susan Douglas, in her influential book *Where the Girls Are*, gives an indication of how the Beatles allowed young girls to feel more comfortable with their newfound sexuality while simultaneously allowing young boys an opportunity to explore their feminine side without being railroaded into the traditional view of militaristic values of manhood, in which self-expression was a taboo. Douglas saw the Beatles as a kind of interfusion of the girl groups of the early sixties, which offered the teen and preteen girls of the time a mirror in which their own inner lives were made manifest and in turn provided role models for these young girls.[37] The males of the time, finding the opposite to be so for them, could emulate malehood through the Beatles but at the same time express their emotions, often through music (e.g., the Four Preps' "A Letter to the Beatles") and their personal appearance, especially long hair.

The Beatles' image and likeness became a significant symbol of the 1960s, and their mop-top haircut came to represent youth, fun, optimism, and hope. The mop-top symbolized a civilized and healthy disrespect and insolence rather than rebellion. Though it was acceptable, it was not conformist. Long hair has traditionally been connected to a notion of clairvoyance that was cut out by the reasoning mind of the Enlightenment, as Danny, a character from the George Harrison–produced film *Withnail and I*, enthuses: "our hair is our aerials to the cosmos." The Essenes, a separatist Jewish sect around the time of Jesus, for example, kept their hair long in order for them to be able to witness the coming of the Messiah, and in ancient Israel, hair was deeply associated with identity, as one of the most famous stories, that of Samson in the Old Testament, suggests.[38] Samson had felt the cosmic power rushing through him but was sapped of it once his hair was cut. Interestingly, Jesus has always been depicted with long hair, even though in conservative Christian countries, long hair has come to be seen as antisocial and rebellious. "What we call ancient clairvoyance," exclaims the nineteenth-century spiritual scientist Rudolf Steiner, "this lighting up of the cosmic secrets within human souls, had to enter the soul somehow."

> We have to picture this as streams flowing into human beings. The ancients did not perceive them, but when these streams occurred and lit up within them, people perceived them as their inspirations. . . . In the distant past, these streams were purely spiritual, and clairvoyants could perceive them as purely astral-etheric streams. But later these purely

spiritual streams dried up, as it were, and condensed to etheric-physical streams. What became of them? They developed into hair. Our hair is the result of these ancient streams. The hair on our body was formerly spiritual streams that flowed from outside into human beings. Our hair is nothing else but dried up astral-etheric streams.[39]

It is for this reason, Steiner explains, that in Hebrew, the words for "light" and "hair" were virtually the same, because the Hebrews were conscious of the relationship between spiritual inspirations through "light" streaming into the human being through the hair.

The artist, particularly during the sixties, in order to identify with the younger generation, needed to have their hair long. "Everyone," remarked the Byrds' Roger McGuinn, "was trying to grow their hair long."[40] Long hair seemed to naturally indicate something individual, antiauthoritarian, and otherworldly. In reference to the Dionysian aspect of the Beatles, hair was significant in that the Satyrs, the followers of the god, still in old clairvoyant consciousness, were covered almost entirely in hair. For Nietzsche, the Satyr was sublime and divine, representing truth and nature in its most primordial form. The Satyr had the power to magically transform the Dionysian reveler into something transcendent. "In this magic transformation," suggests Nietzsche, "the Dionysian enthusiast sees himself as a satyr, *and as a satyr, he in turn sees the god*, i.e., in his transformed state he sees a new vision outside himself which is the Apolline perfection of his state."[41]

Steiner interprets the biblical story of Jacob and Esau in a similar manner. In this story, Jacob dresses himself in goat's skin to impersonate his slightly older twin brother, Esau, who was covered in bodily hair, in order to receive the blessing of the first born from his father.[42] From Steiner's perspective, this is the replacement of old clairvoyant dream-like consciousness (a kind of cosmic consciousness in which we are not fully conscious and, therefore, not free) with "sense-based reasoning," which, similar to Nietzsche's view, brings about a separation of humanity from its spiritual origins. For Steiner, this separation is a stage in humanity's evolution, after which, in full consciousness and freedom, humanity must reunite with its spiritual origins, that is, the Dionysian primordial oneness.[43]

While the Beatles' suits, boots, and cheeky grins made their style and image acceptable across sex, race, and generation, it was their hair that made them unique and progressive. The Beatles, intuitively, knew that their hair gave them a certain power. In their first-ever television appearance, the interviewer asked them more about their hairstyle than he did about their music.

In their first press interview in the United States (February 7, 1964), their hairstyle became a major talking point:

Reporter: Do you feel like Samson? If you lost your hair, you'd lose what you had?
Reporter: How many of you are bald if you have to wear those wigs?
Lennon: We're all bald. And deaf and dumb too.[44]

It was primarily through the hairstyle that a follower of these cultural icons could identify themselves and possibly why Donna Lynn sang "My Boyfriend Got a Beatles' Hair Cut" as a response to the group's arrival in the United States in 1964.

What the Beatles were possibly achieving is the breaking down of the barriers not only of class and race but also between the sexes. Paul McCartney would claim this fact when he stated, "Short hair for men, long hair for women. We got rid of that convention for the Americans."[45] The Beatles pointed to the androgynous nature of the human being, which, if expressed in esoteric terms, is made up of a physical body and also a subtler body known as the etheric body, a spiritual aspect of the human being that is often the opposite sex to the physical body.[46] It might be argued that the Beatles allowed the etheric element of the teenage fan to find an expression in the personality of the physical being and thus created a unified, androgynous, human individual—the "new Adam," as the poet William Blake would name it. Here the human being was, in a nonsexual sense, balancing the yin and yang elements of masculine and feminine within them. "The imagery of sexual warfare," writes Diane Long Hoeveler, is

> central to the vision of apocalypse which Blake proclaims as his poetic mission. The political apocalypse of the earlier work, such as *The French Revolution*, fades as the spiritual gains prominence. . . . By the time he was writing *Jerusalem* the only apocalypse he could endorse was one in which the "sexes must cease and vanish" in the psyche so that humanity can assume its spiritualized "body." It became clear to Blake that political reform of society could not be affected until an individual and spiritual redemption took place in every heart. To become androgynous, to overcome the flaws inherent in each sex, emerges as the central challenge for all Blake's characters.[47]

These poems promise that, after the apocalypse, young men will regain their polymorphously perverse sexuality and live in a state of eternal bliss.

Blake's prophetic poems were enormously popular and influential in the 1960s, while ideas of androgyny would become a major aspect of sixties cultural progression, particularly the latter half of it. (The image, for example, of "Sweet Loretta Martin," who "thought she was a woman" but was, in fact, a man in "Get Back," expresses the androgynous culture of the latter half of the 1960s.) By the 1970s, it was highjacked for promotional reasons by pop stars like Marc Boland and David Bowie and became a mostly commercial and sexual concern. In other words, the spiritual androgyny, which Blake points to and which finds expression in the Beatles, becomes perverted into a purely sexual idea that many pop stars used to further their careers.

Conclusion

Beatlemania was a "religious" experience that, in its Dionysian-like splendor, gave new energy to the dying forces of a world devastated by two world wars. It gave new hope to a postwar generation and allowed for a rebirth of consciousness and of society—spiritually, sexually, socially, and economically. It cast away old ideas regarding race, class, and gender and pointed toward a Utopian vision of the future in which individuals were merging their male and female aspects, where the female intuition was given respect and balanced out the judgmental rationalism of the male energies to enable the individual and community to live in harmony together.

The figure of Dionysus would be consciously expressed in the latter half of the sixties, mainly through figures like Mick Jagger and Jim Morrison, who gladly took on the identity of the god. It was expressed later by individuals like Iggy Pop and more recently in Bono's the Fly and Macphisto characters. But the Beatles' early live performance clearly captured a sense of the Dionysian rites. The Beatles seemed to channel the energy of Dionysus unconsciously and as an intuitive reflection of sixties cultural evolution. The Beatles, in other words, were an authentic vehicle for both the frenetic impulses of the deity, which were completely outside their control, and the rejuvenating force of the same impulse that came through them, often in their early years unconsciously. In fact, it is the very nature of Dionysus to be beyond conscious thought, out of control, and "puzzling to the core."[48] Any attempt by people like Jim Morrison to control it ultimately leads to their destruction.

Whether Beatlemania or the Beatles could ever have achieved such a Utopian state, one that William Blake hoped for, is possibly expecting too much. But, if anything, once the frenzy of Beatlemania quieted down, the Beatles (through their personalities, their image, and their music) did manage to give to the world a brief feeling of what society could be like when in harmony with itself.

NOTES

1. Nietzsche, *Birth of Tragedy*, 19.
2. Padel, *I'm a Man*, 186.
3. Davies, *Beatles*, 277.
4. Langager, "With Our Love."
5. Davies, *Beatles*, 287–88.
6. Woodhead, *How the Beatles Rocked the Kremlin*, 178.
7. Savage, *Faber Book of Pop*, 196–97.
8. McGregor, "Nietzsche," 15–16. See also Bortoft, *Wholeness of Nature*.
9. Kruger, "Sex, Spies, and Rock and Roll."
10. Davies, *Beatles*, 299.
11. Palmer, *All You Need Is Love*.
12. Savage, *Faber Book of Pop*, 195.
13. Nick Jones, *Melody Maker*, July 3, 1965. See also Shaffner, *British Invasion*, 120.
14. Savage, *Faber Book of Pop*, 177.
15. Lambert, *Magical Mystery Tour Memories*.
16. Nietzsche, *Birth of Tragedy*, 18.
17. Kraemer, "Ecstasy and Possession," 73.
18. Kovacs, *Christianity and the Ancient Mysteries*, 31.
19. Stanley, *Yeah Yeah Yeah*, 126.
20. Savage, *Faber Book of Pop*, 177.
21. Howard, *Beatles*.
22. Taich, "Beatlemania."
23. Ibid.
24. Ibid. (emphasis added).
25. Padel, *I'm a Man*, 295.
26. Ibid., 229–30.
27. Garlitz, "Reflection," 6.
28. Hess, "Women," 91, quoted in Taich, "Beatlemania."
29. Padel, *I'm a Man*, 27.
30. Davies, *Beatles*, 290–91.
31. Larkin, *High Windows*, 34.
32. Garlitz, "Reflection," 3–4.
33. Russell, *History of Western Philosophy*, 16.
34. Peebles, "John Lennon."
35. Bradby, "She Told Me What to Say."
36. Ibid., 383.
37. Douglas, *Where the Girls Are*, 113–21.
38. Niditch, *My Brother Esau*.
39. Steiner, *Universal Human*, 42–43.
40. Palmer, *All You Need Is Love*.
41. Nietzsche, *Birth of Tragedy*, 44 (emphasis in original).
42. Genesis 25:25, KJV: "And the first came out red, all over like a hairy garment; and they called his name Esau."
43. Steiner, *Universal Human*, 44.
44. Winn, *Way Beyond Compare*, 123.
45. Turner, *Beatles 66*, 120.
46. Steiner, *Outline of Occult Science*, 39–60.
47. Hoeveler, *Blake's Erotic Apocalypse*, 21.
48. Garlitz, "Reflection," 3.

BIBLIOGRAPHY

Bortoft, Henri. *The Wholeness of Nature: Goethe's Way Toward a Science of Conscious Participation in Nature*. Hudson, NY: Lindisfarne, 1996.

Bradby, Barbara. "She Told Me What to Say: The Beatles and Girl Group Discourse." *Popular Music and Society* 28, no. 3 (2005): 359–90.

Davies, Hunter. *The Beatles: The Authorized Biography*. London: Heinemann, 1968.

Douglas, Susan. *Where the Girls Are: Growing Up Female with the Mass Media*. New York: Three Rivers, 1994.

Garlitz, Dustin. "A Reflection on the Dionysian Spirit of Music in Nietzsche's *The Birth of Tragedy*." Unpublished paper, University of South Florida, 2006. http://www.philosophyofmusic.org/nietzsche_music_garlitz_2006.pdf.

Hess, Elizabeth. "The Women." *Village Voice*, November 8, 1994.

Hoeveler, Diane Long. *Blake's Erotic Apocalypse: An Androgynous Ideal in Blake and Shelley*. Urbana: University of Illinois Press, 1976.

Howard, Ron, dir. *The Beatles: Eight Days a Week—The Touring Years*. London: Apple Corps, 2016. Series.

Kovacs, Charles. *Christianity and the Ancient Mysteries: Reflections on Rudolf Steiner's "Christianity as Mystical Fact."* Edinburgh: Floris, 2017.

Kraemer, Ross S. "Ecstasy and Possession: The Attraction of Women to the Cult of Dionysus." *Harvard Theological Review* 72, nos. 1–2 (1979): 55–80.

Kruger, Li-Da, dir. "Sex, Spies, and Rock and Roll, 1962–1964." Episode 2 of *The 60s: The Beatles Decade*. United Kingdom, 2006.

Lambert, Dave, dir. *Magical Mystery Tour Memories*. London: Wienerworld Limited, 2008. Film.

Langager, Ross. "'With Our Love, We Can Save the World': The Beatles Within and Without the Late '60s Zeitgeist." *Pop Matters*, November 23, 2009. https://www.popmatters.com/115776-with-our-love-we-can-save-the-world-the-beatles-within-and-without-t-2496121406.html.

Larkin, Philip. *High Windows*. London: Faber and Faber, 1974.

McGregor, Damon Paul. "Nietzsche, Unconscious Processes, and Non-linear Individuation." Master's thesis, Louisiana State University, 2011. https://digitalcommons.lsu.edu/gradschool_theses/265.

Niditch, Susan. *"My Brother Esau Is a Hairy Man": Hair and Identity in Ancient Israel*. New York: Oxford University Press, 2008.

Nietzsche, Friedrich. *The Birth of Tragedy and Other Writings*. Edited by Raymond Geuss and Ronald Speirs. Translated by Ronald Speirs. Cambridge: Cambridge University Press, 1999.

Padel, Ruth. *I'm a Man: Sex, Gods and Rock 'n' Roll*. London: Faber and Faber, 2000.

Palmer, Tony, dir. *All You Need Is Love: The Story of Popular Music*. London: London Weekend Television, 1977. Series.

Peebles, Andy. "John Lennon: The Final Interview." *BBC Radio One*, December 6, 1980. https://www.bbc.co.uk/programmes/p00c74jg.

Russell, Bertrand. *A History of Western Philosophy*. New York: Simon and Schuster, 1967.

Savage, Jon. *The Faber Book of Pop*. London: Faber and Faber, 1995.

Shaffner, Nicholas. *The British Invasion: From the First Wave to the New Wave*. New York: McGraw-Hill, 1982.

Stanley, Bob. *Yeah Yeah Yeah: The Story of Modern Pop*. London: Faber and Faber, 2014.

Steiner, Rudolf. *An Outline of Occult Science*. Chicago: Anthroposophical Literature Concern, 1922.

———. *The Universal Human: The Evolution of Individuality*. Hudson, NY: Anthroposophic Press, 1990.

Taich, Allison. "Beatlemania: The Defiance of a Generation." *Pop Matters*, November 11, 2009. https://www.popmatters.com/115702-beatlemania-the-defiance-of-a-generation-2496119961.html.

Turner, Steve. *Beatles 66: The Revolutionary Year*. New York: HarperCollins, 2016.

Winn, John C. *Way Beyond Compare: The Beatles Recorded Legacy*. Vol. 1, *1957–1965*. New York: Three Rivers Press, 2008.

Woodhead, Leslie. *How the Beatles Rocked the Kremlin*. London: BBC, 2009.

CHAPTER 9
A Religion in Fact
The Beatles as Religious Phenomenon Hidden in Plain Sight

GRANT MAXWELL

One of the most striking qualities of the collective narrative told about the Beatles is the consistent use of language describing their discovery of American rock and roll as a mystical revelation, their commitment to rehearsing this genre of music as a devotional spiritual practice, and their concerts as ecstatic religious rituals. Though often mediated by a distancing ironic humor, these rhetorical tropes seem to be more than mere metaphor, indicating a profound convergence between rock and roll and religion in the experience of many of those who participated in the Beatles phenomenon. Robert Bellah defines religion as "a set of symbolic forms and acts that relate man to the ultimate conditions of his existence."[1] This definition seems to be fundamentally true of the Beatles and their audience: it was not school or work or science or institutional religion but rock and roll that expressed the deepest yearnings and intuitions of the Beatles and many people in their generation, evident in their lives as much as in the "spiritual longing" of their music.[2]

John Lennon described his discovery of Elvis Presley as "the conversion," declaring, "Elvis was bigger than religion in my life."[3] And Lennon's encounter with "the spirit of [Presley's] performance" does in fact appear to bear all the signs of religious conversion explicated by William James in *The Varieties of Religious Experience*: Lennon's "self hitherto divided" found in rock and roll a model for relating to his most intimate bodily experience that rendered him "unified and consciously right superior and happy" in his devotion to the genre.[4] Of course, Lennon was not a deliriously happy individual from that moment forward, but this does not appear to be the meaning of happiness that James intends. Rather, James suggests that conversion produces an affect of felicitous and confluent unity of purpose, a higher kind of happiness grounded in a profound sense of significance and destination, a set of felt qualities that seem to have characterized much of Lennon's experience from this point onward, despite his personal struggles.

Paul McCartney expresses this religious quality just as directly, though always with an ironic inflection, describing the Beatles' early sessions listening to rock and roll records as "worshipping" and nominating Presley as "the guru" they'd been waiting for: "The Messiah had arrived."[5] To be precise, the irony generally employed by the Beatles is a double irony, as they often ironically negate with their tone what they are literally asserting, only to negate the negation by communicating, also through subtle tonal inflections as well as facial and gestural cues, that they do in fact mean what they say, performing a critical self-awareness, demonstrating that they are holding the skeptical pole within their encompassing belief. As Jonathan Gould aptly notes, it is a testament to their genuine veneration of Presley that, although the Beatles would cover a number of his songs live, Presley was the only one of their primary initial heroes whose songs never made their way onto a Beatles record, "almost as if he were indeed the reigning deity and they a group of novitiates, proscribed from speaking his name."[6] Or as Mark Lewisohn puts it, "Elvis Presley was God, it was as simple as that."[7]

The Beatles' biographers generally employ such religious rhetoric with a similar irony to that employed by the Beatles themselves. Although Bob Spitz writing that "like an earnest disciple, John reacted with missionary devotion" to his discovery of rock and roll or Lewisohn declaring that when skiffle devotees like the Beatles "heard 'That'll Be the Day,' those eternally uplifting two minutes, they were *converted*" may appear merely metaphorical or hyperbolic to casual reading, the overwhelming prevalence of such rhetoric in relation to the group from numerous sources suggests that these tropes are an acknowledgment of a truth hidden in plain sight: the Beatles really were disciples of Presley, and they really were missionaries for the return of affective intuition mediated by rock and roll.[8] Similarly, Gould writes, "from the start of the Beatle phenomenon, the press had harped on the analogy between the zeal of Beatlemaniacs and that of religious devotees," and although Gould never directly confutes the literal meaning of this statement, his rhetoric creates an ironic distance from such belief: "harped," "zeal," and "Beatlemaniacs" are all drolly overinflated terms, apparently meant indirectly to communicate an elevated critical perspective in relation to the implied credulity of "the press."[9] Rather than contradicting the idea that the Beatles were essentially a religious phenomenon, Gould seems almost to find it slightly distasteful to admit the plain truth of this supposition, enacting a rhetorical operation in reaction to the trivializing attitude often characteristic of modern sophistication. However, in spite of a "disenchanted" modernity that found it necessary hierarchically to disqualify nonrational modes of thought in order to produce a differentiation from nonmodern modes, that the Beatles stayed "faithful to the sounds they loved" is an essential condition for the musical and cultural transformation in which they played a primary role.[10]

On the one hand, it is a mistake to be overly reverential about the Beatles, as one of their most attractive qualities is the self-aware levity with which they approached everything, both themselves and others. As George Martin observed, "they don't take themselves too seriously."[11] On the other hand, however, once the realization has been achieved, it becomes difficult to ignore the overwhelming prevalence of religious rhetoric describing the Beatles' devotion to their music, though always with an irony endemic partially to their Liverpudlian roots and partially to their historical moment. The critical distance that this ironic stance afforded was a significant factor in allowing the Beatles to take up the Promethean torch from Presley and the other original rock and rollers to move the genre toward greater self-consciousness and complexity.

Presley was not really grappling with questions; he generally performed his identity in an uncritical mode. But the numinous vocabulary used to describe the Beatles again and again, masquerading as metaphor or ironic conceit, suggests that the Beatles and their milieu conceived of the phenomenon in which they were participating as something approximating a spiritual awakening. Ultimately, "the secular somehow becomes holy" in the music of the Beatles, the wine of daily life transubstantiated into something sacred.[12]

George Harrison declared in 1966, "To me it seems that Western philosophy is very prejudiced because they look upon mysticism as a magical 'something else,' you know? But after everything the greatest Western philosophers have said, to me it all boils down to the fact that they still haven't hit upon what the Eastern people have."[13] The trajectory of this observation is essentially correct, recognizing that the predominant culture of modernity in the West, including many of its most influential philosophers, has privileged the epistemology implicit in science based exclusively on material and efficient causation, while "mysticism" and "magic" constitute radically different modes of constructing experience, which have generally been developed to a higher degree in Eastern, globally Southern, and Indigenous cultures, based primarily on formal and final causation.

Aristotle delineated four types of causation, which can be divided into two groups of two: *material causation* is the fact that material objects exist at all, which is the precondition for *efficient causation*, which has generally come to mean material objects acting physically on other material objects and which is what we generally think of in the early twenty-first century when we use the word "cause." However, Aristotle also posited two other intertwined types of causation: *formal causation*, the mode of efficacy for potentialities in the nature of process—forms, archetypes, or universals—that are manifest in all actual occasions, while *final causation* is a mode of efficacy lured by teloi, the goals or purposes of these formal potentialities.

Although modernity has often defined itself by a rejection of formal and final causes, in part because teleology seems to preclude free will, a Spinozan "freedom of mind" is conserved in the subtle teleological conceptions developed by philosophers like Leibniz, James, Bergson, and Whitehead, for which final causes are affective inclinations that lure process toward becoming rather than pregiven ends.[14] Occulted domains concerned with religious experience, mysticism, magic, alchemy, and teleology, all closely connected to the lived experience of rock and roll and to most modern countercultural streams, are generally more amenable to explanation through a mode of thought based on formal-final causation rather than only the material-efficient causation privileged in the predominant modern modes of thought. During the Beatles' early years, affective and intuitive epistemologies, the modes oriented toward the discernment of formal and final causes, were severely repressed within the collective English psyche, and as Gould observes, "whatever magic the Beatles possessed lay dormant in the soul of every English boy," a repressed numinosity demanding a catalyst like the Beatles to open the floodgates of the creative vitality simmering below the surface of a largely rationalized British, and ultimately Western, culture.[15]

Lennon, seeking an explanation for his feeling of difference from others, experienced the discovery of rock and roll through Radio Luxembourg as a miraculous epiphany that "gave you plenty to dream about," as one of his contemporaries put it, though whereas dreaming is often associated with unfocused, undisciplined thinking, Lennon, McCartney, and Ringo Starr "observed the [rock and roll] radio broadcast faithfully" as a kind of spiritual discipline.[16]

McCartney described it as "a revelation," and for Lennon, "the broadcast was some kind of personal blessing, like a call from a ministering spirit," as according to Pete Shotton, Lennon "regarded it like scripture."[17] This compounding of religious language from McCartney, Lennon's close childhood friend, and one of the Beatles' primary biographers exceeds the plausible reach of mere metaphor, suggesting that the Beatles and their associates understood what was occurring to them as an essentially religious phenomenon in its broadest sense.

That Shotton describes Lennon as having "behaved distractedly" before the broadcasts recalls a passage from Mircea Eliade's *Shamanism* in which the initiate "becomes absent-minded and dreamy, loves solitude, and has prophetic visions."[18] Lennon certainly possessed a quality that can accurately be described as "vision," as according to an art-school mate, "John had a fantastic imagination that enabled him to see things for what they really were . . . and then jumble them up in a hilarious, thought-provoking way."[19] Lennon possessed an exceptional ability to perceive by means of "imagination," to penetrate to the heart of things and discern connections that others could not, and to express what he saw in engaging ways, qualities that those who witnessed the phenomenon from the inside often describe explicitly in terms of a spiritual calling. To apply Occam's razor, the most straightforward explanation for the phenomenon in question is that Lennon, his friends, and their influences and followers were engaging in what they experienced as a kind of religious practice through their disciplined engagement with rock and roll.[20]

It is clear that all of the Beatles, and Lennon in particular, had a powerful sense of calling in relation to rock and roll; they felt compelled, sensing something that seemed to demand expression through them, something beyond their volition, later experiencing a "confirmation of their calling" at a 1960 concert by Gene Vincent and Eddie Cochran. However, even in Lennon's earliest experiences with a band in the mid-1950s, his bandmates, having never witnessed a live skiffle group, "were obliged by John's special knowledge, unaware that his know-how was for the most part intuitive."[21] While Spitz implies that the fact that Lennon's "special knowledge" was "intuitive" somehow deceived the other boys, just below this level of interpretation, the vocabulary that he employs almost begs for a different explanation.

It is as if Spitz is making (understandable) concessions to the predominant ethos that regards intuitive knowledge as hierarchically less valid than rationally acquired knowledge, but the surrounding rhetoric, and the biographer's general orientation, belies this implication, suggesting that the members of this group perceived Lennon as the recipient of a gift that "effortlessly" produced awe in his compatriots. This subtle, though perhaps unintentional, rhetorical operation expresses the larger cultural significance of the Beatles as a kind of postmodern Trojan Horse for the return of affective knowledge to a position of cultural prominence. According to Lennon's childhood friend Nigel Wally, Lennon "just *knew* what to do, it was right at his fingertips. . . . It wasn't this concept he'd worked out; it came naturally to him."[22]

McCartney was no less devoted to rock and roll. After his mother died, he desperately clung to this music in the same way that many people find solace in religion during difficult times. As Spitz describes, for McCartney, listening to rock and roll and dreaming himself into the imaginal world created by the music was akin to a meditative practice, "a kind of reverie," in which he would float in a womb-like nonrational state of consciousness, "not even thinking," immersed in the "alchemical" quality summoned by the music.[23] These words, thrown out casually, gesture inexorably toward the deeper significance of what is, on the surface, merely an adolescent boy listening to pop music but in fact appears to be the spontaneous development of a transrational spiritual discipline by an individual who lived in a largely disenchanted culture.

The similar claim that McCartney's "talent was at the service of some hidden energy" is characteristic of the language used to describe the Beatles, and rock and roll in general, as what many accounts of this genre's genesis imply is that the great rock and roll singers like Presley, Lennon, and McCartney were vessels for the will of a higher power or an animating force—"whatever they may consider the divine," to borrow James's phrase.[24] All of the religious, mystical, and alchemical metaphors employed to describe these men's relationship to their music indicate that these founding fathers of rock and roll related to the genre as a kind of spiritual practice, but perhaps less dogmatic, more expansive, more epistemologically flexible than the traditional religions, like a spontaneously reemerging form of shamanism, the primal, nearly universal spiritual practice of humanity, in novel conditions.

The tendency toward doubly ironic distancing suggests the collective recognition that these sorts of revelations that the Beatles experienced and enabled are not really about the figures who produced them, as is usually assumed for ancient prophets and messiahs. Rather, for many twentieth-century devotees of rock and roll, while the experience has certainly been mediated through the "rock star" figure, it is the revelation itself, the music itself, or the ecstatic affect that the music evokes in the listener that becomes the primary focus of attention. While Lennon would toy with the idea that he was a messianic figure, it seems that Lennon and his fans self-consciously reenacted, in the kind of differential repetition described by Gilles Deleuze, the roles that Christ and his followers played on a different order of ingression, from Lennon's claiming, "We're more popular than Jesus now," in a 1966 interview and singing, "The way things are going, they're gonna crucify me," in the "The Ballad of John and Yoko," to devoting his life to spreading a gospel of peace and love and being tragically martyred by one of his most devoted and troubled disciples.[25]

As Lennon declared in 1968, "If this scene is [around] in 2012 . . . the masses will be where I am today and I should be as groovy as Jesus by then," indicating an implicit understanding that messianic figures like Christ are not fundamentally different beings than their followers but simply ahead of their time, "untimely" to use the Nietzschean term, a role that Lennon seems to have at least temporarily seen himself as fulfilling.[26] However, Lennon also rejected such suppositions at various points, most notably on "God" from *Plastic Ono Band*, in which he expresses his disbelief not only in "God," "Jesus," and "Buddha" but also in "Elvis," "Zimmerman," and "Beatles," as well as on "Imagine," in which he expresses disbelief in "religion" in general. The spiritual aspiration and sense of election that Lennon clearly felt were also apparently problematic for him, embodying the tension of being a visionary individual in a largely disenchanted culture, enacting a constant negotiation between spiritual intuition and rational skepticism.

Impelling the men's productive conflict, Lennon and McCartney shared a fundamental understanding of the necessity of belief in producing something culturally significant—not faith confined by religious dogma but a Jamesian "will to believe" in the righteousness of their mission and the inspired quality of their music. As McCartney describes the band's approach when they were still struggling in Liverpool, "We had this way of getting over problems—someone would say, 'Well, what are we going to do now?' and we'd say, 'Well, something'll happen,' and the four of us believed that. . . . There was this, like, *faith*." Lennon expressed a similar sentiment, recalling, "we dreamed of being the British Elvis Presleys, and we believed it," elsewhere declaring, "we were the best fucking group in the goddamn world . . . and believing that is what made us what we were," a belief that carried the Beatles through their numerous transformations, including the shamanic Reeperbahn ordeal that produced what Mo Best called "a revelation to behold."[27]

This will to believe is also evinced in the humorous call-and-response that the Beatles would perform when their energy began to flag: "Where are we going, boys?'" Lennon would prompt his bandmates, to which they would respond, "To the top, Johnny! To the top!" "And where is the top?" he would ask, to which the others would reply, "The toppermost of the poppermost!"[28] This incantation, while certainly a parody of the music-business circus, also expressed James's pragmatic insight that a belief's validity "is the process of its valid-*ation*," in this case, though always filtered through layers of irony, that they were headed for great things.[29] In order to achieve something great, one must generally believe that it is possible, even probable, that one will achieve that thing. Although on one level of signification, the Beatles performed this scenario as an ironic parody, on a deeper level, the humor allowed them to express their belief that they would be commercially and artistically successful while simultaneously allowing a deflection from what they perceived as overly sentimental sincerity. In this subtle operation, they could explicitly express their feeling of teleological destination while always maintaining a plausible deniability that they were only joking.[30]

In a purely materialist reading, such an assertion of destiny would have seemed absurd, as the precedent of external circumstances leading up to their Parlophone session in 1962 seemed to suggest that the Beatles would *not* be successful just as they had been unsuccessful in obtaining a recording contract until that point. Although Brian Epstein had taken "a gigantic leap of faith" to believe in the group, later declaring, "I knew they would be bigger than Elvis," he also acknowledged that, "from all evidence so far, the Beatles had nothing going for them."[31] The Beatles and their manager felt that they were destined for greatness, but the only available recording, which Epstein used as a demo when shopping for a record label, was simply not very good. However, the Beatles' unshakable intuitive sense that they had something novel and important to offer impelled them to persevere, a faith that was justified copiously in due course.

It was not just the Beatles and Epstein who possessed this sense of destination, as the milieu in which they were embedded was ripe for such an emergent phenomenon, lifting the Beatles out of the crowd when it became clear that they were the local band most likely to succeed. As the DJ Bob Wooler announced one evening at the Cavern in 1962, "Hey, listen, Cavernites.... The next time the Beatles appear on this stage they'll be wearing their *brand-new suits*. Now, this is going to be a *revelation!*" In this proclamation, we see the mythogenetic machinery gearing up, making anything that the Beatles did part of their mystique. Although there is a sense in which this announcement by Wooler was a cynical marketing move—Wooler himself admitting that "there was a touch of Barnum and Bailey in this"—it seems to have been experienced by the crowd as exactly what Wooler said it would be: a revelation.[32]

Many actions taken by the Beatles could be accurately interpreted in this double way: as evidence of a profoundly significant, essentially religious phenomenon or of merely a trivial pop-culture fad driven by the cynical desire for money and fame. It is one of the primary insights of pragmatism that rationality can find valid and convincing logical arguments for seemingly incommensurable interpretations, the enchanted or the disenchanted in this case, so the difference really amounts to what the participants in the process decide to believe primarily on the basis of their intuitive sense of the situation.[33] In the case of the Beatles, all of the elements converged to allow them to play a central role in the radical shift in attitude of a significant portion of their generation, to provide the conditions under which their audience could choose to believe in what is often described as the spiritual efficacy of the Beatles.

Of course, this belief was only possible because people were hungry for something to believe in, but this fact does not lessen the significance of the belief. It is the Beatles' faith in their mission that allowed the audience to believe, and in turn, it is the audience's faith in the Beatles that spurred the band on to ever-greater heights of creativity in a feedback loop of energy and intention. This is an exemplary case of Alfred North Whitehead's "slightest change of tone which yet makes all the difference," and this reciprocal belief certainly did make a great difference, soon mediating the emergence of culture from a black-and-white world into the full psychedelic Technicolor that still largely defines the aesthetic possibilities of our culture half a century later.[34] To satisfy the dictates of the rational modern mind, it was important that what was believed about the band was at least plausible. However, the phenomenon of the Beatles attests to the value in itself of belief in something that exceeds individuality, evident in the fruits that this kind of belief can bear for lived experience, especially when balanced by a moderate, healthy dose of skeptical rigor.

Epstein describes the band as having "actually glowed" in their new suits, which recalls the halos often depicted around Christian saints or Buddhas.[35] Whether the Beatles were physically emitting light or not is beside the point for this mode of thought, as judging by Epstein's statement, the witnesses to this revelatory instance experienced the moment "as if" the four boys were glowing, and this was what mattered to them, as this perception had a real effect on the crowd's affective state. Whether the Beatles were actually emitting light or whether this is only a metaphor for something harder to define is a question for scientists and skeptics to consider after the fact, just as they have done with the purported miracles of messiahs, sorcerers, and shamans for millennia. Ultimately, there does not appear to be a reliable scientific way of knowing if these kinds of phenomena are literally true or not, as it often seems to be the case that the naively literalist act of measuring the numinous disrupts the collective energetic quality, the "magic," that participants in metaphysical phenomena consistently describe.

The crowd's focus of attention was not on critiquing but on allowing the "miraculous" quality of the moment to produce the kind of positive affect that, in turn, produces measurable benefits for health and happiness that James describes. However, this is not to say that the question of whether the "glowing" quality of the Beatles actually consisted of the emission of photons is not a valid one, just as the question of how many angels can fit on the head of a pin was a valid question to the medieval Christian scholastics. But it is not the correct question if one hopes to understand the experience of the people who participated in this phenomenon on their own terms, rather than violently imposing the materialist, scientific mode on them as academia, and modernity generally, has so often done with groups projectively identified as "other," from ancient and primal cultures to racially or socioculturally marginalized groups in contemporary society.

However, as opposed to the relatively naive quality of most precritical religious belief, the Beatles and their audience generally maintained a critical distance from the mythogenetic narrativizing. That the Beatles are described as having been "slightly embarrassed" in the moment when their new suits were revealed demonstrates that they were still holding the pole of doubt within their circle of belief, a necessary corrective to the violence and oppression that has been perpetrated in the name of unquestioned religious certainty over the centuries. Although there were certainly philosophical and artistic precursors to this integrating dissolution of doubt and belief mediated by the Beatles, the sixties were a pivotal moment in the emergence of this novel mode into collective awareness.[36]

Whereas the predominant modern cultural streams had come to construct this polarity as a choice between belief and skepticism, or between religion and science, the Beatles and many people in their generation implicitly understood that these two dualities are not mutually exclusive but complementary and deeply intertwined poles in a dialectical process. Academia, which might be described as something like the secular priesthood of modernity in reaction to the previous priesthoods dominant in premodernity, is only now beginning to become conscious of this knowledge that many people outside the halls of academic power have been articulating for decades, if not centuries, often the result of institutional biases more than individual beliefs. An emergent mode of relation cannot become explicit in a culture until the authoritative guardians of that culture's highest knowledge are able to create forms of language and institutional structures that can viably articulate and contain the new mode, in this case, what anyone who has ever enjoyed the ecstatic revelation of rock and roll knows intuitively.

Although both academics and priests can certainly be untimely forerunners, they, as the keepers of the deepest beliefs of their cultures, are often among the last to be convinced of a new way of conceiving experience—or perhaps merely the last to admit that they hold heterodox beliefs. But when a sufficient number of these cultural guardians have been publicly converted to a new mode of thought, a novel epoch of human history has generally resulted, visible in the transition from the classical era to the Christian era as much as in the transition from the medieval to the modern. At the core of these transitions, a mythical narrative invariably expresses the character of the transformation, in the stories of Jesus and his disciples as much as in the stories of Copernicus, Kepler, and Galileo. The Beatles may similarly be considered by posterity as one of the primary characters in the transformational narrative currently in the process of composition.

Participating in the enactment of the Beatles' mythogenetic process in 1961, the newly formed *Mersey Beat* newspaper included an absurd story by Lennon titled "A Short Diversion on the Dubious Origins of the Beatles," in which a man descends on a "flaming pie" and pronounces that they shall be called "Beatles—*with an a*."[37] This pseudoreligious origin story is a parody of divine revelation that lets the audience in on the joke. The story seems to suggest that the Beatles are a genuinely religious phenomenon but that one should not let on that one actually believes this, at least not without a wink and an enigmatic grin. This kind of double irony is what allowed the Beatles and their fans to walk the tightrope between belief and skepticism, an inside joke for the young and the hip—a new kind of revelation that, like a gestalt picture or a "magic eye" 3-D image, one can only perceive if one looks in just the right way, not focusing too much on any one detail but softening one's gaze to take in the whole picture, allowing what is genuinely present, though hidden in plain sight, to emerge.

Although new modes of thought are almost always criticized for this kind of "fuzzy logic," an established cultural milieu is deeply informed by the beliefs that have been predominant for generations, while new modes have not yet had time to develop their particulars. As Whitehead understood, "foolishness" is an intrinsic component of novelty, so that a leap of faith is always required to enter into a new way of constructing reality.[38] Copernicus, Kepler, and Galileo experienced a similar sort of resistance and condemnation in the sixteenth and seventeenth centuries to that experienced by Presley, the Beatles, and Bob Dylan in the twentieth. The orthodox image of thought, whatever it may be in whatever domain of activity, has always had a great deal of time to articulate the finer points of its approach, while the emerging mode must stumble in the dark, mapping out radically novel territory and making things up as it goes. Although many members of the generation that first thought of themselves in terms of a "counterculture" learned not to become anti-intellectual but to set critical rationality aside when the intuitive mode is more appropriate to the particular needs of the situation, this mode of relation is still in the process of coming to consciousness in our cultural discourse, so that even now debates are often framed as occurring between the fixed combatants of irrational religious belief and skeptical scientific rationalism, a simplistic binary that musicians have done as much to dissolve as Continental, pragmatist, and process philosophers have.

As catalysts for this fundamental cultural transformation, the Beatles were not content merely to conquer Britain; they felt that they were destined for international recognition. Once the group found success in England, they turned their sights to the United States, which they saw as a kind of "Promised Land." It is hardly necessary at this stage in the analysis to point out the religious imagery, which contains within it a spiritual yearning for the origin of the genre to which they were devoted. Because the Beatles were so profoundly influenced by US rock and roll, their explicit intention was to bring their version of the music back to its place of inception, thereby performing a dialectical synthesis of the genre by carrying their distinctly novel iteration into direct relation with the locus of its original incarnation. Epstein, having been "converted" by witnessing the Beatles at the Cavern, "shared their dream and persisted in his belief that an American tour should happen without delay," a passage that unintentionally provides a rather good definition of religion: the persistence of belief based on a shared vision of reality.[39] And once they made it to the United States in 1964, as Gould writes of their performance on *The Ed Sullivan Show*, it was "a complete revelation," suggesting an initiatory fulfillment of the persistent visionary belief of the Beatles, their manager, and their devotees.[40]

Although the Beatles were a primary catalyst in the metamorphosis of their culture, they did not cause the rising tide that lifted all ships. In the first meeting between the Beatles and the Rolling Stones in 1963, "there were already signs of a musical undertow that was pulling uniquely talented and expressive youths into the onrushing tide of change."[41] Like a tea kettle that climaxes in a change of state as it comes to a boiling point or like the crest of a wave, the Beatles and the Stones were carried by a vital impulse toward novelty, a quality of the moment that these young men embodied in a way that seems to have come from something exceeding their individuality, agency assigned not to the primary actors in the process but to the process itself. In the most spontaneous of manners, a profound transformation of culture was occurring through the Beatles and their contemporaries, and as the momentum built, their exponentially expanding audience directed an unprecedented amount of energy and attention toward the band. For the "fanatics" who merely wanted to touch them or be in their presence, the Beatles radiated an undeniable numinosity. The mostly female Beatles fans who came to scream at their concerts "were engaged primarily in an act of ritualistic confirmation," suggesting a spontaneous mass participatory religious rite with the capacity to produce ecstatic transformation through belief in the numinous power of these four young men.[42]

As in the conversion experiences that James describes, though on a collective scale, "in the miraculous year" of 1963, "suddenly everything the Beatles did resonated with meaning."[43] The surging mass belief in their spiritual significance impelled the renewal of the world that they inhabited as surely as if they were the embodiment of a new force of nature not yet described by physics. As James, Bergson, and Whitehead all understood, the vital impulse toward novelty constitutes a teleological inclination that exceeds the ability of physical science, as it has predominantly been conceived in the twentieth century, to comprehend.[44] The response to the Beatles, particularly in their unprecedentedly massive live performances in the midsixties, was often described as a titanic force of nature surging through the host of humanity participating in the phenomenon of Beatlemania, descriptions that exceed mere metaphor to express the coming to awareness of a previously concealed quality of reality.

The Beatles were enacting a narrative experienced by many who participated in it, particularly the Beatles themselves, as an autonomous process impelling them to ever greater heights of both artistic achievement and mania. According to one journalist, "It was *exactly* the story we'd been waiting for."[45] And according to another writing in mid-1964, "They have become a religion in fact. The days of their ministry on earth seem to be over—they don't seem to perform so much—and they have been taken up into heaven preferring to conserve the Holy Quaternity in a delicious incommunicado. All over the place though there are icons, devotional photos and illuminated missals which keep the tiny earthbound fans in touch with the provocatively absconded deities."[46]

As if in expectation of a messianic dispensation, the press and audience, their genuinely religious passion overflowing the capability of ironic containment, were searching for someone to embody and express their deepest yearnings for revelation.

The language consistently employed in describing Beatlemania, encapsulated in a phrase like "pandemonium on the sidewalk," evokes religious passion at its wildest and most extreme, recalling the maenads of the Dionysian cult in ancient Greece, female fanatics who would achieve ecstasy through intoxication and dancing and, in the case of Euripides's *Bacchae*, hunting down and killing a king in their divine frenzy.[47] The Beatles had little agency in the process occurring around them, as Beatlemania emerged of its own volition, no single person or group possessing the power to manufacture such a response. Rather, this phenomenon embodied the spontaneous expression of a new way of relating to bodily affect within the ritualized setting of the Beatles' concerts, so that, in a very short time, the transgressively ecstatic behavior became the norm. The Beatles and their audience were being carried by a momentum that overflowed any individual participant, so that the four young men found it necessary either to ride the wave or to get off, so to speak, as catalysts for the unconscious drive of their audience to undergo a self-transformation in the fundamental way they were relating to experience.

The "exhilarating," unstoppable "spiritual anarchy" of the shows impelled the eruption of ecstatic affect on a scale never before achieved, and the Beatles' music was the catalyst for this mass awakening of experiential domains rendered largely unconscious by pervasive rationalization. Despite the Beatles' inability to control the phenomenon for which they served as the focus, as the momentum grew, there was increasingly a sense that they possessed the kind of spiritual force usually attributed to prophets, saints, and shamans, "as if they gave off some special juju, as if they would make everything all right, which, in a sense, they actually did."[48] Here Spitz implies that even though there is an ironic, "as if" quality to the essentially religious adoration, the actual effect that the Beatles had on their audience, and on the culture at large, by many accounts was experienced as psychologically healing, enacting an incipient reintegration of modernity's primal wound, the split between subject and object and between affect and intellect.

Although this integration resulted in the collective emergence of something potent and numinous, the Beatles maintained their ironic posture even, or especially, toward their own fame. This holding the pole of doubt within their encompassing belief is what allowed the Beatles to work concretely, on a daily basis, "to keep the fantasy alive."[49] Although "fantasy" is a word, like "myth" or "magic," often trivialized in our era, the word itself does not contain this derogatory sense. Rather, "fantasy" etymologically means to "make visible" that which is invisible, which is strikingly close to the meaning of "revelation."[50] There is no clearer evidence of the pervasive repression of formal and final causation in modern discourse than that the most basic words associated with these causal modes have taken on a veneer of triviality over the centuries of their use.

According to Spitz, the Beatles were "connected to a growing disenchantment with the establishment," his employment of the term "disenchantment" echoing Weber's, though in precisely the opposite context.[51] Whereas modernity had been a long process of epistemological disenchantment, the counterculture rebellion of the sixties embodied a disenchantment with the very disenchanted mode of thought that had resulted from the exclusivist privileging of intellect since the Enlightenment. Much like the phenomenon of double irony, this "double disenchantment" produced not merely a return to premodern enchantment but rather an individuated reembrace of formal and final causation by a world in which rationalist materialism was dominant, producing a novel mode whose nascence was enacted for many millions of people by the Beatles.[52]

NOTES

1. Bellah, *Beyond Belief*, 21.
2. Riley, *Tell Me Why*, 35; Turner, *Gospel*, 10.
3. *Rolling Stone*, June 28, 1970; Lewisohn, *Tune In*, 90.
4. Spitz, *Beatles*, 41; James, *Varieties of Religious Experience*, 177.
5. Lewisohn, *Tune In*, 9, 89; Beatles, *Anthology*, 22.
6. Gould, *Can't Buy Me Love*, 305–6.
7. Lewisohn, *Tune In*, 9.
8. Spitz, *Beatles*, 41; Lewisohn, *Tune In*, 146.
9. Gould, *Can't Buy Me Love*, 341.
10. Weber, *Protestant Ethic*; Stengers, *Cosmopolitics I and II*; Riley, *Tell Me Why*, 41, 18.
11. Lewisohn, *Tune In*, 809; MacDonald, *Revolution in the Head*, xx.
12. Riley, *Tell Me Why*, 33.
13. Turner, *Gospel*, 10.
14. Spinoza, *Collected Works*, 594.
15. Gould, *Can't Buy Me Love*, 179; Lewisohn, *Tune In*, 410.
16. Spitz, *Beatles*, 34.
17. Ibid., 34–41; Beatles, *Anthology*, 22.
18. Spitz, *Beatles*, 34–35; Eliade, *Shamanism*, 19.
19. Spitz, *Beatles*, 105.
20. Turner, *Gospel*, 5–6.
21. Spitz, *Beatles*, 51.
22. Ibid., 51.
23. Ibid., 176, 51, 92.
24. Ibid., 92; James, *Varieties of Religious Experience*, 36.
25. Deleuze, *Difference and Repetition*, 90.
26. Turner, *Gospel*, viii, 1.
27. Lewisohn, *Tune In*, 340, 557, 839; Riley, *Tell Me Why*, 36.
28. Beatles, *Anthology*, 68.
29. James, *Pragmatism*, 77–78.
30. James, *Will to Believe*.
31. Lewisohn, *Tune In*, 499; Spitz, *Beatles*, 284.
32. Spitz, *Beatles*, 274, 284, 354.
33. James, *Pragmatism*, 1.

34. Whitehead, *Science and the Modern World*, 2.
35. Spitz, *Beatles*, 355.
36. Ibid., 355.
37. Gould, *Can't Buy Me Love*, 79; *Beatles, Anthology*, 41.
38. Whitehead, *Science and the Modern World*, 47.
39. Spitz, *Beatles*, 386–87, 269.
40. Gould, *Can't Buy Me Love*, 4.
41. Spitz, *Beatles*, 408.
42. Gould, *Can't Buy Me Love*, 184.
43. Ibid., 142; Spitz, *Beatles*, 422.
44. Bergson, *Creative Evolution*, 22; Whitehead, *Process and Reality*, 28.
45. Spitz, *Beatles*, 428.
46. Gould, *Can't Buy Me Love*, 341.
47. Spitz, *Beatles*, 427.
48. Ibid., 553, 483.
49. Ibid., 492.
50. Simpson and Wiener, *Oxford English Dictionary*, s.v. "fantasy."
51. Spitz, *Beatles*, 519.
52. Whitehead, *Science and the Modern World*, 47, 143–47.

BIBLIOGRAPHY

Beatles. *The Beatles Anthology*. San Francisco: Chronicle Books, 2000.
Bellah, Robert N. *Beyond Belief*. Berkeley: University of California Press, 1970.
Bergson, Henri. *Creative Evolution*. New York: Barnes and Noble Books, 2005.
Deleuze, Gilles. *Difference and Repetition*. New York: Columbia University Press, 1994.
Eliade, Mircea. *Shamanism*. Princeton: Princeton University Press, 1964.
Gould, Jonathan. *Can't Buy Me Love*. New York: Harmony Books, 2007.
James, William. *Pragmatism*. Toronto: Dover, 1995.
———. *The Varieties of Religious Experience*. New York: Vintage Books, 1990.
———. *The Will to Believe, Human Immortality, and Other Essays in Popular Philosophy*. Mineola, NY: Dover, 1960.
Lewisohn, Mark. *Tune In*. New York: Crown Archetype, 2013.
MacDonald, Ian. *Revolution in the Head*. Chicago: Chicago Review Press, 2007.
Riley, Tim. *Tell Me Why*. Cambridge, MA: Da Capo, 2002.
Simpson, John, and Edmund Wiener, eds. *Oxford English Dictionary*. 2nd ed. New York: Oxford University Press, 2009.
Spinoza, Baruch. *The Collected Works of Spinoza*. Vol. 1. Princeton: Princeton University Press, 1985.
Spitz, Bob. *The Beatles*. New York: Back Bay Books, 2005.
Stengers, Isabelle. *Cosmopolitics I and II*. Minneapolis: University of Minnesota Press, 2010.
Turner, Steve. *The Gospel According to the Beatles*. Louisville, KY: Westminster John Knox Press, 2006.
Weber, Max. *The Protestant Ethic and the "Spirit" of Capitalism and Other Writings*. New York: Penguin Books, 2002.
Whitehead, Alfred North. *Process and Reality*. New York: Free Press, 1985.
———. *Science and the Modern World*. New York: Free Press, 1967.

PART 4

RECEPTION OF THE BEATLES

CHAPTER 10

Helter Skelter

Charles Manson's (Supposed) Apocalyptic Reading of the White Album

MARK DUFFETT

On New Year's Eve, at the end of 1968, the petty criminal and commune leader Charles Manson supposedly asked Paul Watkins and his other followers at the Myers Ranch, "Are you hip to what the Beatles are saying?"[1] He continued, "Dig it, they're telling it like it is. They know what's happening in the city; blackie is getting ready. They put the revolution to music. . . . It's 'Helter Skelter.'" Finally, he emphasized, "Helter Skelter is coming down. Hey, their album is about getting the young love ready, man, building up steam."[2] The eccentric clan leader appeared to believe that the Fab Four were alerting the United States' youth to an upcoming race war that he and his followers, the Family, would escape by first hiding underground, then emerging to rule incumbent over the Black population. With a few coded words, he ordered his most dedicated followers to visit Cielo Drive in Hollywood on the night of August 8, 1969, where they killed the pregnant Hollywood starlet Sharon Tate and her friends. The next night, they murdered the supermarket executive Leno and Rosemary LaBianca.

The shocking, grizzly Tate-LaBianca murders are often considered not just a metaphorical end to the 1960s but also a horrific, real-life footnote in the story of the Beatles.[3] As the second decade of the twenty-first century drew to an end, the Fab Four were also becoming a footnote in Manson's story. The investigative journalist Tom O'Neill spent two decades trying to connect its vast universe of facts and cast of characters.[4] Beyond the awful nights in August 1969 on Cielo and Waverly Drive, there was the musician Bobby Beausoleil and Susan Atkins's murder of Gary Hinman, Manson's attack on the drug dealer Bernard "Lotsa Pappa" Crowe, his connections to the Los Angeles music industry via the Beachboy Dennis Wilson and the producer Terry Melcher, and his training in Scientology and links to the Straight Satans biker gang and Process Church. In other words, the Family was connected to a tangled web of figures, suggesting no simple narrative.

At Manson's unprecedentedly long and expensive 1970 show trial, Vincent Bugliosi—who later wrote *the* best-selling true-crime book of all time about the incident—put forward his theory that Manson believed the Beatles had revealed that a global race war was on the way.[5] Bugliosi claimed that Manson believed he was guided by Beatles album tracks, including "Piggies" and "Blackbird."[6] As a premise for the case, "Revolution Number 9" was considered as supposedly corresponding to chapter 9 of the book of Revelation in the Bible and marking the Beatles out as social leaders:

> And out of the smoke came forth locusts upon the earth; and power was given to them, as the scorpions of the earth have power. And the shapes of the locusts were like unto horses prepared for war; and upon their heads as it were crowns unto gold, and their faces were as men's faces [a male rock group]. And they had hair as the hair of women [male hippies], and their teeth were as teeth of lions. And they had breastplates of iron [electric guitars]; and the sounds of their wings was as to the sound of chariots, of many horses rushing to war. . . . And thus I saw the horses in a vision, and them that sat on them, having breastplates as of fire [electric guitars] and of hyacinth and of brimstone: and the heads of lions; and out of their mouths proceedeth fire and smoke and brimstone [amplified sound].[7]

At the LaBianca residence, "Helter Skelter" was written, misspelled, in the victim's blood on a refrigerator door. It was also scrawled on a door at the Spahn Ranch, where the Family had been staying, seemingly linking them to the crime scene.

With both Bugliosi and Manson himself now dead, few informed commentators any longer believe the idea that Manson's apocalyptic reading of the White Album was the *real* reason that he implicitly ordered his most dedicated followers to visit Roman Polanski's residence. If the prosecution's Beatles-based reading of the Manson murders was so suspect, why has it continued to resonate, at least among the less initiated?[8] In this chapter, my aim is neither to pronounce whether the Beatles "really were" religious or how their lyrics could have been misinterpreted nor to reprosecute or exonerate Manson. Instead, I am interested in understanding the cultural logic that has used Manson's purported fascination with the Beatles to score political points about the nature of the sixties.

Bigger than Jesus?

Between 1955 and 1980, US society was characterized by concern about growing secularization and a certain sense of paranoia that invaded both Christian and secular circles.[9] The Beatles had agency and conscience as celebrities. As they matured, they became outspoken on matters both religious and secular. The group's members were never exactly spiritual leaders—even if others sometimes took them that way—but they were very public spiritual seekers. Concerns about the degree of influence that they had over the youth of the United States were prompted by the band's public statements. In the summer of 1966, *Datebook*'s cover quoted John Lennon as saying, "I don't know which will go first—rock 'n' roll or Christianity!"[10] The comments ignited a wave of moral outrage, especially in the South. It should be noted, however, that they came in the context of *Time* magazine asking, "Is God Dead?" in stark red letters on its April 8, 1966, front cover—the first of its covers not to carry a picture. Lennon apologized on air to a WCFL disk jockey in Chicago that August, but his words were ambiguous. He said that what he had said was "wrong or taken wrong," and—reflecting a comparatively New Age sensibility—"I believe that what people call God is something in all of us."[11] The Beatles, as popular musicians, pointed out that Christian traditions were in doubt and helped to challenge the social norms justified with reference to them. In mass culture, rock stars were framed as Christianity's sham alternative—commodity "cult" leaders—when in fact, the Beatles were spiritual seekers who represented the search for alternatives that characterized the era. The band's summer on tour was dogged by their popular disapproval, but Lennon maintained his anti-Establishment stance.

A few weeks after *Datebook* published the tendentious comments, the Beatles released their LP *Yesterday and Today* to great controversy in the United States because it featured them sitting with smiles on their faces in white coats adorned with randomly strewn pieces of raw meat and decapitated baby dolls. The photographer Robert Whitaker's controversial "butcher cover" was quickly stickered over and replaced. The band insisted that it was a misfired protest against the war in Vietnam. Nevertheless, it showed that they could be audacious social rebels. Part of the symbolic link between the Beatles and Manson was that they had already playacted the role of murderers on that LP cover—in their case, to parody the dissociation of a society that could make killing a clinical science.

Michael Kramer has noted that rock was marked by a differentiation of consumer formats, creating a form of music that positioned itself as more adult and knowing than mass-produced pop.[12] The musical content of the White Album was diverse rock. Its cover was the antithesis of the vivid, crowded, multicolored *Sgt. Pepper* design and directly explored questions of mass culture. Fans gazing on the White Album cover could see just a blank, white space, something that—given the politics of the time—might be construed as having racial connotations, but was also associated with the notion of a "blank slate": the idea that consumers could project whatever they wanted onto a disinterested surface. On the album track "Glass Onion," Lennon referenced both *Sgt Pepper* and "I Am the Walrus" from the *Magical Mystery Tour* TV film. By saying that the Walrus had been Paul (McCartney), he began teasing the audience, inviting them into a game in which the group offered clues that deceived their followers, tantalizing them with an ongoing guessing game. In other words, the Beatles were not just world makers; they were puzzle creators.

At this point, it is worth noting a particularly strange aspect of the story. Soon after the Tate-LaBianca murders were announced in the summer of 1969, rumors gained ground that Paul McCartney was dead. The conspiracy theory emerged in *Beatles Book* in February 1967 but spread rapidly from September 1969, when several radio shows were made about it. As Barbara Suczek put it, "The most striking characteristic of the McCartney phenomenon is probably its preoccupation with the covert."[13] "Paul is dead" relocated the paranoia of the Kennedy assassination in the realm of entertainment and, like the references used in the lyrics of "Glass Onion," allowed fans to endlessly speculate, not just about Paul's demise but about how it had been covered up and secretly coded by the Beatles in their music and album artwork—notably for *Abbey Road*. The Manson prosecution's decision to go with a Beatles conspiracy happened in the context of this phenomenon.

(Mis)Reading Manson

Hollywood has always created its own class hierarchy. The glamorous "City of Quartz" has continually lauded its stars as an aristocracy that leads the nation. According to the media scholar Nick Couldry, "It is 'common sense' that the 'media world' is somehow better, more intense, than 'ordinary life,' and that 'media people' are somehow special."[14] The Family's Los Angeles show trial was one in which a group of Hollywood glitterati victims was "upstaged" by an eccentric rabble of hippy misfits. In one way, it had elements that resembled a degraded version of class revolution: as Martin Amis put it, "the revenge of the insignificant on the affluent."[15] This idea positions Manson as a failed celebrity or crazed fan who used cult leadership to take revenge on his own more successful brethren. In the end, the jury did not need a popular-music analogy to understand that Manson could be a charismatic leader; both inside and outside the court room, the behavior of his female followers amply demonstrated the grip he had over them. Their obedient coproduction of Manson's monstrosity almost rendered the question of how he could turn ordinary followers into murderers redundant. Instead, it opened up the possibility of using rock stardom, framed in a quasi-mystical or religious way, as a means of demonstrating the intense *strength* of his powers. If Manson could persuade "innocent girls" to become serial killers, he was—given social assumptions about age and femininity—potent indeed.

Though Charles Manson was a somewhat poor fit for a cult leader, his induction of Family members *did* follow some cult-like practices. Manson combined a number of tactics that better recruited female followers to his clan than just playing music. He complimented girls on their insecurities, positioned himself as their father, did not judge them, and frequently went on the road, effectively creating a traveling bubble of people isolated from society. His ideas and practices "deprogramed" Family members from social norms. These included collective drug trips and group orgies, plus gnostic preaching in which Manson dispersed his identity. At least as he told it, he was somebody *and* nobody, the Devil *and*, perhaps, he implied, Jesus Christ.

Behind the ideas that Charles Manson was a failed rock star who tried to become a cult leader is the notion that he was, at heart, a deranged fan. This was a reading that John Lennon took up. Speaking just before his untimely death, he explained, "Manson was just an extreme version of the people who came up with the 'Paul is dead' thing or who figured out that the initials to 'Lucy in the Sky with Diamonds' were LSD and concluded I was writing about acid."[16] It is easy to see why Lennon would have adopted this dominant, accessible reading. Though the ex-Beatle centrally suggested that Manson was, in effect, arguably an "extreme fan" of his group, the notion remains somewhat problematic. Charles Manson's musical tastes were formed by singers more like Bing Crosby than Elvis or John Lennon. He played Beatles records, but there is little evidence that he enacted associated fan practices, like attempting to go to a concert or convention. What he had in common with a few Beatles "fans" was that he participated in conspiracy theorizing.

Joan Didion's famous reading of the Manson incident in her piece "The White Album" was published almost a decade after the trial. Didion's reading, it has been pointed out, is arguably right of center in orientation. The experimentation with unusual philosophies and communal families that marked out the counterculture as a giant experiment in alternative living is dismissed as the idealist wanderings of broken and distracted youth. While such experiments had largely been closed down by the time she was writing, in part due to the carefully spun publicity around the Manson murders, her essay functioned to make the process seem fateful. In her reading, a pall of chaos descends over Los Angeles, leading to a climate of paranoia that was *fulfilled by* the Manson murders. In other words, the shocking thing about the crimes was not just the disconnected casualness with which they were committed but the notion that they were unsurprising to the cognoscenti of the city. The message is driven home by a mode that was "religious" insofar as it evoked a kind of apocalyptic dread. Replacing politics with *death trip*, such ideas serve to locate alternative lifestyles as part of a bad dream.

While Didion's piece is called "The White Album," she does not mention the Beatles. Here, as in the Manson case itself, the Beatles' famous record takes the Hitchcockian role of the McGuffin: a cipher chased through the narrative, only for readers to find that ultimately it disappears. Just like the White Album was a present absence around which the Manson case cohered, for Didion, it functions as *no-thing*, a disappeared object, standing in for the disconnect between naive idealism and actual carnage.

The irony of readings positioning Manson as cult leader is that so few communes became recognizably religious in the sixties. Hippy communities that sprang up around musicians and other leaders had trouble creating organized religions. Drugs were primarily a gateway to the spiritual or numinous rather than organized forms of worship. The ethics of nonjudgmental communality were obstacles to all but the most tenacious of human gods.

Jailhouse Games

An aspect that appears to fit the dream logic of the Manson case, but not its actuality, was that at least one newspaper report from the time claimed that the defense had requested John Lennon appear at the trial in order to explain "Helter Skelter." A Beatles spokesperson pointed out that Lennon had not actually written "Helter Skelter," adding that summoning him to Los Angeles would have been "like summoning Shakespeare to explain *MacBeth*."[17] Not only was Lennon more prominently associated with the "threat" of secularity than McCartney was, but it was Lennon who sang on "Glass Onion" and who, more so than McCartney, epitomized the sense of inner struggle associated with rock music. Neither Manson nor Lennon had much contact with his parents, and some people have argued that childhood feelings of abandonment were the source of their problems. Such readings reduce personal and social complexity to family matters. Seeing the two characters as "little men" struggling to grow up by evading or playacting the masculinity of father figures locates them on a wider terrain of Oedipal struggle that has become a hallmark of postwar pop culture.

In the immediate postwar years, before rock and roll shook things up, American social commentators were concerned about a different kind of threat: Momism. Arguably emergent as a critique of the wartime social advances made by women, Momism was the arguably misogynistic idea that mothers were in danger of being overbearing and stifling the full development of their children, such that "a mother is to blame for her son's aberrations and crimes."[18] In a Freudian frame, Momism is arguably a displaced version of castration anxiety: a male child is stuck in a dyadic relationship with his mother. He cannot move on from her attention, grow up, and form an equal bond with a woman of his own age. In an infantile state, his pleasure at being "married to mummy" is tinged with paranoia that his father will take revenge. Momism displaces the child's personal sense of fear and guilt onto the figure of the ogress, a domineering mother who "spousifies" her son and keeps him Oedipally entrapped in the absence of an adequate father figure on the scene.

Rock and roll's encounter with Momism initially came in the shape of Elvis Presley, whose mother, Gladys, was his closest friend. The Beatles, too, were not immune from perceptions of being Oedipally entrapped, and—especially in John Lennon's case—they manifest evidence that gave some credence to the theory. There were multiple elements to this. First, especially in its Beatlemania phase, the childlike side of the band was promoted. Here was a set of young men with boyish, mop-top haircuts intent on "larking about," an image not only forwarded in *Help!* and *A Hard Day's Night* but perfected in the daft and seemingly impromptu Christmas recordings that were sent out to fan-club members every year. Meanwhile, the fans called the band "the boys," a term of endearment that was used throughout *Beatles Monthly* even into 1969, when Lennon sported a bushy beard. Second, the Beatles formed a visible, public, adolescent "gang" that could be perceived as a substitute family of sorts, or even an alternative marriage (a "psycho-musical marriage"), displacing Oedipal tensions into homosocial male bonding and forming a refuge against adult life.[19] Third, the group's eventual breakup was blamed on key members forming monogamous couples with women. I am not suggesting here that every Beatle was existentially, Oedipally entrapped but rather that the group played up to an appealing notion of psychological immaturity that made them seem more available to audiences and was hard to jettison, even as they slowly grew up. The importance of the Oedipal frame as a lingering social perception was indicated by the music critic Robert Christgau, who said of Lennon in 1971, "Nobody just screams away his entire Oedipal heritage, and even as John acts out the fierce symbiosis of his marriage, he remains a jealous guy who interrupts his wife on Howard Smith."[20]

Oedipal entrapment was not just associated with rock stars. Other male celebrities of the era also had lifestyles that implied a poor fit with monogamy.[21] The theme entered pop culture in fictional ways, too. In John Frankenheimer's 1962 feature *The Manchurian Candidate*, Lawrence Harvey portrayed Raymond Shaw, an existentially broken US soldier who had fought in the Korean War and has been brainwashed to kill a presidential candidate. His overbearing mother, played by Angela Lansbury, had, it turns out, made a pact with the Russians and Chinese to use her son as an assassin who will oust the inconvenient candidate and leave his stepfather a free route to the presidency. On the way, Harvey shoots both his own young wife and her father. In the end, the film shows that Shaw's route to individual freedom is to reject both his communist captors and his evil mother. It is indicative, however, that not only does he sport an Elvis quiff, but when he carries out his act of assassination, he is disguised as a Christian pastor.

In a sense, the church is a deeply Oedipal institution. On the one hand, it claims to seriously address the social and spiritual issues of adulthood, not least our fear of mortality. On the other, the celibacy of its leaders, and their belief in the virgin birth, makes marriage a human institution allowed to the congregation but not to its leaders and sex in any relationship outside of marriage a shameful sin. From one angle, this spiritual refusal of sex and its opposite—the promiscuous "free love" practiced by Manson and his following—both seem infantile. In the wake of the introduction of the Pill, the "big men" of the church were contradicted *both* by a tidal wave of male lust ushering in the permissive society and by feminists objecting to patriarchy. Marshall McLuhan skewered this relationship between Oedipal Momism and feminism in 1970 when he wrote, "Tiny Tim has a name that expresses a world of grievance. His own act consists of singing like a pre-puberty choir boy and at the same time mocking the mellow tone of a suburban matriarch; i.e., the masculinized woman who has robbed him of his sex."[22] As Jeffrey Melnick notes, "It seems fairly clear that the fear created by the Manson girls was complexly tied up with the social anxieties about women's liberation."[23] Implied in Didion's version of history is a portrayal of Manson as an unloved, illegitimate child turned petty criminal yet, one who—not unlike John Lennon—acted "in the name of the father" to give several girls what was initially a pleasant experience of *social acceptance*. Manson thus both houses society's sexual guilt and arguably takes upon himself the impossible task of expiating the country of it. The horror of the Manson case was that once such guilt appeared to be gone, it returned and got acted out in the killing of an innocent young mother (Sharon Tate).

Based on Vincent Bugliosi's book *Helter Skelter*, the 1976 TV movie of the same name portrays Manson as a dramatic adolescent. When he sees Bugliosi at the end of the trial, Manson is led into the room by two armed guards to see his prosecutor alone. Challenged by the weight not just of the crimes but of the moral certitude that he deserves to be executed or incarcerated for them, he breaks down and goofs around like a teenager, ending the conversation:

Manson: [Hysterical] I almost did it, didn't I? I almost pulled it off. I almost made it, huh?
Bugliosi: [Serious] No, Charlie. You weren't even close. You killed some people. That's what you did. You accomplished murder. You took a bunch of sad kids—human flotsam—and you played jailhouse games on them. That's it, Charlie. You're not even important any more.
[Bugliosi packs up his papers as Manson is led away.]

The scene places Bugliosi in an adult role, modeling composed emotions and making stern judgments, in contrast to Manson's manic exuberance. His role is to remind his charge of the gravity of his crimes. The fictionalized Bugliosi's term "jailhouse games" recalls a history of youth culture stretching back to the 1957 Elvis movie *Jailhouse Rock*.[24] Thus, after Manson's darkly maniacal courtroom performance, which was itself an embrace of a social perception—exacerbated, no doubt, by the December 19, 1969, *Life* magazine cover that showed him high on *all* of his LSD stash—in *Helter Skelter*, the Family's leader is reduced to a child whose infantile nature is signified through his links to music and youth culture ("plenty of time to play my guitar," "jailhouse games"). Such moments continue to position Manson as a kind of Oedipal remainder: the defeated, last residue of a childhood fascination that has to be released when one is reminded that it does no good.

It is important to understand here that the "jailhouse games" reading of Manson helps to situate a version of the 1960s, placing it as an adolescent phase of Sturm und Drang between the innocence of the 1950s and the jaded pragmatism of the 1970s. This reading is not unique to Manson alone: it follows the contours of the idea that Western society childishly repressed that most adult of activities—sex—and then found immature ways to express it (lust and permissiveness) before settling into a more mature "adult" pattern. Such readings freeze the 1960s as the boomer generation's "coming of age," rather than emphasizing it as a time when alternative religious, social, and political movements threatened the established basis of what Kathleen Hannah once called "the bullshit Christian capitalist way of doing things."[25] In this context, the Beatles have to be framed not as mainstream advocates of the underground but as naive dabblers in dangerous alternative lifestyles. Frozen in their era, their investigations have become the childish thing that has to be put away for their generation to grow up.

This idea finds its epitome in Jeff Lieberman's LSD-soaked 1978 disco horror film *Blue Sunshine*, in which there is a slightly comic moment in which two female friends are chatting casually with each other, having shared their youth and now become housewives.[26] One admonishes the other for her inability to let the Beatles go. It was as if, by then, the Fab Four had become part of collective memory: a symbol of both 1960s idealism and the baby boom generation's failure to embrace the more "adult" stresses of life in a turbulent economy.

In sum, when news of the Manson Family crimes emerged, not only was its leader framed as a variable and vicious career criminal who ordered his followers to commit grave deeds, but he was also positioned as a failed music star, a cult leader, and a deranged "Beatlemaniac" who thought he saw apocalyptic messages in the White Album, or at least used that idea to mislead his own clan. Such readings further lend themselves to suggest that Manson was *playing* with cult leadership and was in that sense a kind of adolescent figure. What is at stake in these (mis)readings of Manson is that they also, to some degree, cast doubt on the credibility of the Beatles as political radicals and spiritual seekers. By rendering the late 1960s as a phase of *adolescent* experimentation, they help to debase the credibility of role models who were exploring radically different lifestyles, challenging the status quo, making societal critiques, and seeking social justice. The new versions of society and subjectivity that they were creating through living experiments could be written off as immature and potentially protofascist cells with egomaniacal leaders.

Manson was used to deal a blow to "free love" because he could so easily be framed as an inadequate son playing at being a permissive father. My point is that this then reflects back on the Beatles and the world of alternative positions that they helped broach in the cultural mainstream. If Manson could be seen as a deranged fan *playing* at being a star musician, who then *dabbled with* being a cult leader (with deadly consequences that he could never fully own), his connection to the Beatles could then make *them* more easily seem like figures who mistook their totemic roles (as the front men of mass commodities) for positions of social leadership.

Fixing a Hole: The Issue of Race

At different times, African Americans have been seen as *both* a threat to civilization—given to sensual abandon—and the United States' "motherless child": a social group that has experienced centuries of oppression and gives a "great nation" much to feel guilty about. In *Soul on Ice*, the Black Panther dissident Eldridge Cleaver perceived the Beatles as smuggling out a Black sound to the white youth of the United States and using intellectualism as a smoke screen.[27] This makes the White Album not a warning but something that, for Cleaver was "injecting Negritude by the ton into whites in this post–Elvis Presley–beatnik era of ferment."[28] He concluded:

> For Beatle fans, having been alienated from their own Bodies so long and so deeply, the effect of these potent erotic rhythms is electric. Into this music, the Negro—as it were, drained off, as pus from a sore—a powerful sensuality, his pain and lust, his love and his hate, his ambition and his despair. The Negro projected into his music his very Body. The Beatles, the four long-haired lads from Liverpool, are offering up as their [musical] gift the Negro's Body, and in so doing establish a rhythmic communication between the listener's own Mind and Body. Enter the Beatles-soul by proxy, middlemen between the Mind and the Body.[29]

Cleaver is constantly dismissive of the Beatles for not being heterosexual, "real men." Not only does he talk about their "hordes of Ultrafeminine fans."[30] One of the things that Cleaver, correctly, I think, points out is the comparative cultivation *and* perceived relative infantilism of the Beatles. Speaking of the way that their content prioritized a whimsical version of affectionate love over the searing urgency of sex, Evan Davies claimed, "The Beatles, probably unconsciously, are servants of the white Goddess. She is elaborately catered to in their poetic content."[31] It is indicative that race is mentioned here. If rock and roll was for teenagers, there was a sense in which the Beatles' pop was for everyone, including older people and children. Take, for example, the sing-along nature of some of their songs or their animated adventures. This does not mean that the band never tackled "adult" themes but rather that its approach was characterized by a certain level of displacement or dissociation. They were often whimsical, satirical, innocent, knowing, indirect: "Fixing a Hole," as opposed to "Awopbopaloobop." As one commentator put it in 1972:

> The Beatles had, over the years, moved from straightforward, comprehensible statements of the "I Want to Hold Your Hand"–"I Saw Her Standing There" period of 1963 to the confusing and seemingly unintegrated verbal streams that are characteristic of many 1967 songs: "Lucy in the Sky with Diamonds," for example, and "I Am the Walrus." The "absurdity" of the songs was reflected in the style of album cover decorations, those of the later years being typically designed as collages of apparently unrelated and randomly selected items. Randomness can create fertile field for subjective interpretation: one man's nonsense is another's apocalypse.[32]

The White Album marked a moment when any semblance of a straightforward approach was no longer tenable. In its place was a dissociated howl of raw affect—"Helter Skelter"—a lively example of rock, a music that effectively submerged the blues and saw young white males *get serious*, allowing Mick Jagger to be accepted as an acolyte of Muddy Waters.[33] Within the Beatles, the move was epitomized in a handover between Paul McCartney, who was conventionally romantic and "nice," and John Lennon, who, arguably, was not. On the first disk of the album, Lennon's cryptic audience games on "Glass Onion" are followed on the next side by songs that supposedly inspired Charles Manson ("Blackbird" and "Piggies"). The first disk ends with "Julia," a number that explored "Lennon's semi-Oedipal obsession with his mother . . .

heavy baggage."³⁴ The next disk included McCartney's lost screams on "Helter Skelter" and the tracks "Revolution 1" and "Revolution 9" on side 4.

The Manson trial was important because it symbolically reformulated social problems as matters of personal ethics. As an evident villain, Charles Manson could also be used as a scapegoat in relation to other debates without issues of wider culpability needing to be examined. He was both/and. If one symbolic function of the trial was to reject "free love"—with all its liberal political connotations—as infantile, Oedipal misadventure, another function was arguably to reduce racial injustice to a matter of immediate personal ethics. Never mind centuries of racial oppression and material inequality. The "Helter Skelter" reading of the Family's motives drew attention to *personal paranoia* rather than systemic racism.

One theory of the Tate-LaBianca murders is that once Manson shot the drug dealer Bernard Crowe, he thought that the Black Panthers were coming after him. This led him to encourage the planting of clues at the murder sites that a race war was "coming down" and that Black radicals were responsible for the killings. Whatever his reasons for guardedly ordering the crimes, however, they were likely to be fairly mundane and immediate. This complicates the "race revolution" reading, as it means that Manson cannot quite fulfill the jester side of his role: direct murderer or not, the vile core of his being was reflected in race hatred that, ironically, caused white drifters to kill their own, more affluent compatriots. Equally, this complicates the religious signification of the White Album. The question comes home to roost in the song "Blackbird," which supposedly tackles injustice toward Black women with empathy but which Manson perverts into an indication of imminent Black discontent. In other words, though the Beatles eventually came to hover between the underground and glitterati, one way they were rendered distinct and arguably more "adult" than Manson was that they rejected racism outright and, in a sense, therefore took a degree of mature responsibility for the United States' burden. The group took an ethical stance in favor of racial equality: taking guidance from Little Richard, refusing to perform at segregated venues, and commenting on race in some of their music.³⁵ While the politics of *musical* miscegenation arguably complicate this ethical stance, it is worth remembering that from March 1969, John Lennon was in the United Kingdom's most prominent mixed-race marriage and was subject to what he called an "outpouring of race-hatred."³⁶

It is indicative there that Tom O'Neill tried his hardest to connect Charles Manson back to the US secret services and locate him as one of their assets. One irony of the apocalyptic reading and its claim about a race war is that while Manson was stirring up the specter of interracial violence in order to help his followers commit real, white-on-white bloodshed, *the US secret services had plants inside the Panthers encouraging Black radicals to create social mayhem*.[37] In other words, Manson *purportedly* succeeded in brainwashing his female "fans" to commit murder where the CIA faltered, but the intelligence services had a degree of success in demonizing Black radicalism where Manson failed.

Manson was a career criminal. In his brief period of late-sixties freedom, he also became something of a budding recording artist and commune leader. Casting him in certain ways positions him as a *vanishing mediator* who could help to lay the sixties, and a version of the Beatles with it, to rest by *explaining away* the challenge of the era's pervasive radicalism. After all, locating the decade as a period of youth culture suggests that it was simply the moment when the United States *grew up*.

And what of the Beatles? Somewhere between Manson's indictment and the trial, they split up. John Lennon later explained, "When I met her [Yoko], I had to drop everything. . . . It was 'Goodbye to the boys in the band.'"[38] He walked away from his audience, his band, and his God.

NOTES

1. The credibility of Watson's testimony has been doubted. Kelly, "Neil Sanders."
2. N. Sanders, *Now Is the Only Thing That's Real*, 67.
3. Two items appear, for example, in Mike Evan's 2004 edited volume *The Beatles Literary Anthology*: E. Sanders, "1969: Helter Skelter"; and Blake, "All You Needed Was Love," 301–4.
4. O'Neil, *Chaos*.
5. Bugliosi and Gentry, *Helter Skelter*.
6. N. Sanders, *Now Is the Only Thing That's Real*, 67–69.
7. Ibid., 70.
8. O'Neil, *Chaos*, 46.
9. The feared decline in the size of church congregations had countertrends, such as the continuing popularity of Billy Graham's crusades, the wider explosion of the Pentecostal movement, and the success among hippies of the Jesus movement (the "Jesus People"). See Hunt, "Were the Jesus People Pentecostals?"
10. Cleave, "How Does a Beatle Live?"
11. Beatles, *Anthology*, 223–26; Gould, *Can't Buy Me Love*, 346–47.
12. Kramer, *Republic of Rock*, 12.
13. Suczek, "Curious Case," 69.
14. Couldry, "Media Power," 353.
15. Amis, "Joan Didion's Style," 3–4.
16. Sheff, "Playboy Interview."
17. "Lennon Wanted for Manson Trial."
18. Oever, *Mama's Boy*, 5.
19. Bannister, "Where We Going Johnny?," 42; Weber, "Some Other Kind of Mind."
20. Christgau, "Now That We Can't Be Beatles Fans Anymore," 48.
21. Some British examples include Cliff Richard, Dick Emery, and Jimmy Savile. The notion of the arrested male as philanderer or bachelor also appeared more widely in pop culture–in Hitchcock's films or the James Bond series, for example–because it reflected contemporary issues like sexual permissiveness, women's liberation, gay rights, abortion, and rising divorce rates.
22. McLuhan, *Culture Is Our Business*, 244.
23. Melnick, *Charles Manson's Creepy Crawl*, 15.

24. Thorpe, *Jailhouse Rock.*
25. Hannah, "Riot Grrrl Manifesto."
26. Leiberman, *Blue Sunshine.*
27. Cleaver, *Soul on Ice,* 224.
28. Ibid., 233.
29. Ibid., 235.
30. Ibid., 235.
31. Davies, "Psychological Characteristics," 276.
32. Suczek, "Curious Case," 70.
33. Hamilton, *Just Around Midnight.*
34. Madmanmunt, "On the White Album."
35. Harris, "Story of Why the Beatles Refused to Play."
36. Cott, *Days That I'll Remember,* 50.
37. I am thinking here, for example, of the Bureau of Special Services and its efforts to infiltrate the Panthers in New York. Its agents unsuccessfully tried to frame the local chapter—as one newspaper explained at the time—as plotting to set off bombs and fire guns in January 1969 inside five crowded midtown Manhattan department stores, including Macy's and Bloomingdale's. Torgoff, *Lords of the Revolution.*
38. Coleman, *John Ono Lennon,* 28.

BIBLIOGRAPHY

Amis, Martin. "Joan Didion's Style." *London Review of Books* 2, no. 2 (1980): 3–4.
Bannister, Matthew. "'Where We Going Johnny?' Homosociality and the Early Beatles." In *The Routledge Research Companion to Popular Music and Gender,* edited by Stan Hawkins, 35–47. Abingdon, UK: Routledge, 2017.
Beatles. *The Beatles Anthology.* San Francisco: Chronicle Books, 1996.
Blake, John. "All You Needed Was Love." In *The Beatles Literary Anthology,* edited by Mike Evans, 301–4. London: Plexus, 2004.
Bugliosi, Vincent, and Curt Gentry. *Helter Skelter: The True Story of the Manson Murders.* London: Arrow, 2018.
Christgau, Robert. "Now That We Can't Be Beatles Fans Anymore." *Village Voice,* September 30, 1971.
Cleave, Maureen. "How Does a Beatle Live?" *Evening Standard,* March 4, 1966.
Cleaver, Eldridge. *Soul on Ice.* New York: Delta, 1999.
Coleman, Ray. *John Ono Lennon.* Vol. 2. London: Sidgwick and Jackson, 1984.
Cott, Johnathan. *Days That I'll Remember: Spending Time with John Lennon and Yoko Ono.* New York: Anchor, 2013.
Couldry, Nick. "Media Power: Some Hidden Dimensions." In *Stardom and Celebrity: A Reader,* edited by Su Holmes and Sean Redmond, 353–59. London: Sage, 2007.
Davies, Evan. "Psychological Characteristics of Beatlemania." *Journal of the History of Ideas* 30, no. 2 (1969): 273–80.
Didion, Joan. *The White Album.* New York: Farrar, Straus and Giroux, 2009.
Gould, Jonathan. *Can't Buy Me Love: The Beatles, Britain and America.* London: Piatkus, 2008.
Hamilton, Jack. *Just Around Midnight: Rock and Roll and the Racial Imagination.* Cambridge: Harvard University Press, 2016.
Hannah, Kathleen. "Riot Grrrl Manifesto." *Bikini Kill Zine* 2 (1991). History Is a Weapon. https://www.historyisaweapon.com/defcon1/riotgrrrlmanifesto.html.
Harris, Sonya. "The Story of Why the Beatles Refused to Play in Front of Segregated Audiences." *My Modern Met,* August 1, 2020.
Hunt, Stephen J. "Were the Jesus People Pentecostals?" *PentecoStudies* 7, no. 1 (2008): 1–33.
Kelly, Tim. "Neil Sanders on His Book *Now Is the Only Thing That's Real.*" *Our Interesting Times* (podcast), December 18, 2017.
Kramer, Michael. *The Republic of Rock: Music and Citizenship in the Sixties Counterculture.* New York: Oxford University Press, 2013.
"Lennon Wanted for Manson Trial." *Daily Kent Starter,* October 29, 1970.
Lieberman, Jeff, dir. *Blue Sunshine.* Cinema Shares International, 1978. Film.
Madmanmunt. "On the White Album." *The Beatles White Album Project* (blog), March 19, 2005. https://www.thewhitealbumproject.com/reviews/on-the-white-album/.
McLuhan, Marshall. *Culture Is Our Business.* Eugene, OR: Wipf and Stock, 2014.

Melnick, Jeffrey. *Charles Manson's Creepy Crawl: The Many Lives of America's Most Infamous Family*. New York: Arcade, 2018.

Oever, Roel van den. *Mama's Boy: Momism and Homophobia in American Culture*. Basingstoke, UK: Palgrave, 2012.

O'Neil, Tom. *Chaos: The Truth Behind the Manson Murders*. London: Windmill Books, 2019.

Sanders, Ed. "1969: Helter Skelter." In *The Beatles Literary Anthology*, edited by Mike Evans, 298–300. London: Plexus, 2004.

Sanders, Neil. *Now Is the Only Thing That's Real: A Re-examination of the Manson Murders, Motives and Mythos*. Nottingham, UK: Number Six Dance, 2017.

Sheff, David. "Playboy Interview with John Lennon and Yoko Ono." *Playboy*, September 1981.

Suczek, Barbara. "The Curious Case of the Death of Paul McCartney." *Urban Life and Culture* 1, no. 1 (1972): 61–76.

Thorpe, Richard, dir. *Jailhouse Rock*. Beverly Hills, CA: Metro-Goldwyn-Mayer, 1957. Film.

Torgoff, Martin. *Lords of the Revolution: The Black Panthers Documentary*. VH1 Productions, 2009. Film.

Weber, Erin Torkelson. "Some Other Kind of Mind: Book Review, *The Beatles with Lacan*, by Henry Sullivan, 1995, Part 1." *The Historian and The Beatles* (blog), June 19, 2018. https://beatlebioreview.wordpress.com/2018/06/19/some-other-kind-of-mind-book-review-the-beatles-with-lacan-by-henry-sullivan-1995-part-i/.

CHAPTER 11

Sanctum or Artifact?

The Beatles' Music in *Yesterday*

CHRISTIANE MEISER

Fictitious music films and the lives of real, famous musicians often overlap: we know many successful music films about, for example, Mozart, Ray Charles, Eminem, and many others. Films like these often show a turning point in the life of a famous musician or give a biographical overview of that life.[1] Only rarely does one see a narrative configuration as in the movie *Yesterday*.[2] In this film, the story is not primarily about the Beatles, although the movie is full of their music. As I will show in this chapter, *Yesterday* presents above all the *music* of the Beatles as something sacred. Fittingly, the supposed genius behind the music, Jack, is perceived as a messiah on one level, while on another level, the events of the film turn him from impostor to medium of the sacred music of the Beatles.

The plot's inciting incident is a global blackout, after which the music of the Beatles is wiped from history. Every memory of them, all material proofs of their existence, and every digital footprint on the internet are gone. The protagonist, Jack, believes that he is the only one who remembers the Beatles' songs, and he's determined to bring them back to the world—while passing them off as his own. This narrative constellation brings together two different kinds of film-viewing experiences on two different media levels: whereas *Yesterday*'s viewers are likely to be well versed in the Beatles' music—they already know the songs and may even connect them with their own cultural commemoration—the intradiegetic (that is, in-story) characters hear this music for the very first time. These two levels operate at once. While some disparity in knowing about the success of a group is common to films about real-life musicians, it is far less common in the genre of music films to tell the story of an altogether different act (Jack) while ignoring the real-life phenomenon that made it possible. The Beatles' story is never fully addressed in *Yesterday*, because the movie is not a retelling of the band's history.[3] If we keep these two layers of narration in mind, the movie constantly plays with what the film viewers recognize and the intradiegetic listeners newly come to appreciate. So, to viewers of *Yesterday*, the Beatles are, at the same time, existing and extinct.

Because the story erases the Beatles from history, the movie can't directly deal with the extraordinary cultural phenomenon that the Beatles were—which would be the conventional way for a music film relating to existing music stars. This dramaturgical peculiarity certainly reflects the Beatles' special sense of humor. As a consequence of this narrative unpossibility, the focus shifts toward the songs and only the songs. They have to be recollected by Jack, and in doing this act of restoration, Jack makes it his first priority to remember everything correctly and not to reprocess all the artistic work and various influences that originally were part of the songs' creation. The result of this setting is that we hardly see any artistic confrontation with the songs and their possible meanings. At the same time, the movie suggests, it is only the music that affects the masses, to the extent that Jack becomes as famous as Ed Sheeran.

What we do see in relation to the music is that it has an existential meaning for Jack and his fans. This reading can be taken from different scenes that are deliberately staged to show Jack's rise as a music star in filmic shortcuts: cheering fans resembling Beatlemania crowds, visuals of rising numbers of fans illustrated by internet clicks, "likes," and a journalist calling Jack "the Shakespeare of pop music." So, the film uses many external symbols in order to show that Jack is, in fact, very famous and successful thanks to the Beatles' music. However, at the same time, the film, which operates as both a comedy and a music film, doesn't explore the artistic performance and the meaning of the songs. As Owen Gleiberman explains in his review of the film, "In 'Yesterday,' the greatness of the Beatles is like a trump card that Jack, and the filmmakers, keep playing. Yet the greatness of the Beatles is never something the film invites us to discover." It's narratively posited that the music *is* great—and many film viewers would naturally agree—while the narration doesn't provide answers for how Jack or the listeners might interpret the songs or how it affects them. As the film is nevertheless convincing that Jack's (or, rather, the Beatles') music is most successfully conquering the world (again), one can ask from a narratological point of view how the film manages to let the music appear so brilliant when, at the same time, there's a lack of narrative engagement in the music's meaning. In my view, the film is able to conjure this effect by staging the music as sacred, but something *indifferently sacred*, as I show below.

Act One: The Sin

The first turning point in the movie's narrative structure is when Jack realizes that the Beatles never existed in this kind of displaced reality. He comes to realize that, somehow, since the blackout, the Beatles were erased from the world; he finds no traces of them online or in his carefully curated LP collection. As soon as this news sinks in, the camera displays Jack's list of unsuccessful songs to set up his idea to use the Beatles' songs to further his own career. After his closest friend, Lily, promises him that she doesn't know the Beatles, Jack walks through the raining city, sees his reflection in a window, and asks himself, "Am I gonna do this? Can I do this?" This sequence takes place at night, a thunderstorm visually and acoustically enhancing the dramatic impact in addition to the increasingly speeding-up electric sounds conveying Jack's inner stress. By creating this sequence within this apocalyptic atmosphere, the movie frames this narrative thread of passing off the Beatles' music as his own as Jack's personal fall of humankind. Insofar as Jack knowingly chooses to do wrong and thus betrays his idealized music gods—the Beatles—the film's narrative logic presents this decision as a kind of original sin. Only with the help of John Lennon's transcendent figure will he find a way back to do right. In contrast to Jack's confession at the end of the film, which is visually dominated by light, the story's triggering sequence puts Jack in the dark and alone.

Once Jack has been introduced to the music-industry world with a little help from his newest friend, Ed Sheeran, he makes acquaintance with his soon-to-be manager, Debra, who actively adds a religious aura around Jack and his music to the narrative. Her character functions as a kind of Mephistophelian figure, as Richard Brody points out in his film review.[4] This characterization seems to be quite accurate given the fact that she promises him the fulfillment of his dreams in exchange for what turns out to be his soul. While Debra's diabolical side is easily found to be ruled by capitalistic impulses, she also conjures a religious disposition both around stardom and then around Jack as a star. This can be seen, for example, in a scene in which Debra and Jack decide to work together. Debra wants to make sure Jack is willing to give everything in order to become a music star. She shows him his opportunities. Defying Jack's indecision, she says, "Buddy, what I'm offering you is the great and glorious poisoned chalice of money and fame. If you don't want to drink it, which I would understand, go back and have a warm beer in little, bonny England. If you do want to drink it, I need to hear you say, 'Debra, I'm so thirsty. Give me the goddamn chalice.' So, which is it?" Jack answers, "I'll take the chalice."

With this metaphor, not only is the pact between Debra and Jack sealed, but also the narration foreshadows Jack's upcoming success. As the dialogue uses the specifically religiously significant noun "chalice," it postulates a transcendent element in a music star's career. As the story progresses, Debra mystifies Jack's public persona by releasing five songs online without showing him in person. The marketing strategy to evoke "the enigma Jack Malik" pays off immediately; the public excitedly awaits Jack's appearance, as film viewers learn in a montage of enthusiastic reactions to the first released songs. The expectation of the fans is also religiously significant insofar as the rising star is Jack *Malik*; the word *malik* is a Semitic expression for "king."[5] So, another religious motif is displayed here: people are in earnest expectation of Jack as a game-changing, pop-music king.

Stepping back from the plot point of view, the film shows its audience that the Beatles' music immediately becomes a global success, even though the public excitement seems to be in equal parts about the enigma Jack and the upcoming album. But again, as Gleiberman states, the film shows the audience excitement as a given, whereas it doesn't explore what is so great about the songs, why people connect with them, and why they are an immediate success. This may show that *Yesterday*'s screenwriter and director consider the Beatles' music powerful enough on its own, but the film does not by itself establish this impression. Rather than belaboring the point, however, in this section, I'm interested in analyzing the result of this narrative strategy. Insofar as Debra frames Jack's image for the intradiegetic audience, she also frames the film audience's impression of Jack. Her praising of his enormous influence on the music world culminates in referring to Ed Sheeran as "John the Baptist," because it was his role to recognize Jack's potential and make him known. In this picture, Sheeran only paves the way for "the Messiah," Jack. The frantic masses of fans confirm that prospect.

The "major marketing meeting of meetings" scene underscores the idea that both music and musician are treated as sacred. In this meeting, Jack and a ridiculously large number of marketing employees discuss the cover of Jack's album. Whereas Jack tries to apply some of the original album titles and parts of the visuals from the Beatles' album covers, the marketing department, unified against Jack's misunderstood suggestions, settles on the album title *One Man Only*. Thus, the focus on the ingenious element of Jack writing all his songs on his own (as he claims) intensifies, in reference to both Jack's image and his inner doubts. The momentum of Jack's genius also surfaces when Sheeran wants to talk about Jack's artistic process. The story uses Sheeran to uphold the narrated assumption that Jack is an unprecedented musical genius such that one of the current most successful songwriters bows before this greatness. Bracketing out Jack's increasing desperation caused by his authorship-lie, *Yesterday* clearly presents the music and its creator(s) as ingenious and religiously significant.

Act Two: Craving for Salvation

Jack's personal suffering stands in stark contrast to his shining image. From the beginning of his newly invigorated career with the Beatles' songs, Jack rarely seems actually happy despite having his lifelong dream at hand. He suffers from the knowledge that he is a fraud, taking credit for the work of his idols, the Beatles. A part of his struggle is also to reconstruct some of the songs he wants to put on his album, especially "Eleanor Rigby" and "Penny Lane." Here again the movie shows an unconventional musical situation: Jack doesn't actually compose the songs himself. To stimulate his memory and legitimize the references to Liverpool in his songs, he travels to Liverpool—a Mecca of sorts for Beatles fans—and visits some of the iconic Beatles locations. These, of course, are only iconic to Jack and the film's viewers; Jack's roadie and friend, Rocky, doesn't understand the significance of the locations they visit or why Liverpool deserves his respect. Of course, Jack's main task is it to remember as many songs as completely as he is able, and from this perspective, the movie is more concerned with cultural heritage than with the creative artistic process (more on this below).

Jack's inner conflict, due in part to his miserable love life and in part to his public deception, reaches a climax as his album release, accompanied by a rooftop concert, comes closer.[6] His desperation finds expression in the song "Help!," which Jack performs at the concert and can be understood quite literally in this context. After the show, Jack actually does get help when he meets a man and a woman who also remember the Beatles. But instead of exposing his deceit, they thank him for preserving the music, because, as the woman says, "a world without the Beatles is a world that's infinitely worse. So, thank you. And use it well." This line encapsulates the essential meaning the movie gives to the Beatles' music. So, surprisingly, Jack is celebrated not only by the masses who believe he is the genius behind the music but also by the only other two people who have retained knowledge of the Beatles after the blackout. They value the Beatles' music in their lives so highly that it doesn't seem to matter to them that Jack lies about the authorship. In addition to their appreciation, Jack gets help from them in another way: they give him the address of the John Lennon who is still living in this parallel universe.

Jack immediately sets out to find Lennon, who has become a sailor, pursues his painting, and apparently has not engaged in a musical career. Lennon is bewildered by Jack's reverence toward him. As they talk about life, love, and happiness, Lennon turns to Jack and tells him, "You want a good life? It's not complicated. Tell the girl you love that you love her. And tell the truth to everyone, whenever you can." Visually, the scene takes place at a beach in front of Lennon's house on a bright, sunny day; a very calm atmosphere is set. The culmination of this sequence is Jack hugging Lennon after this advice. They rise from a sitting position while the camera is positioned slightly lower, which creates a low-angle shot. In addition, the two men stand directly between the camera and the light of the sinking sun, resulting in a silhouetted image of them as shadows over which sunlight refracts. In the construction toward this final image, John stands up reluctantly while the camera is already in the low-angle shot position. The effect of this cinematographic technique is that Lennon almost can't be recognized because of the bright ray of sunlight, while the already standing Jack is being shot from the opposite site, that is to say, behind Lennon. This sequence is accompanied by soft, increasingly intensifying and ethereal organ sounds that climax when Jack hugs Lennon. The effect of this mise-en-scène is the impression that the figure of John Lennon has a transcendent power and by hugging him, the earthly Jack is able connect with that kind of power.

In my view, the staging of this scene shows an epiphany on different levels. First, it completes the arc that began in the dark moment of Jack's decision to pass off the music of the Beatles as his own. Whereas in the stormy night, he chooses a path of false witnessing, with the help of the godlike figure of Lennon, Jack finds his way back to light and happiness. The narrative of the fight between dark and light, both as external entities and internal impulses, is a common religious cipher in narrations that are being unfolded visually throughout the movie.[7] As Matthias Fritsch, Martin Lindwedel, and Thomas Schärtl explain, the dualism of dark and light harks back to gnostic texts representing the dualism of being close to a godly entity or not.[8] For viewers, it is possible to decode the essential meaning of this scene on the basis of the visuals alone.

Before this scene, Jack believed John Lennon to be dead, murdered in 1980. His resurrection, therefore, is a transcendent moment, and Jack's getting to know one of his idols seems to be an experience that is not of this world. Again, both narrative levels are operating at once: the film's audience is in Jack's position of having extradiegetic knowledge of Lennon's death, while the intradiegetic situation means that Lennon is alive in this parallel universe. Even without the context of the initializing "dark scene," the significant use of light can be understood as a symbol for a religious experience. According to Fritsch et al., having an experience with God is commonly represented in Platonic philosophy with light-related metaphors that have long been continued in filmic arrangements.[9] The figure of Lennon surrounded by glistening light and Jack's embrace of him gives Lennon a transcendent, godlike aura that is consistent with the existential meaning Jack puts into this encounter: "The vision of light-flooded existence stands as a cipher for the transformation of the material into spirit, for boundary expanding and transcendence."[10] In the moment when Lennon is being light-flooded, he is both revealed and concealed from clear view, which indicates the transcendent as being "something that underlies the visible but remains elusive," as Natalie Fritz et al. describe representations of transcendence.[11] In this context, the transcendent experience empowers Jack to follow Lennon's instructions. But the scene's transcendence is about more than the light; in fact, the entire set collaborates to religious effect. As noted by Fritz et al., not only light but also sun, ocean, and wind are symbols of transcendence.[12] The encounter with Lennon, moreover, brings to the fore the name of the protagonist: insofar as "Jack" is a derivative form of "John," the film already marks Jack's discipleship with the transcendent figure, Lennon. Jack's redemption is well on its way when he says that he no longer needs psychiatric therapy now that he has met and spoke with Lennon. The effect is comedic, but this does not detract from Jack's actual, existential relief.

Jack is now encouraged to end his episode of defrauding his most revered sanctuary. As Lennon counsels him to tell Ellie about his love and also to tell the truth, he makes Jack aware of the things that existentially matter to him.

To sum up, the scene of the epiphany gives the protagonist a new belief set and an instruction for action. By doing so, *Yesterday* closes the dark chapter of Jack's taking credit for an artistic work that has become sacred to every listener. For Jack, acting as a stand-in for the extradiegetic viewer, the encounter becomes *super*natural when he meets the figure of John Lennon.

Act Three: The Confession

Jack worships John Lennon so much that he follows his instructions exactly. In order to obey Lennon's commandments, Jack uses a concert of Ed Sheeran for a last appearance, in which he plays a few of the most popular songs, including "All You Need Is Love." During this song—which, in this context, can be seen as a hymn that follows Lennon's advice—the listeners in the audience create a sea of lights with their phones. After the song, which also may serve as a reassurance for Jack of what Lennon advised him to do, Jack makes a confession to Ellie, and the stadium acts as a *pars pro toto* for the world. He says:

> This is Ellie. And when I had no fans, Ellie was my only fan, the only person in the world who believed in me. And that's why tonight I asked Ed if I could come on and play, because I want to tell her, and you, what I've done. Darn it, Ellie, I've been untrue. All the songs I've sung tonight were really written and performed by four men called John Lennon, Paul McCartney, George Harrison, and Ringo Starr, the Beatles. They were the real geniuses. Me, I'm just a sort of go-between to, well, get their astonishing stuff into the world. And I passed their amazing work off as my own so I could look like I was amazing, too. [The crowd starts jeering.] I want you all to know that I'm not going to take any money for this work that isn't mine. So, you can have all the songs for free. Rocky, do it.

"Right," Rocky says. "Here goes," as he uploads the songs. Jack then says, "They're being released, for free, online now. And I'd love to not take any more praise for it. So, um, I'm so sorry. And while I'm at it, there's one other thing to say as well, because I've been a fool twice over. And I want to thank Ellie for her love. And, Ellie, Elle, I love you. I always have, always."

After the announcement of the free songs and especially after the confession of love, the crowd cheers again and sees Jack off with a tremendous applause. There are shouts of praise and a reactivation of the sea of lights, invoking again the spiritual connotation of light mentioned above. This eruption of the mass is shown from an extreme high-angle shot so that the look of the shot conveys the impression of unified forgiveness and appreciation for the music and the love confession.

A closer look at Jack's confession speech demonstrates that he not only does everything Lennon told him but also finds a solution to the strange reality that makes him one of only three people who know the Beatles' songs. In the form of a "go-between," Jack wants to serve as a medium between the world and the music, a person bringing something to this world to which no one else has access. In this sense, Jack can be understood as a prophet. The story points out how important the music has become for the masses of fans, but Jack's confession releases him from his secret. Consequently, Jack's mission becomes to preserve the Beatles' cultural heritage. This dissolves the question of Jack's artistic contribution, as he always has been remembering and not creating the music. Jack can act as a medium to a pop-cultural sanctum (Beatles music), without betraying his gods, John, Paul, George, and Ringo.

The end of the film shows the implementation of Lennon's commandment about love. In a montage, the images alternate between Jack singing "Ob-La-Di, Ob-La-Da" with schoolchildren and prolepses of the happy married life of Jack and Ellie, who become a family much like Desmond and Molly Jones. The future of the Beatles' music fades into the background, which brings us to the last issue.

A Tame Beatles-Religion of Love

Reflecting the different types of narrative strategies described so far, this text faces a problem, as mentioned earlier: *Yesterday* uses narrative and cinematographic strategies to mark the music of the Beatles and the musicians themselves, represented by the figure of John Lennon, as sacred. The music is pictured in so brilliant a manner that even Ed Sheeran admits his inferiority to the genius behind it, calling himself Salieri to Jack's Mozart. Yet, at the same time, and here I'm following Gleiberman, the film doesn't explore the music.[13] The film mainly shows the emotion induced by the music before Jack's big breakthrough, for example, when he plays "Yesterday" to his friends. As soon as Jack has become a star, the story doesn't engage in telling why the music has this decisive effect on so many people. One could argue that the movie postulates a self-sufficiency of the music, meaning that the songs themselves are powerful enough to affect the masses. The movie strips off all the cultural knowledge and myths about the Beatles, as it puts only their music in the spotlight. According to the story, it is not the glamorous person of Jack (or anything other than the music) that leads to its enormous success. What matters is the music, not the context. The assumption here is that the music itself could generate a worldwide phenomenon close to the historic "Beatlemania." *Yesterday*, therefore, features plenty of examples to show that the Beatles' music could reach the same level of religious significance in this parallel universe as in ours, but the film also provides no explanation for why or how the music becomes sacred for this new audience that receives the music under completely different cultural circumstances.

To reflect on one of the central questions of this book, whether the Beatles had a religious or antireligious message, *Yesterday* doesn't allow an easy answer, so I offer two conjectures: first, regarding the movie as a discrete work of art, it seems that in fact it isn't a specific music-related (substantial) message that the film wants to convey; instead, the aura created by the film's inclusion of the Beatles music and the figure of John Lennon seems to be religious itself. In the way the narrative enfolds, *Yesterday* seems to present the Beatles and their music *as a religious heritage* rather than a message within the music itself. From that perspective, Jack can be seen more as a preserver of a cultural heritage that would have been lost after the blackout. By tuning out the political, social, and religious aspects of the Beatles and focusing only on the music, the viewer receives a clean, bourgeois, and tame version of the Beatles. Similar to the concept of "patchwork religion," the postmodern culture—in the form of this film—doesn't insist on immersing itself in the phenomenon of the Beatles in its entirety. Instead, the priority is to feel good, which becomes increased by the love-story arc. Because the story does not address the interpretation of the music, *Yesterday* turns the extraordinary phenomenon of the Beatles into a legacy, an artifact. In this story, the Beatles become a cultural heritage, which means the nostalgic perspective becomes the dominating one. So, it appears that the first message is that the Beatles' music has a religious power, but *Yesterday*'s story isn't very keen to explore a religious message in the music itself; hence, it presents the Beatles and their music as something *indifferently sacred*.

With that said, a closer look at the figure of John Lennon in the film is revealing and religiously significant. By telling Jack to always tell the truth and to tell Ellie about his love, Lennon presents a religious message not in the sense of dogmatic or denominational truths but for Jack's individual belief system. Lennon's message offers Jack a way back into a contented and happy life. Since the story links "All You Need Is Love" to Jack's confession, both in reference to the music's authorship and to the confession of love, this song can be understood as a spiritual guideline that Jack received from Lennon. This perspective would be in line with Steve Turner's suggestion that the Beatles advocated for the religious idea of love.[14] According to Turner, it was Lennon who'd make "great shaman material," so in addition to his mythical aura, his figure is well suited to be a spiritual leader to Jack—even if their meet-up happened as involuntarily and casually as in the film.[15] What is more, one finds Zen influences in Lennon's intradiegetic minimalism, shared by the real John Lennon.[16] Lennon imparts to Jack the insight that having a good life "isn't complicated." Moreover, connecting "All You Need Is Love" with Lennon's advice opens links to a biblical perspective of love, thus underlining the religious impact of Lennon's counsel.[17] In promoting a religion of love, the Beatles proved to be ahead of their time, taking into account that sociologists claim an earthly religion of love at the beginning of the twenty-first century.[18] But while during the sixties, the Beatles strived to global peace through love (and, for a while, through hallucinogenic drugs), the phenomenon of a love religion, as described by Beck and Beck-Gernsheim, turned out to relocate the center of the belief system toward the inwardness of a couple's individuals.[19] This shift is mirrored in *Yesterday*'s ending, as the movie concentrates the happy end entirely on the marriage of Ellie and Jack and the founding of their family. *Yesterday*, of course, is not only a music film but also a romantic comedy, and the film is committed to this genre as well. Taking into account the screenplay writer, Richard Curtis, who is most known for his romantic comedies, it's not surprising that the religious message of the film turns out to be about romantic love between two people and not the utopian counterculture idea of a power of love that brings peace to the world. Nevertheless, *Yesterday* also tells us something about how the music of the Beatles is pictured in the twenty-first century.

In conclusion, Danny Boyle's *Yesterday* implies two sanctities: First is the commandment of love and truth that is being declared by the intradiegetic transcendent figure of John Lennon toward his follower, Jack. Second, the Beatles' music appears as a sacred artifact worth saving. However, the music's sacredness is presented as a given, without need for reflection or vindication.[20]

NOTES

1. Kuhn, "Biopic."
2. Boyle, *Yesterday*. The narrative of Gurinder Chadha's *Blinded by the Light*, also a movie released in 2019, operates similarly, by telling a story about a young man for whom the music of Bruce Springsteen has a life-changing effect. In the movie, the pop star and the protagonist never meet in person, but the extrafictional knowledge of Springsteen's music and career cannot be separated within the viewing process.

3. The film *Yellow Submarine* by the Beatles also tells of a parallel universe in which the band does not exist. But *Yellow Submarine*, as Gary Mulholland writes, "is all about the overall mise en scène, not the plot," which is the main focus here (*Popcorn*, 78).

4. Brody, "Danny Boyle's Comedic Fantasy."

5. Hoch, *Semitic Words in Egyptian Texts*, 144–45.

6. This is, of course, another one of the countless references to the Beatles. Within this chapter, however, I only take them and also the many wordplays into account when needed for the specific argumentation, as there could surely be an entire book about following every intradiegetic clue to the Beatles.

7. Fritsch, Lindwedel, and Schärtl, *Wo nie zuvor ein Mensch gewesen ist*, 95–98.

8. Ibid., 95.

9. Ibid., 99.

10. Ibid., 100. My translation; originally, "Die Vision lichtdurchfluteter Existenz steht als Chiffre für die Verwandlung des Materiellen in Geist, für Entschränkung und Transzendenz."

11. Fritz et al., *Sichtbare Religion*, 86. My translation; originally, "Transzendenzdarstellungen als der Ausdruck von etwas, das dem Sichtbaren zugrunde liegt, aber entzogen bleibt."

12. Ibid., 85.

13. The film *Bohemian Rhapsody*, for example, can be used as a counterexample. Here, too, songs already known to film audiences are presented in a new way through the film. The film, which tells the story of the band Queen, is devoted in detail to the significance that music has, especially for the protagonist, Freddie Mercury. Another example is the film *A Star Is Born*, a romantic drama and a music film in which a singer searches for the way to her own sound. In both films, music is decisively elaborated on by addressing music in general and also specific songs in terms of their significance for the protagonists. This makes it clear to the film audience *why* certain songs are so important intradiegetically and not just *that* they are important.

14. Turner, *Gospel*.

15. Ibid., 6.

16. Ibid., 160.

17. Ibid., 11.

18. Beck and Beck-Gernsheim, *Das ganz normale Chaos der Liebe*.

19. Turner, *Gospel*, 127; Beck and Beck-Gernsheim, *Das ganz normale Chaos der Liebe*, 231–36.

20. In comparison to the daunting essential questions that the Beatles process in their art, which entails love as well as transcendence but also drugs and destructive drives, the movie evades this profundity in order to create a romantic comedy. Whereas the Beatles' albums had been burned because John Lennon made the well-known Jesus comparison, there is no such spiritual and aesthetic conflict within the narration. Without questioning the legitimacy of that, one can ask if the movie actually does the cultural heritage of the Beatles a favor.

BIBLIOGRAPHY

Beck, Ulrich, and Elisabeth Beck-Gernsheim. *Das ganz normale Chaos der Liebe*. Frankfurt am Main: Suhrkamp, 2005.

Boyle, Danny, dir. *Yesterday*. Written by Richard Curtis, featuring Himesh Patel, Lily James, Ed Sheeran, and Kate McKinnon. Cantley, UK: Universal Pictures, 2019. Film.

Brody, Richard. "Danny Boyle's Comedic Fantasy About a World Without the Beatles." Review of *Yesterday*. *New Yorker*, June 29, 2019.

Chadha, Gurinder, dir. *Blinded by the Light*. Burbank, CA: New Line Cinema, 2019. Film.

Cooper, Bradley, dir. *A Star Is Born*. Beverly Hills, CA: MGM, 2018. Film.

Fritsch, Matthias J., Martin Lindwedel, and Thomas Schärtl. *Wo nie zuvor ein Mensch gewesen ist: Science-Fiction-Filme: Angewandte Philosophie und Theologie*. Regensburg, Germany: Pustet, 2003.

Fritz, Natalie, Anna-Katharina Höpflinger, Stefanie Knauß, Marie-Therese Mäder, and Daria Pezzoli-Olgiati. *Sichtbare Religion: Eine Einführung in die Religionswissenschaft*. Berlin: de Gruyter, 2018.

Gleiberman, Owen. Review of *Yesterday*. *Variety*, May 4, 2019.

Hoch, James E. *Semitic Words in Egyptian Texts of the New Kingdom and Third Intermediate Period*. Princeton: Princeton University Press, 1994.

Kuhn, Markus. "Biopic." In *Filmwissenschaftliche Genreanalyse: Eine Einführung*, edited by Markus Kuhn, Irina Scheidgen, and Nicola Valeska Weber, 213–39. Berlin: de Gruyter, 2013.

Mulholland, Garry. *Popcorn: Fifty Years of Rock 'n' Roll Movies*. London: Orion, 2010.

Singer, Bryan, dir. *Bohemian Rhapsody*. Century City, CA: Twentieth Century Fox, 2018. Film.

Turner, Steve. *The Gospel According to the Beatles*. Louisville, KY: Westminster John Knox Press, 2006.

CHAPTER 12

Necrolennonolatry

The Postmortem Adventures of John Lennon

MURRAY LEEDER

So often we hear John Lennon evoked through absence. At *Come Together: A Night for John Lennon's Words and Music* (2001), a tribute concert held less than a month after the September 11 attacks, a not-yet-disgraced Kevin Spacey described himself as "incredibly pissed off." He said, "I'm outraged because this passionate prophet of peace and so many others are not with us, because we live in an all too violent world. . . . It's up to all of us to do what we can to not only keep John's songs alive but to help rebuild New York." Lennon provided a particularly good example of the "illusion of intimacy" between a celebrity and their audience, and the crime of December 8, 1980, not only robbed Lennon of the remainder of his life but deprived the public of his continued presence as a singer/songwriter, as a social actor, and, critically, as a living symbol.[1] The sociologist Fred Fogo has written about how Lennon came to represent the Utopian aspects of the 1960s, with his death signifying their final demise.[2]

It can equally be said, however, that Lennon's tragic death secured his legacy, or at least a particular benign and institutionalized version of it. It is hard to imagine that official sites of memorialization like Strawberry Fields in Central Park or the Liverpool John Lennon Airport existing without his death. Though Lennon had been subject of much debate in the years after his death,³ time has seen him solidify into a largely uncontroversial cultural icon, fit even for children's books.⁴ But his presence has been felt in other, less official ways, as some people claim that he has been a frequent visitor to séances both private and public, repeatedly spotted at sites of personal significance, and has even authored a number of books from beyond the grave. If the course of Lennon's life made him, as Steve Turner puts it, "great shaman material," then after his death, he has also made great ghost material.⁵ This phenomenon fits into a much more extensive phenomenon of what Helen Sword refers to as "necrobibliography," books that claim provenance from the afterlife through channeling. Playing on Sword's coinage "necrobardology" for the veneration of the spectral Shakespeare, I use "necrolennonolatry" to draw together the disparate claims of contact with the ghostly or spiritual postmortem John Lennon, especially when they involve creative production.⁶ This chapter argues for the importance of this spectral legacy, examining it within the historical practices of spiritualism as they intersect with authorship, religion, celebrity, and entertainment.

In My Afterlife

Lennon's murder became a paradigmatic example of a sudden, shocking death of a beloved (if also controversial) celebrity. In particular, it is associated with the galvanizing of the public into spontaneous mass mourning, represented by widely distributed image of crowds surrounding the Dakota.⁷ Memorialization of Lennon tends to center around the date of his death—this was dramatically the case for its forty-year anniversary in 2020—rather than his birthday or another landmark. If Lennon the individual famously struggled with his star image—and that tension between fame-loving rock star and hermetic recluse ironically *became* his star image for his last years—he has provided a decidedly polysemic signifier in death.

Directly across the street from the Dakota sits the headquarters of the American Society for Psychical Research (ASPR); my research trip there in 2011 also facilitated a pilgrimage to the site of the assassination of a childhood idol of mine, who happened to die around fifteen months before my birth. Founded in 1884, the ASPR was one of numerous organizations of the period designed for the sober and scientific investigation of ghosts, psychic powers, haunted sites, and the like. This only partially successful scientification of the supernatural came at a time of mass interest in the topic of communication with the dead and the relative mainstreaming of spiritualism as a complicated religious, scientific, and entertainment phenomenon. Spiritualists often claimed that knowledge of their contact with the spirit realm would usher in a glorious spiritual awakening on Earth, and its claims to put mourners in contact with the deceased led to spikes in its popularity during major conflicts like the US Civil War and World War I. Spiritualism was tied closely to the explosion of media culture in the nineteenth century, and many scholars have examined the entanglement of spiritualism with the invention of the telegraph, photograph, and other new technologies of inscription and transmission.[8] Simone Natale has shown the extent to which spiritualism was also imbricated with the emergence of mass celebrity and entertainment cultures. Though "belief in ghosts, haunted houses, and spirit communications existed . . . long before the advent of spiritualism," Natale writes, "the spiritualist movement succeeded in incorporating those beliefs into the growing market for entertainment and spectacular attractions. The extent to which spiritualism participated in this market is a distinctive characteristic of the movement that most sets it apart from previous forms of belief in supernatural and ghost entities."[9] That market is still alive, as evidenced by the robust industry of purportedly nonfiction supernatural books and the popularity of ghost-hunting reality television programs like *Most Haunted* (2002–20) and *Ghost Hunters* (2004–20).

A loose parallel can be drawn between Lennon and Abraham Lincoln, another figure whose favorable legacy was secured by his assassination. The level of Lincoln's personal interest in spiritualism has been debated, but after his death, he became a favorite visitor to séances.[10] In 1922, the ghost of Lincoln was reported as having been spotted on the set of the prospiritualist film *The Bishop of the Ozarks* (1923), acting as a kind of postmortem acting coach.[11] In life, the magpie-ish Lennon apparently had a periodic interest in contacting the dead, though in typical form, he seems to have vacillated between the role of hopeful believer and scoffing cynic. His own life was famously shaped by grief and loss, and according to his childhood friend Nigel Whalley, he attempted a séance to contact his dead mother, Julia, just months after her death.[12] More larkishly, he hosted a séance by a pair of professional mediums in the Dakota and satirized them in a story called "The Incredible Mediocre Rabbits," itself published posthumously in *Skywriting by Word of Mouth* (1986).[13] Lennon and Yoko Ono were also alleged to have held a séance with Jessie Ryan, the wife of the actor Robert Ryan, who had earlier lived and died in their apartment in the Dakota.[14]

Anthony Elliott writes, "We have been told that John Lennon 'is the spirit of a generation.' As a transcendent hero, Lennon haunts our culture."[15]

Although Elliott is speaking metaphorically, this haunting has also been quite literal. It did not take long after Lennon's death for supernatural encounters with him to begin. A medium named Bill Tenuto, it is claimed, channeled him in 1983, as did an anonymous Boston couple who allowed the author Arthur Myers to speak with him.[16] Myers also cataloged some manifestations of Lennon at the moment of his death and the apparent prognostication of his death by the psychic Eugenia Macer-Story.[17] One person even claims to have seen the figure of Lennon on the cover of a Beatles album come to life, look at him, and say, "Let it be"—citing a McCartney song, curiously enough.[18] Lennon's ghost is claimed to "roam the Dakota building, appearing to bandmates and family," even appearing to Ono at their famous white piano, and also to manifest on the West Coast.[19] The model Robin Givens encountered it in the West Hollywood apartment that he once occupied.[20] Back in Liverpool, a dog walker claimed to have spotted the ghosts of Lennon and Aunt Mimi outside Strawberry Field.[21] There are numerous other examples. Lennon's ghost is as geographically unbound as his fame.

Another persistent motif is postmortem interactions between Lennon and other musicians, often linked with the creative process. In 1987, the tabloid *National Enquirer* claimed that Michael Jackson interacted with Lennon's ghost on multiple occasions after Jackson purchased most of the Beatles catalog and that Lennon gave him a green light to license "Revolution" to Nike.[22] In 1981, Carl Perkins wrote a song called "My Old Friend," performed as a duet with Paul McCartney during the sessions for *Tug of War* (1981), McCartney's first album fully recorded after Lennon's death; Perkins reportedly believed that "John had written the song from beyond and given it to him for Paul."[23] Liam Gallagher of Oasis has repeatedly spoken about seeing Lennon's ghost, including while recording with McCartney.[24] During the production of the *Beatles Anthology*, the three surviving Beatles faced the intrinsically spectral task of reworking Lennon's "Free as a Bird" into a brand-new Beatles song (with Lennon's home-demo-quality vocals suggesting someone singing from another world). Says McCartney, "We even put one of those spoof backwards recordings on the end of the single for a laugh, to give all those Beatles nuts something to do. . . . Then we're listening to the finished single in the studio one night, and it gets to the end, and it goes 'zzzwrk nggggwaaahh joooohn lennnnnon qwwwwk.' I swear to God. We were like, 'It's John. He likes it!'"[25] Here again, Lennon's spirit is understood to provide a techno-spectral assent that is beyond question, such as Lincoln's ghost bestowed on *The Bishop of the Ozarks*.

These claims may not be entirely earnest. When McCartney describes imagining Lennon as a sort of judge to arbitrate whether his lyrics are any good, it is clearly just an embellishment when the headline writer refers to him as "summon[ing] Lennon's ghost," and to the best of my knowledge, Perkins did not add Lennon's name as a cowriter for "My Old Friend."[26] In other cases, however, it is meant to be understood literally. The British Library has a collection from the Balham medium Rosemary Brown, who claimed to channel reams of new pieces by composers like Chopin, Liszt, Schubert, and Rachmaninov, as well as Lennon, Fats Waller, and Gracie Fields.[27] Even more dramatically, the North Dakota resident Linda Polley's website, Voices from Spirit, credits more than 150 songs as "By; John Lennon. Channeled Through; Speaker Linda J. Polley." She also lists songs similarly credited to Johann Sebastian Bach, George Harrison, Kurt Cobain, Frank Sinatra, and "Jesus of Nazareth, Called the Christ," including a tribute to "Heaven's Earthly hero, Jimmy Kimmel."[28]

This unique repertoire has attracted some press interest, and one track bearing the Lennon attribution, a Christmas song called "Listen to the Angels," was remixed by Moby and got some radio play as a peculiar seasonal novelty track; reportedly, all proceeds were donated to the charity Save the Children, per Lennon's request.[29] Linda and her husband, Gerald "Gerry" Polley, who died in 2012, practiced a unique form of Spiritism, which they claimed originated on the defunct planet Hades. Gerald even launched a presidential campaign in 2007.[30]

The Polleys are the topic of the documentary short *Where Has Eternity Gone?* (2002) by Barney Snow. Interviewed there, the Polleys claim that the Kingdom of God itself has been endangered by the failure of the United States Congress to remove President Bill Clinton from office. Mary and Jesus Christ have abandoned Earth, and Lennon's spirit, they hold, sends them new songs to help combat Al Gore and Hillary Clinton; to them, the stakes of the 2000 election were nothing less than the future of all life on Earth. They describe Lennon collaborating with Bach as performance director of the one-thousand-person angelic choir. Gerald claims:

> John Lennon's views have changed considerably. We've talked quite a bit about that, . . . as he puts it, that man died on the sidewalk of New York. . . . That man got into the spirit realm, and he heard from Mary, he heard from Jesus, . . . and he realized that he was very, very naïve. He also wanted it known that though he was much into the drug culture, it cost him a great deal, and he warns people now that he was gravely mistaken and that drugs lead to nowhere but pain. That's what John told me.

On October 1, 2016, Linda Polley uploaded a video of herself to YouTube singing "Vote for Trump (Stop the Pervert)," credited to Lennon and featuring lines like:

> If you want your sons wearing skirts and pantyhose,
> with lipstick on their faces and shining nail polish that glows,
> Then vote for Hillary and she'll import the panty hose!

and:

> If you want your children to go out there to the stars,
> then vote for Trump and they'll be goin' pretty far!
> Vote for Trump and they'll be flyin' out passed [sic] Mars![31]

The Polleys represent an extreme example of how the postmortem Lennon becomes a floating signifier available to any conceivable position. One wonders why they did not simply channel a more conservative musical icon like Elvis Presley, but clearly the narrative of Lennon having seen the light and changed his position after death is part of the appeal.

In His Own Ghostwrite

Numerous book-length accounts of Lennon's afterlife exist. These include Jason Leen's *Peace at Last: The After-Death Experiences of John Lennon* (1984), Linda Deer Domnitz's *John Lennon Conversations* (1984), Linda Keen's *John Lennon in Heaven: Crossing the Borderlines of Being* (1994), Jewelle St. James's *All You Need Is Love: The Incredible True Story of One Woman's Search, Discovering Her Past Life with John Lennon* (2003), Ronald Ritter and Sussan Evermore's *Conversations with John Lennon* (2015), Ryuho Okawa's *John Lennon's Message from Heaven: On the Spirit of Love and Peace, Music, and the Incredible Secret of His Soul* (2020), Caroline Oceana Ryan's *Lennon Speaks: Messages from the Spirit of John Lennon* (2020), and Alaina Feather's *John Lennon: Spirit in the Sky* (2021). They range from extended question-and-answer sessions to detailed memoirs; a number of them offer afterlife travel narratives akin to Dante's *Divine Comedy*, C. S. Lewis's *The Great Divorce* (1945), or Richard Matheson's *What Dreams May Come* (1978). Almost all of them are first-person accounts, in which the author details personal and sometimes very intimate contact with Lennon's spirit.

In *Peace at Last*, for example, Leen claims to have been visited by Lennon three days after his death, his arrival announced by an angelic force. Over the coming days, Lennon's etheric form came again, and a few weeks later, on Christmas Eve 1980, he declared that they would go together on a "great adventure."[32] The bulk of the book is written from Lennon's perspective, starting with a first-person account of his death; he leaves his bullet-riddled body and sees it lying in a pool of blood. He is greeted by the original figure of loss in his life, his mother, Julia, who tells him, "John, your greatest work is yet to come. But first, all your pain must be surrendered; you must be completely healed and totally at peace."[33] Three angels then usher them to "the borderlands of Heaven," at which point Julia explains seven levels of Creation, the unification of which creates the eighth realm, Heaven. She tells him his purpose: "The decree has been given: '*No longer shall mankind fear death!*' You are being asked to help the people of Earth understand that death is only an illusion. They must release their fear of death in order to know the truth of their own immortality. Only then can they fully embrace the joy of living and the blessing of life."[34]

Lennon is guided by Julia on what a self-referencing Lennon characterizes as "a *real* Magical Mystery Tour," showing a succession of realms and meeting a succession of angels.[35] In this eclectic version of the afterlife, there is much talk of crystals, Akashic records, and chakras. Late in the process, Lennon meets the Creator, who appears to him as the conventional figure of Jesus and declares himself "totally united with the Lord of Creation."[36] The book ends with a few poems and a Q&A-style interview between Leen and Lennon. Here Lennon passes on individual messages (like "I love you, Yoko") but also announces plans to send music to Earth in the form of several albums, designed to "help raise the vibrations on Earth." He says, "I want to help restore everyone's faith in life."[37]

Where Leen's version of the deceased Lennon parallels Dante, Linda Keen's *John Lennon in Heaven* has Lennon play Virgil to Keen's Dante—her personal guide on a tour of the afterlife. This 280-page memoir provides a guided tour of another lush and intricate version of the afterlife, with appearances by Mozart and King Arthur, Julia Lennon and Brian Epstein, aliens and a talking lion named Mashoe. It claims that Lennon and Ono were reincarnations of Robert and Elizabeth Barrett Browning and that Sean Lennon is a "new expression" of their son Robert Barrett Browning; it also reveals that Lennon, incarnated as a Black American woman named Gracie, was the author's mother.[38] Similarly concerned with reincarnation, Jewelle St. James's *All You Need Is Love* is written in a memoir/novel style.[39] It reveals that the author and Lennon were lovers in a past life, in seventeenth-century England. One of the psychics presented in the book asserts that Lennon was also the reincarnation of Bramwell Brontë, brother of Charlotte, Emily, and Anne, another example of supernaturally tethering Lennon to canonical English writers, a recurring theme throughout the body of necrolennonolatry.[40] Others do the opposite, showing him acting through his successors, for instance, by inspiring Radiohead's "Karma Police" (2007) to explain his feelings about his assassination.[41]

"For a Séance in the Dark": The Spirit of John Lennon

Though numerous, these books about supernatural contact with Lennon are relatively obscure works, either self-published or coming from extremely small presses. Their profile is dwarfed by *The Spirit of John Lennon*, a television special that became available at the cost of US$9.95 per view on April 24, 2006. Purportedly demonstrating contact with Lennon, it reportedly drew five hundred thousand viewers.[42] This was not the first TV séance with a celebrity; in 1989, the Halloween special *In Search of Haunted Hollywood* staged a jokey séance with Marilyn Monroe, and the same producer behind *The Spirit of John Lennon*, Paul Sharratt, earlier made *The Spirit of Diana* (2003), featuring a séance with Diana, princess of Wales.

The Spirit of John Lennon features two séances. One is performed by the Liverpudlian medium Joe Power at the La Fortuna Café in New York City, and the other by Patricia Bankings in her Los Angeles business, the Crystal Matrix.[43] The latter, we are told, is accomplished with the help of Bankings' ascended master, St.-Germain. The sitters for both séances include a mix of personal friends and people who only knew Lennon by reputation. Power delivers answers secondhand as if he is receiving them from Lennon, often in a slightly confused, fragmentary fashion, whereas Bankings adopts an unplaceable accent and allows Lennon to communicate directly.

The special also has elements of a travelogue, visiting significant sites in Liverpool and New York City, though it features neither Lennon's childhood home on Menlove Avenue nor the interior of the Dakota. Locations are tied in with the putative attempt at contact and provide "evidence" of the mediums' powers. For example, when visiting the Cavern Club in Liverpool, Powers says he hears Lennon shouting the name "Eddie Cochran." A caption helpfully tell us that "Lennon was a big fan of the American musician Eddie Cochran," while the barman at the Cavern searches old records to confirm that Cochran played Liverpool in 1961. Later, a talking-head documentary-style interview with the Beatles' first manager, the late Allan Williams, references Cochran, at which time the program flashes back in black and white to Powers's earlier mention of Cochran in the Cavern. This is an example of what Bill Nichols calls "evidentiary editing," where cutting in documentary formats is designed to make a logical case—in this case, the legitimacy of Powers's talents and thus of mediumship in general.[44]

The Spirit of John Lennon also visits India, another site of significance to the Beatles, which the narration casually exoticizes as "perhaps the world's most mysterious and spiritual land." The filmmakers trek into the wilderness to find a guru who, we are told, regularly channels Lennon. When they find him, he plays a tune on a sitar and provides a series of lyrics in Hindi that allegedly make a new Lennon song. Once translated, the lyrics are reworked by the Los Angeles musician Brad Stanfield into a Lennonish idiom for the program's final set piece. The resultant song, "Peace," has the chorus "Peace / Make peace / Make peace / Peace."

Advocacy for peace, albeit in a rather toothless and unsystematic way, is a unifying theme in *The Spirit of John Lennon*, playing to that particular dimension of Lennon's posthumous profile. When Lennon is asked if he would rather be remembered for his music or for his message of peace, the answer comes via Power: "Peace and music. Music is peace." A message is also delivered outside the mouth of a medium, since we are told that an apparent audio error during the first séance is actually the words, "Peace. The message is peace." The narration suggests that the recording is an example of EVP, "electronic voice phenomena," whereby spirit voices are captured by audio recordings.[45] Within the special, EVP is explained by Sandra Belanger, captioned as "Anthropologist & EVP Expert," who classifies this recording as a "Class A EVP," invoking professional expertise to justify these supernatural events.

The second séance also is subject to a series of technical "errors," this time visual in character—a sudden disruption of the live tape recording registering as a burst of color and vaguely resembling a human form. In a gesture familiar to many viewers of ghost-hunting reality television shows, technical accident—or photo manipulation resembling accident—becomes an index of the spirit world. The technical director appears on TV describing it as a "technical disturbance. . . . Clearly, it looks like a face," and as something that cannot be explained technically. The narration suggests that it's a visual form of EVP and then asks, "Was what occurred that evening a glitch, a technical disturbance, or a vision from a mischievous spirit, or even John Lennon himself? You must decide yourself."

This is a familiar phrase throughout *The Spirit of John Lennon*. Throughout, the narration maintains a slightly skeptical tenor, asking questions like, "Did this song actually come from the spirit world? Now, you can decide for yourself." In fact, it starts with a disclaimer declaring the show to be "for entertainment purposes only": "Starcast, Inc., makes no representations of authenticity of the events recorded in this program. You must decide for yourself." No doubt there are legal reasons for these evasions through recourse to entertainment and viewer's choice, but they also place the program within a long tradition wherein spiritualism and antispiritualism coexist in a sort of feedback loop.

Responses to *The Spirit of John Lennon* were decidedly mixed. It was evidently taken seriously by some people, however; the Lennon fan site run by "Zoe" at johnlennonlyrics.faithweb.com includes "Peace" on the lyrics page, with a note indicating its supernatural origins.[46] But Yoko Ono refused to participate, and her spokesman, Elliot Mintz, lambasted the program as "tasteless, tacky and exploitative." Mintz also asserts, "John Lennon was an amazing communicator of heart, mind and spirit. He still speaks to those who choose to listen to his recordings. That was the medium he chose to speak with us."[47] Of interest here is that Mintz's phrase could have slotted comfortably within the program itself but here frames "spirit," "medium," and "speak with us" as metaphors instead of facts. "Tasteless" and "unofficial" though it may be, *The Spirit of John Lennon* ultimately furthers the project undertaken by Lennon's estate, of securing his reputation as an uncontroversial and commodifiable cultural hero.

Long Lost John

"I believe in everything until it's disproved. So I believe in fairies, the myths, dragons. It all exists, even if it's in your mind. Who's to say that dreams and nightmares aren't as real as the here and now?" This quote appears as the header for Zoe's aforementioned lyrics website, plus on goodreads.com and brainyquote.com, and a search on Google Books finds it quoted in *Fairies: An Informative and Whimsical Guide* (2018) by Toni Klein and *The Dream Recorder* (2015) by Bryan Kolar.

But did Lennon say that? It sounds vaguely "Lennonish." I certainly cannot prove that he did not say it, but without an original source, it seems likely to be either a misattribution or an outright fabrication. There is no shortage of comparable examples; Lennon's posthumous profile, like that of George

Carlin and Abraham Lincoln, has resulted in numerous fake "no-nonsense wisdom" quotes attributed to him. Snopes.com debunked one meme circulating in 2017 that paired a photo of Lennon toward the end of his life with the text, "I honestly beleive [sic] that the only way we are going to get ourselves out of the messes we've created for ourselves is to find strong and independent leaders. It's going to take a revolution. Electing someone that isn't a politician is the only way. Perhaps a business man."[48] Its caption, "John Lennon, 1981," may mean that the meme is actually a facetious intelligence test, but this retroactive Lennon endorsement of Trump bears an obvious comparison to Linda Polley using channeling to do the same. In truth, it's impossible to say if the mercurial Lennon might have evolved into a right-wing Trump supporter (witness Jon Voight); it seems almost fortunate that he died well before we needed to find out. The floating signifier of the postmortem John Lennon can serve the bland and anodyne messages of peace of *The Spirit of John Lennon* or the eccentric but largely apolitical cosmic revelations of Leen or Keen but also right-wing discourses that establish him as a sort of prodigal son set right by death.

The spectral Lennon gets so many things that the real Lennon never did: maternal absolution, access to the secrets of the universe, emotional stability, shelter from the ravages of fame, and the ability to dictate messages of wisdom and peace that are effective and understood. Part of the appeal of necrolennonolatry is that it putatively permits an extremely intimate mode of fan-artist interaction. We see a variation on this in Danny Boyle's film *Yesterday* (2019), in a scene in which Jack (Himesh Patel), one of the few people who remember the Beatles in an alternate timeline, makes a pilgrimage to meet a seventy-eight-year-old Lennon (Robert Carlyle), a retired sailor now living a quiet rural life. This Lennon was denied fame and fortune but also spared a violent and untimely death. He dispenses simple wisdom that has a weight for Jack that this Lennon himself cannot appreciate; *Yesterday* also deigns to give Lennon a sense of humor, something so many of the texts mentioned here fail to do.

Yesterday's scenario echoes some home-movie footage in the documentary *Imagine: John Lennon* (1988), in which Lennon meets with a drifter at his Tittenhurst Park residence and firmly but humanely dispels the young man's delusions that Lennon was singing directly to or about him. So many of us have been that seeker who finds something of personal significance in Lennon's music—even some of us born after his death. Unfortunately, the same was true of Mark David Chapman, whom the tabloid *National Inquirer* claims talks daily "with John's ghost." Chapman says, "He visits me and we talk about music and stuff. He's forgiven me."[49] Such a claim resembles mediums' reports in the 1870s that Lincoln and John Wilkes Booth were reconciled in the purifying space of the afterlife.[50] Most works of necrolennonolatry, however, simply downplay or ignore Chapman, mentioning him in passing at best, refusing to let him usurp his victim's fame.

A tiny incident in Shunji Iwai's segment of the anthology film *New York, I Love You* (2008) draws together numerous themes from across the phenomenon of necrolennonolatry. As the bedraggled composer David (Orlando Bloom) speaks to his assistant, Camille (Christina Ricci), by cell phone in Central Park, he notes that he can see the Dakota. "John Lennon is my god," he asserts, and he expresses admiration for the song "Mother" (1970), a lament over Lennon's separation from Julia. David texts Camille a selfie, and she jokes that she sees Lennon behind him. The mise-en-scène places the Dakota in the background of the image and the "Imagine" memorial at Strawberry Fields in the front. In mere seconds, it provides a remarkably concise restatement of the entanglement of Lennon with spectrality, celebrity worship, authorship, mourning, place, tourism, and technology.

Like Lennon's life itself, his afterlife has proved to be a contested space. Conservative voices imagine him as an apostate to 1960s culture (Rosemary Brown channeled the message "Don't mess around with drugs") and enlist him in their culture war as they try to reframe themselves as the new counterculture.[51] Even though the official curators of Lennon's legacy disavowed *The Spirit of John Lennon*, it is largely consistent with their association of Lennon with inert and vague message of peace, his dalliances with militant radicalism conveniently forgotten. Others see Lennon as ushering a gateway into a mind-bending cosmology that leaves earthly politics far behind. Through it all, there is the fantasy of contact—like that drifter at Tittenhurst Park, earning an audience with the figure who simultaneously seems so accessible and so unknowable.

NOTES

1. Schickel, *Intimate Strangers*, 4.
2. Fogo, *I Read the News Today*.
3. Elliott, *Mourning of John Lennon*; Mäkelä, *John Lennon Imagined*, 218–35.
4. Rappaport and Collier, *John's Secret Dreams*; Sánchez Vergara, *Little People, Big Dreams*.
5. Turner, *Gospel*, 6.

6. Sword, *Ghostwriting Modernism*. Other deceased celebrities have inspired similar books, like *Nirvana in the Spirit: Kurt Cobain* (2018) by Jacqueline Howard. It should also be noted that other supernatural treatments of Lennon are not sacralizing but demonizing. Joseph Niezgoda's *The Lennon Prophecy* argues that Lennon sold his soul to the Devil. To make his case, Niezgoda sifts through Beatles lyrics and cover art in the manner of the "Paul is dead" myth, which

should itself be accepted as a major significant strand of the Beatles' cultural legacy.

7. Studies of celebrity deaths and their aftermaths include Brown, Basil, and Bocarnea, "Social Influence of an International Celebrity"; Magee, "Rest in Mediated Peace"; Radford and Bloch, "Ritual, Mythology, and Consumption."

8. Peters, *Speaking into the Air*; Sconce, *Haunted Media*.

9. Natale, *Supernatural Entertainments*, 8.

10. Monaghan, "Was Abraham Lincoln Really a Spiritualist?"; Lande, *Spiritualism*, 99–108.

11. "Lincoln's New Job," 16.

12. Goldman, *Lives of John Lennon*, 78.

13. Guiliano, *Lennon in America*, 81; Green, *Dakota Days*, 19–21; Lennon, *Skywriting by Word of Mouth*.

14. Birmingham, *Life at the Dakota*, 79. A different chapter could be written about Lennon and occultism; according to the tarot reader John Green's *Dakota Days*, Lennon based important business decisions on tarot spreads and once planned a quest for the Spear of Destiny that pierced the side of Jesus (22).

15. Elliott, *Mourning of John Lennon*, 4.

16. Myers, *Ghosts*, 88–91, 93–94.

17. Ibid., 100–101.

18. Ibid., 103.

19. Jones, *Celebrity Ghosts*, 37, 38.

20. Ogden, *Haunted Hollywood*, 270.

21. Swayne, *Haunted Rock and Roll*, 54–55.

22. "Michael Jackson and Ringo Starr."

23. Edward, *Crossing Over*, 151.

24. Jones, *Celebrity Ghosts*, 38.

25. O'Hagan, "Macca Beyond." Birds are another persistent motif. The surviving Beatles were photographed with a white peacock during the photo shoot for the "Free as a Bird" single; apparently it walked into the frame of its own accord and was taken as a sign of Lennon's presence (Jones, *Celebrity Ghosts*, 38). Julian Lennon's philanthropic White Feather Foundation is named for a gift given to him by a Mirning elder in Australia, which he regarded as a message from his deceased father ("How It All Started").

26. Italie, "McCartney Summons Lennon's Ghost."

27. Perry, "Music from Beyond."

28. Voices from Spirit, "Messages and Songs from the Afterlife."

29. Wherry, "You May Say She's a Dreamer."

30. Rivoli, "Candidate Running on Divine Inspiration."

31. Polley, "Vote for Trump!"

32. Leen, *Peace at Last*, xiv.

33. Ibid., 4–5.

34. Ibid., 8.

35. Ibid., 16.

36. Ibid., 129.

37. Ibid., 139, 137.

38. Keen, *John Lennon in Heaven*, 68–69, 162.

39. St. James, *All You Need Is Love*.

40. Bob Dylan's tribute song "Roll On John" (2012) similarly blends references to Lennon and William Blake.

41. Feather, *John Lennon*, 146.

42. Strachan, "Psychic Dabblers," 50.

43. In Power's own book (*Man Who Sees Dead People*), he describes prior communications with Lennon and receiving Lennon's permission to appear in Sharratt's special.

44. Nichols, *Introduction to Documentary*, 18.

45. Sconce, *Haunted Media*, 85–91.

46. John Lennon Lyrics, accessed September 14, 2023, http://www.johnlennonlyrics.faithweb.com/.

47. Strachan, "Psychic Dabblers," 50. Mintz also had a significant role in shaping Lennon's legacy, curating his unreleased recordings through the radio show *The Lost Lennon Tapes* (1988–92).

48. Mikkelson, "Did John Lennon Anticipate the Election of Donald Trump?"

49. "John Lennon's Killer."

50. Lande, *Spiritualism*, 104.

51. Gurierri, "Rosemary Brown."

BIBLIOGRAPHY

Birmingham, Stephen. *Life at the Dakota: New York's Most Unusual Address*. New York: Random House, 2016.

Brown, William J., Michael D. Basil, and Mihai C. Bocarnea. "Social Influence of an International Celebrity: Responses to the Death of Princess Diana." *Journal of Communication* 53, no. 4 (2003): 587–605.

Edward, John. *Crossing Over: The Stories Behind the Stories.* New York: Sterling, 2010.

Elliott, Anthony. *The Mourning of John Lennon.* Berkeley: University of California Press, 1999.

Feather, Alaina. *John Lennon: Spirit in the Sky.* N.p.: Ibis, 2021.

Fogo, Fred. *I Read the News Today: The Social Drama of John Lennon's Death.* London: Littlefield Adams Quality Books, 1994.

Goldman, Albert. *The Lives of John Lennon.* New York: William Morrow, 1988.

Green, John. *Dakota Days: The True Story of John Lennon's Final Years.* New York: St. Martin's, 1983.

Guiliano, Geoffrey. *Lennon in America: 1971–1980, Based in Part on the Lost Lennon Diaries.* London: Robson, 2001.

Gurierri, Matthew. "Rosemary Brown." *Red Bull Music Academy Daily*, March 15, 2017. https://daily.redbullmusicacademy.com/2017/03/rosemary-brown-feature.

Italie, Hillel. "McCartney Summons Lennon's Ghost: 'I'm Using Him as a Sort of Judge.'" *CTV News*, December 18, 2014.

Iwai, Shunji, et al., dirs. *New York, I Love You.* Los Angeles: Grosvenor Park Media, 2008. Film.

"John Lennon's Killer: 'I'm Possessed by His Ghost!,'" *National Inquirer*, December 8, 2016.

Jones, Marie D. *Celebrity Ghosts and Notorious Hauntings.* New York: Visible Ink, 2019.

Keen, Linda. *John Lennon in Heaven: Crossing the Borderlines of Being.* Ashland, OR: Pan, 1994.

Lande, R. Gregory. *Spiritualism in the American Civil War.* Jefferson, NC: McFarland, 2020.

Leen, Jason. *Peace at Last: The After-Death Experiences of John Lennon.* Bellingham, WA: Illumination Arts, 1982.

Lennon, John. *Skywriting by Word of Mouth.* New York: Harper and Row, 1986.

Lennon, Julian. "How It All Started." 2009. White Feather Foundation. https://whitefeatherfoundation.com/how-it-all-started/.

"Lincoln's New Job." *Kansas City Kansan*, July 9, 1922.

Magee, Sara. "Rest in Mediated Peace: How *Entertainment Tonight*'s Coverage of Natalie Wood's and John Belushi's Deaths Helped Shape Celebrity Death Coverage Today." *Celebrity Studies* 5, no. 3 (2014): 291–304.

Mäkelä, Janne. *John Lennon Imagined: Cultural History of a Rock Star.* New York: Peter Lang, 2004.

"Michael Jackson and Ringo Starr Both Claim They've Seen John Lennon's Ghost." *National Enquirer*, 1987.

Mikkelson, David. "Did John Lennon Anticipate the Election of Donald Trump?" *Snopes*, February 6, 2017.

Monaghan, Jay. "Was Abraham Lincoln Really a Spiritualist?" *Journal of the Illinois State Historical Society* 43, no. 2 (June 1941): 209–32.

Myers, Arthur. *Ghosts of the Rich and Famous.* Chicago: Contemporary Books, 1988.

Natale, Simone. *Supernatural Entertainments: Victorian Spiritualism and the Rise of Modern Media Culture.* University Park: Pennsylvania State University Press, 2016.

Nichols, Bill. *Introduction to Documentary.* 3rd ed. Bloomington: Indiana University Press, 2017.

Niezgoda, Joseph. *The Lennon Prophecy: A New Examination of the Death Clues of the Beatle.* New York: New Chapter Press, 2008.

Ogden, Tom. *Haunted Hollywood: Tinseltown Terrors, Filmdom Phantoms, and Movieland Mayhem.* Guilford, CT: Globe Pequot, 2009.

O'Hagan, Sean. "Macca Beyond." *Guardian*, September 18, 2005.

Perry, Frankie. "Music from Beyond: The Rosemary Brown Collection." *Music Blog: The British Library*, October 31, 2018.

Peters, John Durham. *Speaking into the Air: A History of the Idea of Communication.* Chicago: University of Chicago Press, 1999.

Polley, Linda. "Vote for Trump!" YouTube, October 1, 2016. https://www.youtube.com/watch?v=rls3bL7J83I.

Power, Joe. *The Man Who Sees Dead People*. London: Penguin, 2009.

Radford, Scott K., and Peter H. Bloch. "Ritual, Mythology, and Consumption After a Celebrity Death." In *Death in a Consumer Culture*, edited by Susan Dobscha, 108–22. Abingdon, UK: Routledge, 2016.

Rappaport, Doreen, and Bryan Collier. *John's Secret Dreams: The Life of John Lennon*. Los Angeles: Disney-Hyperion, 2016.

Rivoli, Jonathan. "Candidate Running on Divine Inspiration." *Bismarck Tribune*, October 27, 2007.

Sánchez Vergara, Maria Isabel. *Little People, Big Dreams: John Lennon*. London: Frances Lincoln Children's Books, 2020.

Schickel, Richard. *Intimate Strangers: The Culture of Celebrity*. New York: Doubleday, 1985.

Sconce, Jeffrey. *Haunted Media: Electronic Presence from Telegraphy to Television*. Durham: Duke University Press, 2000.

Snow, Barney, dir. *Where Has Eternity Gone?* Self-financed, 2002. Film.

Solt, Andrew, dir. *Imagine: John Lennon*. Burbank, CA: Warner Bros., 1988. Film.

St. James, Jewelle. *All You Need Is Love: The Incredible True Story of One Woman's Search, Discovering Her Past Life with John Lennon*. Revelstoke, BC: St. James, 2003.

Strachan, Alex. "Psychic Dabblers Give John Lennon Last Word." *Star-Phoenix*, July 15, 2006.

Swayne, Matthew L. *Haunted Rock and Roll: Ghostly Tales of Musical Legends*. Woodbury, MN: Llewellyn, 2014.

Sword, Helen. *Ghostwriting Modernism*. Ithaca: Cornell University Press, 2002.

Turner, Steve. *The Gospel According to the Beatles*. Louisville, KY: Westminster John Knox Press, 2006.

Voices from Spirit. "Messages and Songs from the Afterlife for Jimmy Kimmel." http://www.voicesfromspirit.com/sb/jimmy.htm.

Wherry, Aaron. "You May Say She's a Dreamer." *National Post*, January 22, 2002.

Conclusion

All Together Now—Seeking and Finding Meaning in Community

MICHAEL MCGOWAN

In the introduction and throughout this book, the contributors and I have argued that the Beatles were instrumental in collapsing distinctions, seeing others as a "Thou" and not an "it." They brought people together, and we would do well to remember the value of seeing things through others' eyes as the march toward individualized experiences threatens to convince us of a very dangerous proposition: we are "lords of our tiny skull-sized kingdoms, alone at the center of all creation."[1] As Robert Putnam argues in *Bowling Alone*, "The Beatles got it right: we all 'get by with a little help from our friends.' In the decades since the Fab Four topped the charts, life satisfaction among adult Americans has declined steadily.... Young and middle-aged adults today are simply less likely to have friends over, attend church, or go to club meetings than were earlier generations."[2] With the rise of social media's algorithmic customization, hyperpartisan news intake, and lingering effects of pandemic isolation, the problem of division continues to worsen.

And herein lies the paradox at the heart of the Beatles and religion: they promoted the religious self-exploration and expression of a younger generation, but these activities are only possible within a highly protected set of unbending democratic political institutions about which the Beatles were ambivalent. In 1968's "Revolution," Lennon says, "When you talk about destruction, don't you know that you can count me out," but in another version, we can count him "in." By the following year, Lennon doubled down on peace, not destruction. Youthful idealists struggle to see the larger context, that their very questioning cultural and religious norms is only possible in a political system in which Lockean rights are strictly protected: free speech, freedom of the press, and, of course, the free exercise of religion. In other words, both modern and postmodern forms of religion require strong democratic institutions to protect them. Liberal societies can survive and even thrive—creating globally appreciated art—in tough times, but they cannot survive if *all* of society's institutions are abandoned. Strong democratic political institutions are the condition for the possibility of religious exploration.

In Nietzsche's last, unfinished work, he conceded that Christianity provided a source of moral and social stability for centuries. It "prevented man from despising himself as man, from taking sides against life; from despairing of knowledge; it was a *means of preservation*."[3] But he worried about the negative consequences when certainty in Christianity's dogma erodes. If the 1960s pushed a common religion further from the center of public life, and if the recent rise of political extremism pushes common democratic political institutions further from the center, we may be running out of shared institutions that facilitate harmonious living. That is to say, the selfsame impulse to abandon historic religious institutions in favor of increased personal autonomy must not be permitted to run roughshod over the institutions that make possible the questioning of the former. At some point, historic institutions must be recognized as valuable in and of themselves for their staying power and their ability to make possible that for which the Beatles stood: unity and the preservation of peace. We should robustly condemn any revolution that threatens our ability to question our norms, whether that talk comes from the far right or the far left. If we are to live well together, to seek and find meaning in community, we must remain "all together now," devoted to a set of common principles. On this much, the Beatles and the world's great wisdom traditions, even Christianity, agree. Or, as Lennon put it, "For reasons known only to themselves people do print what I say. And I'm saying peace. We're not pointing a finger at anybody. There are no good guys and bad guys. The struggle is in the mind. We must bury our own monsters and stop condemning people. We are all Christ and all Hitler. We want Christ to win. We're trying to make Christ's message contemporary. What would he have done if he had advertisements, records, films, TV and newspapers? Christ made miracles to tell his message. Well, the miracle today is communications, so let's use it."[4]

NOTES

1. Wallace, *This Is Water*, 114.
2. Putnam, *Bowling Alone*, 334, 335.
3. Nietzsche, *Will to Power*, 10.
4. Turner, *Beatles*.

BIBLIOGRAPHY

Nietzsche, Friedrich. *The Will to Power*. Translated by Walter Kaufmann and R. J. Hollingdale. Edited by Walter Kaufmann. New York: Vintage Books, 1968.

Putnam, Robert. *Bowling Alone: The Collapse and Revival of American Community*. New York: Simon and Schuster, 2000.

Turner, Steve. *The Beatles: The Stories Behind the Songs, 1967–1970*. London: Carlton Books, 2009. Apple iBooks ed.

Wallace, David Foster. *This Is Water: Some Thoughts, Delivered on a Significant Occasion, about Living a Compassionate Life*. New York: Little, Brown, 2009.

Contributors

David Bedford (UK) grew up in the Dingle, Liverpool, by the bottom of Madryn Street, where Ringo Starr was born, and attended the same school as Ringo, though many years later. With his wife, Alix, they left the Dingle for Penny Lane. They have three daughters who were born in the same hospital as John Lennon, and they attended Dovedale School, where John Lennon and George Harrison began their education. Bedford is the author of *Liddypool: Birthplace of the Beatles* and *The Fab One Hundred and Four: The Evolution of The Beatles*. He was a coauthor with the Beatles biographer Hunter Davies on *The Beatles Book*, with fellow authors Keith Badman and Spencer Leigh. He has published *Finding the Fourth Beatle* and *The Country of Liverpool: Nashville of the North*. He was also the associate producer and historical consultant for the documentary *Looking for Lennon*, a podcaster, and a Beatles tour guide in Liverpool.

Kenneth Campbell (USA) is a professor of history at Monmouth University in West Long Branch, New Jersey, where he has taught a variety of undergraduate and graduate courses in British, Irish, and European history, as well as for the past decade or so, the interdisciplinary courses "The Beatles" and "American Popular Culture and the Beatles." In 1995, he received the Monmouth University Distinguished Teacher Award. He is the author of *A History of the British Isles: Prehistory to the Present*, *Ireland's History: From Prehistory to the Present*, *Western Civilization: A Global and Comparative Approach*, vols. 1–2, and most recently, *The Beatles and the 1960s: Reception, Revolution, and Social Change*. He has presented and published regularly on the Beatles in recent years and is the editor of *American Popular Culture and the Beatles*.

John Covach (USA) is the director of the University of Rochester Institute for Popular Music. He is the principal author of the college textbook *What's That Sound? An Introduction to Rock Music*, has coedited *Understanding Rock*, *Sounding Out Pop*, and *The Cambridge Companion to the Rolling Stones*, and is editor of the forthcoming *Cambridge Companion to Prog*.

Melissa Davis (USA) was a member of the world's first graduate program focusing on the Beatles' impact on popular music and society, at Liverpool Hope University. Her dissertation, "A Contextual Analysis of the Beatles'

Reception in America," examined the unique milieu the group found when it debuted on US television two months following the assassination of President Kennedy. She coauthored *The Beatles Bibliography: A New Guide to the Literature* with Michael Brocken and a supplement; a new edition is forthcoming. She lives in Colorado—home to championship football, hockey, and fourteen-thousand-foot snowcapped peaks.

Anthony DeCurtis (USA) is a distinguished lecturer at the University of Pennsylvania and the author of the recently published *In Other Words: Artists Talk About Life and Work*, as well as *Rocking My Life Away: Writing About Music and Other Matters*. He is also the editor of *Present Tense: Rock and Roll and Culture* and coeditor of *The Rolling Stone Illustrated History of Rock and Roll* and *The Rolling Stone Album Guide* (3rd ed.). He is a contributing editor at *Rolling Stone*, where his work has appeared for twenty-five years, and he occasionally writes for the *New York Times* and many other publications. His essay accompanying the Eric Clapton box set *Crossroads* won a Grammy Award in the Best Album Notes category.

Mark Duffett (UK) is an associate professor in media and cultural studies at the University of Chester. He completed his PhD on the fans of Elvis Presley and remains interested in popular music, fan culture, and cultural theory. He has teaching experience at the University of British Columbia and at the University of Wales. He has published several articles in academic journals and has also worked for Sony Music, the BBC World Service, and the Discovery Channel. He has also written numerous articles and book chapters, edited several projects, and authored three monographs: *Understanding Fandom*, *Counting Down Elvis*, and *Elvis*. He has been an invited speaker at events in Russia, Finland, Holland, and the United Kingdom. He is currently editing a new book on Elvis.

Scott Freer (UK) is an independent researcher and an associate lecturer at the University of Lincoln. He is the author of *Modernist Mythopoeia: The Twilight of the Gods* and coeditor of *Religion and Myth in T. S. Eliot's Poetry*. His book *American Disaster Movies of the 1970s: Crisis, Spectacle and High Modernity*, as well as an edited volume, *The Transmedia Legacies of T. S. Eliot's Poetry*, were published recently. He is currently writing two books: *American EcoHorror* and *The Problem of Evil in Postwar British Catholic Women Writers*.

Murray Leeder (Canada) is an adjunct professor in the Department of English, Film, Theatre and Media at the University of Manitoba. He is the author of *Horror Film: A Critical Introduction*; *The Modern Supernatural and the Beginnings of Cinema*; and *Halloween* and editor of *Cinematic Ghosts: Haunting and Spectrality from Silent Cinema to the Digital Era* and *ReFocus: The Films of William Castle*. He has published in such journals as *Horror Studies*, *Canadian Journal of Film Studies*, *Journal of Popular Culture*, and *Journal of Popular Film and Television*.

Sean MacLeod (Ireland) is a musician, songwriter, author, and teacher from Dublin, Ireland. To date, he has produced five albums of his own music and has written a number of books relating to popular music and culture, including *Behind the Wall of Illusion: The Religious, Esoteric and Occult World of the Beatles*. He currently teaches music and music technology at the Limerick College of Further Education and is finishing an arts practice PhD at the University of Limerick. He has been a Beatles fan since the age of eleven and also has a keen interest in the work of the spiritual scientist Rudolf Steiner, which informs much of his writing and music.

Grant Maxwell (USA) is the author of *Integration and Difference: Constructing a Mythical Dialectic*; *How Does It Feel? Elvis Presley, the Beatles, Bob Dylan, and the Philosophy of Rock and Roll*; and *The Dynamics of Transformation: Tracing an Emerging World View*. He has served as a professor at Baruch College and Lehman College in New York, and he has written for *Deleuze and Guattari Studies*, the *American Philosophical Association* blog, *American Songwriter* magazine, the *Journal of Religion and Popular Culture*, and *Interalia Magazine*. He is an editor of the *Archai* journal, he holds a PhD from the City University of New York's Graduate Center, and he lives with his wife and two sons in the Virgin Islands, where he plays in a band called Lovewolf.

Michael McGowan (USA) is a professor of philosophy and religion at Florida Southwestern State College. He is the coeditor of *David Foster Wallace and Religion: Essays on Faith and Fiction* and author of *The Bridge: Revelation and Its Implications*. His writing has appeared in Blackwell's "Philosophy and Pop Culture" series, *Christianity Today*, *International Journal of Systematic Theology*, *Journal of Religion and Film*, *Journal of Human Rights*, *Christian Scholar's Review*, *Teaching Philosophy*, *Theological Book Review*, *Reviews in Religion and Theology*, and the *Teaching Ethics* journal, where he also served on the Editorial Board.

Christiane Meiser (Germany) is a doctoral candidate under Oliver Jahraus at the Ludwig-Maximilians-Universität Munich. Her dissertation deals with religious codes in music films. Previously, she completed the interdisciplinary master's program in Media and Cultural Studies at LMU Munich with a thesis on the narratological problem of ending so-called epic series, after completing her bachelor's degree in German studies (minor in theater studies and musicology). In addition to her university education, she has worked for the theaters in Hamburg and Munich, the Bavarian Broadcasting Company, and the publishing company Suhrkamp. Her main academic interests are media and film theories and contemporary popular culture, as well as research in the context of the "religious turn." Alongside her doctorate, she works at the Bavarian Institute for New Media.

Eyal Regev (Israel) is a professor of Jewish studies in the Department of Land of Israel Studies and Archaeology and the director of the Helena and Paul Schulmann School for Basic Jewish Studies at Bar-Ilan University. His areas of research focus on the social history and archaeology of Second Temple Judaism and early Christianity. His books include *The Sadducees and Their Halakhah*; *Sectarianism in Qumran*; *The Hasmoneans: Ideology, Archaeology, Identity*; and *The Temple in Early Christianity: Experiencing the Sacred*.

Index

AA (Alcoholics Anonymous), 121
  See also recovery programs
Abbey Road (1969), 13, 188
Abbey Road Studios, 60
academia, epistemology of, 175–77, 179–80
"Across the Universe," 89, 144, 146
Advaita Vedanta, 101, 107
Alice in Wonderland (Carroll), 142
"All My Loving," 69
"All My Trials," 77–78
All Starr Band, Ringo Starr and, 128
All Things Must Pass (album), 108, 140
"All Things Must Pass" (song), 139
"All Together Now," 229–30
All You Need Is Love (St. James), 220–21
"All You Need Is Love," 4, 7, 44, 89, 90, 107, 208, 210–11
America Divided (Isserman and Kazin), 6
Amis, Martin, 189
Ancient Chapel of Toxeth Park. *See* Toxeth Unitarian Chapel
androgyny, 159–63
Angadi, Ayana, 100–101, 110n18
An Gorta Mór. *See* Great Irish Famine
Annunciation, Mary's, 134, 137
"Annus Mirabilis" (Larkin), 158
Another Day In the Life (Starr), 127
Anthology (Beatles), 3, 4, 10, 67, 77, 217
antisemitism, 41
Archbishop of Canterbury, 17
Aronowitz, Al, 120
Asher, Jane, 70
Asiatic Music Circle (London), 100
ASPR (American Society for Psychical Research), 215
Astavakra Samhita, 98
"At the Mercy," 78
atman, 14, 21
Autobiography of a Yogi (Yogananda), 102–3, 109
avant-garde art, 20–21

Bach, Barbara, 120–21, 125, 127
"Back in the USSR," 9–10
Bailey, David, x
Bailey, Robert (Rev), 17
"Ballad of John and Yoko," 172
Bangladesh, Concert for, 45
Bankings, Patricia, 221

Barrow, Tony, 138, 141
Barth, Karl, 8
Battle of the Boyne, 52, 54
Baur, Michael, 21
BBC (British Broadcasting Corporation), 3, 4, 52, 87
Beach Boys, 12
Beatlemania, xi, 1, 7, 13, 22, 98, 114, 116, 191–92
  as Dionysian, 156–59, 179–80
  as religious phenomenon, 2–3, 84, 163–64, 166–81
  represented in *Yesterday*, 202, 210
Beatles, The (1968), 12, 15, 89, 108, 118, 185–200
Beatles and Ireland, The (Smyth), 61
Beatles for Sale (1964), 13, 68
Beatles Monthly, 192
Beck-Gernsheim, Elisabeth, 211
Beck, Ulrich, 211
"Being for the Benefit of Mr. Kite," 107
Bellah, Robert, 166
Best, Mona, 62
Big Book of Alcoholics Anonymous, 123
Birth of Tragedy, The (Nietzsche), 150
Bishop of the Ozarks, The (film), 216, 217
Black Forty-Seven, The, 35
Black Panthers, 195, 199n37
"Blackbird," 45, 140, 186, 196, 197
Blake, William, 137, 162–64
"Blind Men and the Elephant" (Saxe), 16
Bloody Sunday massacre, 52, 57, 60
"Blue Jay Way," 107
Blue Sunshine (film), 194
Bohemian Rhapsody (film), 212n13
Boland, Mark, 163
Book of Common Prayer, 51
Boulding, Kenneth, 8
Bow, Clara, 38
Bowie, David, 163
Bowling Alone (Putnam), 229
Boyd, Pattie, 12, 101, 103
Boyle, Danny, 204, 224
Bradby, Barbara, 159
Brahman, 14, 21
Brainwashed (Harrison), 62, 140, 146
Brody, Richard, 203
Brown, Callum, 7
Brown, Rosemary, 225

Buddhism, xi, 16, 73, 79, 84, 91, 134
Bugliosi, Vincent, 186, 193
butcher cover, 188

Cage, John, 8, 20
Carlin, George, 223–24
Carlin, Peter Ames, 76
Carroll, Lewis, 142
Casbah Coffee Club, 62
Catholics vs. Protestants, 31–64
causation, Aristotelian metaphysics of, 169
Cavern Club, 3, 173, 177, 221
Chandogya Upanishad, 15, 107
Chaos and Creation in the Backyard (McCartney), 78
Chapman, Mark David, 83, 95n4, 214–15, 224–25
"Christabel" (Coleridge), 141
Christgau, Robert, 192
Christianity, xi
    and Beatlemania, 17–18
    declining numbers of, 7, 10–11, 16–17, 21
    Lennon on, 85–87
    Nietzsche on, 5–7, 9
Christology, 134
Church of England, 33, 49, 51, 87
Cirque du Soleil, 4
civil rights movement, x, 10, 151, 195–98
Cleave, Maureen, x, 5, 68, 83–84
Cleaver, Eldridge, 195–96
"Cold Turkey," 140
Cold War, 9–10, 23n8, 24n43, 153
Coleman, Ray, 85, 90
Coleridge, Samuel Taylor, 141
Come Together: A Night for John Lennon's Words and Music, 214
communism, 9, 85–86
    See also Cold War
Communist Manifesto (Marx), 93
Complete Illustrated Book of Yoga, The (Vishnu-devananda), 100
Couldry, Nick, 189
counterculture, ix, 1, 8, 177, 180, 190, 225
Coupe, Lawrence, 138–39, 145
Crosby, David, 100, 105, 110n15
"Cry Baby Cry," 108
Curtis, Richard, 204

Dakota Days (Green), 226
Datebook, 18, 187
Davies, Evan, 196
Davies, Hunter, 75, 117, 151, 158
Davis, Carl, 77
"Day in the Life, A" 51, 136

"Daydream" (Lovin' Spoonful), 72
"Dear One," 109
Deleuze, Gilles, 172
Dickie Lewis, 41
Didion, Joan, 190, 193
Dionysus, cult of. See under Nietzsche
disenchantment (Weber), 92, 168, 171–74, 180
Doggett, Peter, 119–20
"Don't Bother Me," 69, 106
"Don't Pass Me By," 114, 116–18
Donovan, 12
Doors of Perception, The (Huxley), 86
Doors, The, 5
Double Fantasy (Lennon and Ono), xi
Douglas, Susan, 160
Driving Rain (McCartney), 76
drugs, 11, 13, 19–20, 71, 111n53, 120, 211, 218
    See also LSD
dualism (metaphysical), 124
Dylan, Bob, ix, 91, 120, 177

Eastman-McCartney, Linda, 75
Ed Sullivan Show, The, 2, 3, 10, 20, 155, 159, 177
Eddie Clayton Skiffle Group, 50
Education Act (1944), 42
ego death, 5, 134–36, 142–44
Eisenhower, Dwight, 8
"Eleanor Rigby," 45, 68–72, 127, 137, 205
Eliade, Mircea, 170
Elizabeth I, Queen, 52
Elliot, Anthony, 216
Elliot, T. S., 140–41, 143–44
Elwood, Robert, 7
Emerick, Geoff, 120
EMI. See Abbey Road Studios
"End, The" 13, 44
Epstein, Brian, ix, 12, 41, 83, 104, 173–74, 177
Epstein, Isaac, 41
Epstein, Jacob, 41
EVP (electronic voice phenomena), 222

Fact or Fantasy? (BBC Program), 3
famine. See Great Irish Famine
Farrow, Mia, 12
Farrow, Prudence, 12
fashion, x, 38, 159–63, 174–75
Feminine Mystique, The (Friedan), 10
feminism, 10, 24n48, 193, 196
"Fine Line," 78
Firth, Simon, 159
"Fixing a Hole," 137, 196

flower power movement, 87
Fogo, Fred, 214
"Follow Me," 78–79
Fonda, Peter, 110n15, 141
"Fool on the Hill," 72
"For No One," 70–71
"4'33"" (Cage), 21
Frankenheimer, John, 192
"Free as a Bird," 217
Freeman, Morgan, 17
French, John, 61
Friedan, Betty, 10
Fritsch, Matthias, 207
Fritz, Natalie, 207

Gambaccini, Paul, 153
"Garden of Love, The" (Blake), 137
Gellar, Larry, 105
Gerry and the Pacemakers, 50
Get Back (docuseries), 118
"Get Back," 4, 163
"Getting Better," 108
Getting Sober (Taylor), 122, 125, 127
Gibberd, Sir Frederick, 56
Gibbins, Ronald, 17
Gilbert-Scott, Sir Giles, 55
Ginsberg, Allan, 19
"Give Ireland Back to the Irish," 52, 58–60
"Give Peace a Chance," 18, 45, 91, 109
"Glass Onion," 144, 188, 191, 196
Gleiberman, Owen, 202–3, 209
God, death of, 5–7, 17, 187
"God," xi, 83, 91, 145–46, 172
God: The Almighty Question (film), 123, 126, 127
Goldberg, Philip, 99, 103
Goldberg, Whoopie, 155
Golden Rule, 87
"Golden Slumbers," 107
"Good Day Sunshine," 68, 71–72
Goodnight Vienna (Starr), 120
Gorbachev, Mikhail, 10
Gospel According to the Beatles, The, 77
Gotnip, Adam, 16
Gould, Jonathan, 23, 167–69, 177
Government of Ireland Act (1920), 52
"Govinda," 108
Graham, Billy, 154, 198
Graves, Harry, 115
Great Depression, 38
Great Irish Famine, 32, 34, 35–37, 54–55
Great Society, 9
Green, John, 226

Haight-Ashbury, 13

Hair Peace, Bed Peace, 18, 89–91, 134
hairstyles, 159–63, 174–75
Hamburg, 13, 120
Hamilton, William, 8–9, 20
Hannah, Kathleen, 194
"Happiness is a Warm Gun," 108
Happy Xmas (War Is Over)," 91
Hard Day's Night, A (film), 8–9, 136, 158, 192
"Hard Day's Night, A" (song), 126
"Hare Krishna Mantra," 108
Hare Krishna Movement. *See* ISKCON
Harrison, George, xi, 1, 3, 4, 11, 76
  agnosticism of, 44
  family background of, 32–3, 38–40, 43, 60–61
  at Haight-Ashbury, 13–14, 102, 103
  and India, 12, 15, 20–21, 84, 98–113, 168
  on Indian music, 99–101
  on LSD, 102–3, 105, 108
  on Lennon's lyrics, 143
  and shaman model, 19
  religious journey of, 67–68, 98–113, 138–40, 146
Harrison, Harold, 41, 61
Harrison, Louise, 39, 61, 98
Harvard College, 51
Harvard Psychedelic Club, 19
Hastings, Adrian, 7
hedonism, 13
Help! (album), 100, 114
Help! (film), 4, 12, 99–100, 158, 192
"Help!" (song), 69, 140, 205
Helter Skelter (Bugliosi), 193–94
"Helter Skelter," 185–200
Henry VIII, King, 50–51
"Here Comes The Sun," 44, 68
"Here Today," 76
"Here, There, and Everywhere," 72
Heswall Children's Hospital, 116
"Hey Jude," 45
higher power. *See* recovery programs
Hilliard, David, 7
Hinduism and the 1960s (Oliver), 16
Hinduism, xi, 11–16, 20
  atman, 14
  Brahman, 14
  and Harrison, 98–113, 135
  karma in, 13, 103
  maya/illusion, 14-15, 139
  miracles in, 103
  path of desire, 13
  path of renunciation, 14
Hoeveler, Diane Long, 162

Hungry Thirties. *See* Great Depression
Huxley, Aldous, 86

"I Am the Walrus," 85, 188, 196
"I Found Out," 83–84, 92
"I Me Mine," 102, 108
"I Saw Her Standing There," 196
"I Want to Hold Your Hand," 196
"I'll Follow the Sun," 68, 79
"I'm a Loser," 69
"I'm Only Sleeping," 141
"I'm the Greatest," 122
"I've Just Seen a Face," 69
ideological monism, 21
"If I Needed Someone," 106
Imagine (album), 86
"Imagine" (song), 18, 45, 58, 83, 92, 93–94, 135, 172
Imagine: John Lennon (film), 224
In Hardship and Hope (Quiery), 54–55
"In My Life," 5
"Incredible Mediocre Rabbits, The" (Lennon), 216
Indian philosophy. *See* Hinduism
Indica Bookshop, 5
"Inner Light, The" 45, 106–8, 139
International Times, 138
IRA (Irish Republican Army), 40, 52, 57
Irish Famine. *See* Great Irish Famine
Irish Fever, 36
Irish Rebellion (1798), 34
ironic distancing, double, 171, 176
ISKCON (International Society of Krishna Consciousness), 15, 92, 95n9, 99, 104–5, 108, 135, 138
Islam, 43
Isserman, Maurice, 6
"It's All Too Much," 107, 139
Iwai, Shunji, 225

Jackson, Michael, 217
Jackson, Peter, 118
Jagger, Mick, ix, x, 163, 196
Jailhouse Rock (film), 193
James II, 33–34
James, William, 21, 166–67, 172–75, 178
Janov, Arthur, 88, 91, 145
Jarry, Alfred, 73
jazz, 38
Jesus Controversy, x, 5, 11, 17–18, 23, 83–84, 87, 172, 187–88, 212n20
Jesus Freaks, 86
Jesus. *See* Christianity
Jewish Historical Society, Liverpool, 41
John Lennon in Heaven (Keen), 220

John, King, 33
Johnson, Paul, 152
Jude (patron saint), 45
"Julia," 196–97
Julian of Norwich, 135

Kane, Larry, 45–46
karma, 13, 103, 110n37
Kazin, Michael, 6
Keats, John, 141–42
Keen, Linda, 220
Kennedy, John F., 91, 151, 153, 156, 188
kenosis, 133–49
KKK (Ku Klux Klan), 23
Kozinn, Allan, 77
Kramer, Michael, 188
"Kubla Khan" (Coleridge), 141

LaBianca, Leno and Rosemary, 185
Lady Chatterley's Lover (Lawrence), 6, 158
"Lady Madonna," 45, 59, 137, 139
Langager, Ross, 151–52
Lao Tzu, 140
Larkin, Philip, 158
Leary, Timothy, 5, 19, 20, 89, 106, 134, 140, 142–43, 146
Led Zeppelin, 5–6
Leen, Jason, 219–20
Lennon, Fr. William, 39
Lennon, James, 56
Lennon, John, x, 1, 5, 10, 23
  agnosticism of, 44, 135, 146
  on Christianity, 85–87, 92–94
  and drugs, 20–21, 82, 86–87, 90–91, 94n1, 135–36, 141, 144, 189–90
  ennui in lyrics, 140–41
  on errant interpretations, 18
  family background of, 33, 37, 39–40, 43, 56
  on Harrison's faith, 104
  imagination of, 170–71
  on Manson, 189–91
  meeting McCartney, 3
  murder of, 214–15
  on origin of band's name, 176
  peace campaign, 89–91, 134, 222
  poetry of, 142
  postmortem appearances, 217–25
  religious journey of, 82–97, 140–46
  and Romantic poets, 141–46
  and shaman model, 19, 211, 215
  solipsism of, 135, 141
  in *Yesterday*, 206–11
Lennon, Julia, 40, 56, 58, 216, 220
Leno, Jay, 10

240 \ Index

Lester, Richard, 136
Let It Be (album), 76
"Let It Be" (song), 45, 59, 73, 136–38
Lewis, Arnold, 41
Lewisohn, Mark, 3, 12, 18, 20–21, 32, 37, 75, 115, 167
Lieberman, Jeff, 194
Life magazine, 194
Lincoln, Abraham, 216, 217, 224, 225
Little Richard, 197
Liverpool Institute, 51, 61
Liverpool Mercury, 36
Liverpool Oratorio (McCartney), 68, 77
Liverpool Resurgent, 41
Liverpool Royal Philharmonic Orchestra, 77
Liverpool Standard, 32
Liverpool, 4
    Everton vs., 42, 49
    Irish Catholics in, 33–34, 35–37, 40, 54–55
    Jewish Community in, 40–41
    pilgrimage to, 4, 205
    religious buildings in, 49–51
    religious life in, 11–12, 31–64
    and World War II, 8, 39
Locke, John, 230
Lockwood, Sir Joseph, 60
London Evening Standard, x
"Lonely Road," 76
"Long and Winding Road, The" 136
"Long Long Long," 108
long sixties, 6–7
Love (Cirque du Soleil), 4
"Love You To," 100, 106, 108, 109n7
Love, Mike, 12
Lovin' Spoonful, 72
Loyal Orange Institute. *See* Orange Lodge
LSD, xi, 5, 11, 20, 21, 71, 82, 86–87, 89–91, 102–3, 108, 134, 137, 141
    and Manson family, 189, 190, 194
"Luck of the Irish, The" 56–58
"Lucy In the Sky With Diamonds," 108, 142, 189, 196
Lynn, Donna, 162

mad women of Dionysus (Nietzsche), 156–59
magic, xii, 86, 91, 168, 175, 179–80
Magical Mystery Tour (1967), 7, 72
Magical Mystery Tour (film), 188
Maharishi Mahesh Yogi, 7, 12, 14–15, 62, 71, 99, 103–4, 108, 135
    Harrison on, 108–9
    Lennon on, 14, 83, 88
    McCartney on, 15

    Starr on, 123, 126
Mahesh, Maharishi. *See* Maharishi Mahesh Yogi
Malik, Jack (character), 201–11, 224
Manchurian Candidate, The (film), 192
Manson, Charles, 185–200
Marsden, Gerry, 50
Martin, George, 4, 5, 14, 20, 100, 168
Mary, Queen, 52, 54
Mascaro, Juan, 111n63
Masons, 54
Mather, Cotton, 51
Mather, Increase, 51
Mather, Richard, 51
"Maxwell's Silver Hammer," 71, 73
McCartney III (McCartney), 79
McCartney, Jim, 39, 59
McCartney, Mary, 42, 45, 59–60, 74–76, 137
McCartney, Mike, 59–60
McCartney, Paul, xii, 1, 4, 10
    agnosticism of, 44, 69, 74, 135
    and avant-garde art, 20–21
    on death, 68, 70, 73–76
    family background of, 33, 39–41, 42–43, 58–60
    on Mahesh, 12
    meeting Lennon, 3
    on prayer, 74
    on rock and roll, 171
    "Paul is dead" conspiracy, 188, 189, 225n6
    realism of, 136–37
    religious journey of, 67–80, 136–38
McConville, Jane, 56
McDonald, Ian, 139, 141, 144
McGovern, Gerry, 116
McGuinn, Roger, 100, 105, 110n15, 161
McKinney, Devin, 70
McLeod, Hugh, 6–7, 13
McLuhan, Marshall, 8, 193
McRobbie, Angela, 159
meaning-making model, 8–9, 16–18
meditation. *See* TM
Meeting the Beatles in India (film), 12, 18
Melnick, Jeffrey, 193
Melody Maker, 154
Mercury, Freddie, 212n13
Mersey Beat, 176
message-giving model, 18–20
Miles, Barry, 5, 71, 80, 138
"mixed" marriages/families, 32, 33, 39–40, 53, 59, 61, 69, 197
modernism, literary, 135
Mohan, Owen, 58

moksha (liberation), 14, 102
Molyneux, Sir Richard, 50
momism, 191; *See also* Oedipal entrapment
"more popular than Jesus." *See* Jesus Controversy
Morrison, Jim, 5, 163
Mozley, Charles, 40
Mālamadhyamakakārikā (Nāgārjuna), 134
"My Boyfriend Got a Beatles Hair Cut" (Lynn), 162
"My Old Friend," 217, 218
"My Sweet Lord," 45, 135, 138–39
Myers Ranch. *See* Manson, Charles
Myers, Arthur, 217
Myrtle Street Children's Hospital, 116
mystical union model, 20–21, 85, 169
mysticism, psychedelic, 134

Nāgārjuna, 134
Natale, Simone, 216
National Enquirer, 217, 224
"negative capability," (Keats), 142
neoorthodoxy, 8
"New Adam" (Blake), 162
New Age spirituality, xii, 186, 214–25
New Republic, 9
New York Times, The, 2, 77
New York, I Love You (film), 225
New Yorker, The, 16
Nhất Hạnh, Thích, 124
Nichols, Bill, 222
Niebuhr, Reinhold, 8
Nietzsche, Friedrich, 5, 9–11, 143, 155
    on Christianity, 5–7, 9, 230
    on cult of Dionysus, 150–65
    eternal recurrence, 11
    last man, 11
    satyrs, 161–63
nihilism, 6, 9–11, 151
nirvana, 134
"No No Song," 120
No One's Gonna Change Our World (Milligan), 145
"Norwegian Wood (This Bird Has Flown)," 12, 100, 106
"Nowhere Man," 11, 140–42

"O My Soul," 79
O'Brien, Ray, 61–62
O'Neill, Tom, 186
"Ob-La-Di, Ob-La-Da," 209
Oedipal entrapment, 191–93, 196–97, 198n21
Oh My God (film). *See* God: The Almighty Question

Oliver, Paul, 16
"Only a Northern Song," 107
Ono, Yoko, 57, 90–91, 105, 134, 145–46, 159, 198, 216, 220, 223
oral tradition, Irish, 55
Orange Lodge, 34, 43, 49, 53–54, 57, 62
Orange Order. *See* Orange Lodge
Orangeism, 37; June 1909 violence, 37–38
Our World (BBC), 7

Padel, Ruth, 150–51, 157
papist, 32
pataphysics, 73
Paul (Apostle), 73, 89
Peace at Last (Leen), 219–20
Penniman, Richard Wayne, 197
"Penny Lane," 7, 136–37, 205
Perkins, Carl, 98, 217, 218
Peter, Paul, and Mary, 77
Photograph (Starr), 127
"Piggies," 107, 186, 196
Pius XII, Pope, 135
Plant, Robert, 5
Plastic Ono Band (Lennon), 91, 145, 172
Playboy, xi, 44
Polanski, Roman, 187
Polley, Gerald, 218
Polley, Linda, 218–19, 224
Portable Nietzsche, The (Nietzsche), 5, 143
postsecularism, 146
potato famine. *See* Great Irish Famine
Powell, Cynthia, 41
Power, Joe, 221
Prabhupada, A. C. Bhaktivedanta Swami, 99, 102, 104–5, 108–9, 140
Pressley, Elvis, x, 105, 119–20, 153, 155, 177, 191, 193, 219
    Beatles' view of, 166–68, 173
Pressley, Gladys, 191
Profumo Affair, 6, 151
Protestants vs. Catholics, 31–64
Prothero, Stephen, 10
Psychedelic Experience, The (Leary), 5, 20, 89, 106, 143
Psychedelic Prayers after the Tao Te Ching (Leary), 140, 146
Puritans, 50–51
Putnam, Robert, 229

Q magazine, 75
Quarrymen, The, 3, 43
Quiery, Greg, 54–55, 58–59

radical theologians, 5, 8–9, 20
Radio India, 62, 109n1

Radio Luxembourg, 169–70
"Rain," 106
Rainhill Asylum, 36
Raja Yoga (Vivekananda), 101–2, 105, 109
Ramakrishna, 101
Ramsey, Ian (bishop), 17
recovery programs, xi, 115, 119–28
    and agnostics/atheists, 123
    concept of "God" in, 122–24
Reformation, The, 6
Regev, Eyal, 141
religion, definitions of, 25n100, 166, 177
Religious Crisis of the 1960s (McLeod), 6, 13
religious epiphany, 206–8
religious experience, 2, 133–81, 207
religious experimentation, 87, 187, 229–30
religious hybrids, 15, 122–23, 210
religious impulse, 9, 17; toward novelty, 178
Religious Literacy (Prothero), 10
religious violence, 57
"Revolution Number 9," 186, 197
"Revolution," 89, 92, 134, 186, 197, 230
Revolver (1966), 70, 72, 89, 106, 141, 143
Righteous Brothers, The, 79
Riley, Tim, 74, 136, 142
Rishikesh (India), xi, 12–15, 63, 72, 99, 104, 135
Rodger, Peter, 123
Rolling Stone magazine, 62, 127
Rolling Stones, ix, 152, 177–78
Romanticism, 141–46
Royal Liverpool Children's Hospital, 116
Rubber Soul (1965), 12, 88, 100, 106, 140
Russell, Bertrand, 159

Salem Witch Trials, 51
Salewicz, Chris, 75
Saltzman, Paul, 12, 18
Samson, 160–62
Saturday Evening Post, 120
"Savoy Truffle," 107–8
Saxe, John Godfrey, 16
Scott-James, Anne, 18
secular saints, 72
secularization, 7, 9, 83–84, 88, 94, 187
seeker churches, 17–18
Sempiternus Rex Christus (Pius XII), 135
Serenity Prayer, 8, 124
Sgt. Pepper's Lonely Hearts Club Band (1967), 7, 14, 22
    concept of, 118, 188
    cover, 11, 102, 188
    song selection, 107, 139
    Lennon on, 18
    Starr's involvement, 117

shaman model, 19–20, 25n86, 170–72, 211
Shamanism (Eliade), 170
Shankar, Ravi, xi, 12, 15, 62, 99–104, 108, 110n15, 110n34
Sharratt, Paul, 221
Shaw, Major Thomas, 62
"She Said She Said," 141–42
"She's Leaving Home," 136
Sheeran, Ed, 202–9
Sheff, David, 135
Sheffield, Rob, 136
Shelden, Michael, 3
Shelley, Percy Bysshe, x, 141
Sheppard, David, 55
Shipley, Morgan, 134, 143–44, 147n17
"Short Diversion on the Dubious Origins of the Beatles, A" (Lennon), 176
Shotton, Pete, 58, 82, 170
Simon, Paul, ix
sitar explosion, 100
Sixties Spiritual Awakening (Elwood), 7
sixties, religious shifts in, 7
Skywriting by Word of Mouth (Lennon), 216
Smith, George, 43
Smith, Huston, 13–14, 19
Smith, Mary Elizabeth (Aunt Mimi), 32
Smyth, Damian, 61
Snapp, Charles, 3
Soling, Cevin, 73
solipsism, 135
"Something," 108
Sometime in New York City (Lennon), 56
"Soul And Inspiration" (Righteous Brothers), 79
Soul on Ice (Cleaver), 195
"Sour Milk Sea," 108
Spahn Ranch. *See* Manson, Charles
Spirit of John Lennon, The (film), 221–25
Spiritualism, 215–25
spirituality vs. religion, 25n100
Spitz, Bob, 71, 167, 179–80
Springsteen, Bruce, 211n2
SRF (Self-Realization Fellowship), 102–3, 105, 109, 111n53
St. James, Jewelle, 220–21
St. Patrick's Day, 34, 55, 63
St. Peters Church (Woolton), 3, 43, 58
Stace, Walter, 21
Stanley, Bob, 155
Star Is Born, A (film), 212n13
Starkey-Gleave, Elsie, 63, 115–16, 120
Starkey, Richard Sr., 115
Starkey, Richy. *See* Starr, Ringo
Starr, Ringo, xi, 1, 11
    agnosticism of, 114–16, 127, 140

Starr, Ringo (*continued*)
    and Beatles' breakup, 118–19
    and Lennon, 119–20
    drumming of, 128n20
    evangelism of, 45, 126–27
    faith of, 63, 114–30
    family background of, 33–34, 39–40, 43, 50, 53, 62–63, 115
    introduction to drums, 116
    medical issues, 115
    on prayer, 123, 126
    on songwriting, 117
    on the afterlife, 124
    rock bottom, 121
Steiner, Rudolf, 160–63
Stockhausen, 20–21
Story of God, The, 17
Strawberry Fields (memorial), 214, 225
"Strawberry Fields Forever," 7, 107, 136, 142–43
Suczek, Barbara, 188
Summer of Love, 7, 13, 22
"Sun King," 68
"Sunday Bloody Sunday," 56–57
Sunyata, 124
Sutcliffe, Stuart, 74–75
Svetaketu (*Upanishads*), 15, 102
Sword, Helen, 215
Sylvan, Robin, 17

Taich, Alison, 156–57
Tao Te Ching, 107, 140, 146, 147n22
Taoism, 16, 25n72, 140, 147n22
tape loops, 20–21, 217
tat tvam asi, 13–14, 102, 107
Tate, Sharon, 185, 193
"Taxman," 106–7
Taylor, Derek, 122, 154
Thatcher, Margaret, 77
theology of crisis. *See* neoorthodoxy
"Think For Yourself," 106
Thus Spoke Zarathustra (Nietzsche), 143
Tibetan Book of the Dead, 5, 20, 106
Tillich, Paul, 16, 24n43
Time Magazine, 5, 186
Tittenhurst Park, 95, 224, 225
TM (Transcendental Meditation), 12, 89, 99, 111n43, 136, 141, 144
    and Boyd, 103–4
    as raja yoga, 108
    criticism of, 15–16
    Harrison on, 43
    McCartney on, 71–72
    vs. prayer, 126

"Tomorrow Never Knows," 5, 20–21, 86, 89, 106–7, 126, 143
Tonight Show, 10
Townshend, Pete, 154
Toxeth Unitarian Chapel, 50–52
Traces of the Spirit (Sylvan), 17
Transport Strike of 1911, General, 38
Trilling, Lionel, 8
"Troubles, The," 55
Trump, Donald, 219, 224
Tug of War (McCartney), 217
Turner, Steve, 19–21, 77, 86, 91, 211, 215
"Twelfth, The," 34
Twelve Steps. *See* recovery programs
"Two of Us," 76

Unger, Art, 18
Upanishads, 15, 107

Valentino, Rudolph, 38
Varieties of Religious Experience, The (James), 166–67
Vatican, 83
Victoria, Queen, 35
Vietnam War, x, 10, 45, 153, 157, 188
Vishnu-devananda, Swami, 100, 102
Vivekananda, Swami, 99, 101–5, 108–9

Wallace, David Foster, 123, 229
Walnut Ridge, Arkansas, 2–3
Walsh, Joe, 127
Waters, Muddy, 196
"We Can Work It Out," 44
Weber, Max, 88, 92, 180
Weiner, Jon, 144
Wesley, John, 40
Whalley, Nigel, 216
Where Has Eternity Gone? (film), 218
Where the Girls Are (Douglas), 160
"While My Guitar Gently Weeps," 25n72, 108
Whitaker, Robert, 188
Whitehead, Alfred North, 174, 176, 178
William of Orange, 33–34, 52, 54
Williams, Allan, 222
Williams, David T., 134
Wings, 60, 80, 146
"Winterbird / When Winter Comes," 79
"With A Little Help from My Friends," 4
With the Beatles (1963), 69
"Within You, Without You," 14, 105–8, 138–40
Womack, Kenneth, 24n48, 69
Wonderwall Music (Harrison), 108
Woodhead, Leslie, 23n8, 152

Wooler, Bob, 173
"Word, The" 18, 88, 89
"Working Class Hero," 58
World War I, 32, 216
World War II, 8, 39, 49-50, 58
Worlock, Derek, 55
wu wei, 147n22
Wynne, David, 105, 111n52

Yellow Submarine (album), 139
Yellow Submarine (film), 23, 212n3
Yesterday (film), 201–13, 224
Yesterday and Today (1966), 187
"Yesterday," 4, 69–71, 209

Yoga Sutras (Patanjali), 101
Yoga Sutras, 12
yoga, 100, 101, 108–9
    bhakti yoga, 104, 108
    jnana yoga, 108
    karma yoga, 108
    Kriya technique, 103
    raja vs. TM, 108
    raja yoga, 101–2, 108
Yogananda, Paramahansa, 99, 101–5, 109, 110n32
You Never Give Me Your Money (Doggett), 119